The Southern Version of **CURSOR MUNDI**

Volume II

**The Southern Version of
CURSOR MUNDI**

General Editor, Sarah M. Horrall

Already published
Volume I. Lines 1–9228. Edited by Sarah M. Horrall
Volume II. Lines 9229–12712. Edited by Roger R. Fowler
Volume III. Lines 12713–17082. Edited by Henry J. Stauffenberg
Volume IV. Lines 17289–21346. Edited by Peter H.J. Mous

Forthcoming
Volume V. Lines 21347–23898 and General Introduction

OTTAWA
MEDIAEVAL
TEXTS AND STUDIES

The Southern Version of CURSOR MUNDI

Volume II
Lines 9229-12712

Edited by
Roger R. Fowler

et exaltabitur sicut
unicornis cornu meum

University of Ottawa Press

© University of Ottawa Press, 1990
ISBN 0-7766-0206-3
Printed and bound in Canada

Canadian Cataloguing in Publication Data

[Cursor mundi]
   The Southern version of Cursor mundi

(Études médiévales de l'Université d'Ottawa = Ottawa mediaeval texts
   and studies; 16)
Volume 1 is no. 5 of series, vol. 2 is no. 16, vol. 3 is no. 13 and
   vol. 4 is no. 14.
Includes bibliographies.
Contents: v. 1. Lines 1–9228 / edited by Sarah M. Horrall –
   v. 2. Lines 9229–12712 / edited by Roger R. Fowler –
   v. 3. Lines 12713–17082 / edited by Henry J. Stauffenberg –
   v. 4. Lines 17289–21346 / edited by Peter H.J. Mous.
ISBN 0-7766-4805-5 (v. 1) – ISBN 0-7766-0206-3 (v. 2) –
ISBN 0-7766-4814-4 (v. 3) – ISBN 0-7766-0107-5 (v. 4).

   I. Title.   II. Series: Publications médiévales de
l'Université d'Ottawa.

PR1966.A35   821'.1   C79-2580-9 rev.

IN MEMORIAM

With the death of Dr. Sarah Horrall in July 1988, the *Cursor Mundi* project suffered an enormous loss. Her knowledge of the entire poem, the related scholarship, and the intricacies of manuscript relations, dialect, and variants was unrivalled, the product of years of painstaking research. As the General Editor of the series, she was patient, scholarly, encouraging, and totally committed to seeing the project through to completion. Her heroic determination was such that she continued to work on the *Cursor Mundi*, proofreading, advising, and submitting corrections, to within two months of her death. It is thus a matter of deep personal grief that she will not be present to share in the joy of the publication of this volume of the *Cursor Mundi*.

REQUIESCAT IN PACE

DEDICATION

This volume is fittingly dedicated to my wife, Aline, and our two young children, Chantal and Sean. Aline gave up honeymoon time to allow me to examine the manuscript in the College of Arms, London. She subsequently generously shouldered my parental and domestic duties so that I could concentrate on finishing this volume. Chantal and Sean, in their turn, have unwittingly helped me keep a proper balance between scholarship and day-to-day family life.

Nepean, 17 June 1989

TABLE OF CONTENTS

ACKNOWLEDGEMENTS

First of all, I would like to thank those teachers who fostered my love of things medieval: L. A. Cummings, University of Waterloo; R. MacG. Dawson, King's College, Halifax; R. St.-Jacques and L. M. Eldredge, University of Ottawa; and, in particular, the late A. P. Campbell, University of Ottawa, under whom I began my *Cursor Mundi* studies.

I am also grateful to Dr. Conrad Swan, Ph.D., M.A., F.S.A., York Herald of Arms, for granting me access to Arundel LVII, and to his accommodating staff for providing favourable conditions in which to study it. I am also indebted to the friendly, understanding, and knowledgeable staff at the University of Ottawa Press, who patiently endured a lengthy but unavoidable delay in the completion of this work. In particular, I owe immense gratitude to Jenny Wilson, who proofread the entire manuscript with exemplary diligence, patience, and cheerfulness.

To the late Dr. Sarah Horrall, the General Editor of this series, I am deeply indebted for help with a multitude of matters. The successful completion of this volume is due in large part to her unstinting labour, constant support, and extensive knowledge of the poem. I must also thank Professor George Kaiser, Kansas State University, for generously proofreading Dr. Horrall's transcription from MS Additional 31042, a task her untimely death interrupted. As well, Professor Kaiser kindly supplied me with xerox copies from his microfilm of Additional 31042 so that I too could proofread the transcription.

This book has been published with the help of a grant from the Canadian Federation for the Humanities, using funds provided by the Social Science and Humanities Research Council of Canada.

GENERAL EDITOR'S INTRODUCTION

In the present volume, the Introduction, the text of MS H, the Explanatory Notes, and the Bibliography have been prepared by Dr. Roger R. Fowler. The General Editor is responsible for the transcription of the variants, the text of MS Add, and the list of errors in Morris' edition (Appendices A and B).

The General Editor wishes to thank the Social Sciences and Humanities Research Council of Canada for a research time stipend and travel grant which made possible the completion of this volume.

INTRODUCTION TO THIS VOLUME

LIST OF MANUSCRIPT SIGLA

H	Arundel LVII, College of Arms, London
T	Trinity College, Cambridge, R.3.8
L	Laud Misc. 416, Bodleian Library, Oxford
B	Additional 36983, British Library, London
C	Cotton Vespasian A iii, British Library, London
F	Fairfax 14, Bodleian Library, Oxford
G	Göttingen University theol. 107^r
E	Edinburgh, Royal College of Physicians
Add	Additional 31042, British Library, London

STRUCTURE OF THIS SECTION

Lines 9229–12712 of *Cursor Mundi* cover the "fifth age" of salvation, a period that includes the birth, temple service, and marriage of the Virgin, the birth of Jesus, his childhood wonder-deeds in Egypt, and the years from adolescence to the beginning of his public life. Since most of this material is not found in the Bible, the *CM* poet employs apocryphal sources for many of the 3500 lines he devotes to this portion of his narrative.

The apocryphal basis of the narrative has, in turn, determined the nature of the Explanatory Notes. Exegetical traditions and patristic commentaries, for example, are not very relevant for source materials that were rejected as non-canonical by such people as Augustine,

Jerome, Innocent I, Gelasius I, and Fulbert of Chartres.[1] Accordingly, my principal concerns are to identify the poet's probable sources, to explain his use of them, and to clarify the text.

A convenient table of contents for this section is available in the textual headings supplied by Richard Morris in his edition. Where these captions are unsatisfactory, however, or where I felt additional ones were required, I have provided my own and placed them in parentheses.

---

1. AUGUSTINE, *Contra Faustum*, *PL* XLII 472; JEROME, *Adversus Helvidium*, *PL* XXIII 200–201; INNOCENT I, *Epistola* vi, *PL* XX 502, where he states of such apocryphal works: "et si qua sunt alia, non solum repudianda, veram etiam noveris esse damnada"; GELASIUS I, *De Libris non Recipiendis*, *PL* XIX 787–94; FULBERT OF CHARTRES, *Sermo i: De Nativitate Mariae*, *PL* CXLI 324–25. An explanation of the abbreviations used in these notes will be found on p. 117.

SOURCES

In composing this section of his poem, the poet ranged quite widely in manner and matter. As he saw fit, he rearranged, translated, paraphrased, summarized, expanded, conflated, and drew selectively from portions of at least a half-dozen works in Latin and Old French. His eclectic method precludes positive identification of all his sources but the following can confidently be cited as his major ones:

Le Château d'amour

Le Château d'amour[2] by Robert Grosseteste (called "seynt Robardes boke" by the poet at l. 9516) supplies the material for about one-fifth of the section edited here. The debt is in the form of careful and extensive translation.[3]

Herman's *Bible*

The *Bible* of Herman de Valenciennes,[4] another important source, is handled more freely. The poet deletes, expands, rearranges, paraphrases, and only occasionally translates phrases or entire lines.

2. See J. MURRAY, ed., *Le Château d'amour de Robert Grosseteste* (Paris, 1918). In addition to the Anglo-Norman versions, Middle English versions were available from the second half of the thirteenth century. See K. SAJAVAARA, ed., *The Middle English Translations of Robert Grosseteste's Château d'amour*, Mémoires de la Société Néophilologique de Helsinki, 32 (Helsinki, 1967). The debt to Grosseteste was first noted by Dr. HAENISCH in *CM*, pp. 23*–31*.

3. Kari SAJAVAARA, "The Use of Robert Grosseteste's *Château d'amour* as a Source of the *Cursor Mundi*: Additional Evidence," *Neuphilologische Mitteilungen*, LXVIII (1967), 186, says "the translation is close and usually matches couplet for couplet." In his longer study (see note 2 above) Sajavaara remarks that the *CM* "reproduces the message of the *Château d'amour* more faithfully than the [four] other [Middle English] versions."

4. The relevant portion has been edited in *La Bible von Herman de Valenciennes*, Vol. II by O. MOLDENHAUER, Vol. III by Hans BURKOWITZ (Griefswald, 1914). See L. BORLAND, *The Cursor Mundi and Herman's Bible*, Diss. Chicago, 1929, and "Herman's *Bible* and the *Cursor Mundi*," *Studies in Philology*, XXX (1933), 427–44; and P. BUEHLER, "The *Cursor Mundi* and Herman's *Bible*—Some Additional Parallels," *Studies in Philology*, LXI (1964), 485–99. A newer edition of Herman's *Bible* by Ina SPIELE, *Li Romanz de dieu et de sa mere* (Leyden, 1975), contains valuable information and a bibliography.

L'Établissement de la fête de la conception Notre Dame dite la fête aux normands

Wace's *L'Établissement de la fête de la conception Notre Dame dite la fête aux normands*[5] is the source for the extensive treatment of the family background and early life of the Virgin. The *CM* poet is generally content to translate and paraphrase this source, rarely altering it in other than minor ways.

Pseudo-Matthaei Evangelium

Pseudo-Matthaei Evangelium,[6] although similarly interested in the pre-biblical Marian history, is chiefly important as an uncanonical gospel containing the wondrous exploits of Christ's childhood that the *CM* poet used extensively in places, selectively in others. Less probable as direct sources but worth mentioning nonetheless as part of the apocryphal tradition are *The Protevangelium of James*, *The Infancy Story of Thomas*, and *De Nativitate Mariae*.[7]

Historia Scholastica

Petrus Comestor's *Historia Scholastica*[8] was a well-known work in the period and one that the *CM* poet used, as Dr. Haenisch observed.[9]

---

5. Ed. G. MANCEL and G. S. TREBUTIEN (Caen, 1842). See E. PÉTAVEL, *La Bible en France* (1864); J. BONNARD, *Les Traductions de la Bible en vers français au moyen âge* (Paris, 1884). HAENISCH, *CM*, pp. 13*–20*, first noted this source. G. L. HAMILTON, in his "Review of Gordon Hall Gerould, *Saints' Legends*," *Modern Language Notes*, XXXVI (1921), p. 238, has suggested that the *CM* poet found much of his apocryphal material in an interpolated copy of Wace, such as that found in BL Add 15606. Comparison with *CM* shows that Add 15606 was not its source, and no more suitably interpolated manuscript of Wace has yet come to light.

6. Ed. K. von TISCHENDORF, *Evangelia Apocrypha* (1876; rpt. Hildesheim, 1966). See O. CULLMANN, "Infancy Gospels," trans. A.F.B. Higgins, in E. HENNECKE and W. SCHNEE-MELCHER, eds., *New Testament Apocrypha* (English trans. R. McL. Wilson) (Philadelphia, 1963), I 363–69; A. F. FINDLAY, *Byways in Early Christian Literature: Studies in the Uncanonical Gospels and Acts* (Edinburgh, 1923); J. HERVIEUX, *What are Apocryphal Gospels?*, trans. Dom W. Hibberd (London, 1960). This source was first noted in HAENISCH, *CM*, pp. 31*–34*.

7. The *Protevangelium* and *The Infancy Story* are translated in HENNECKE's *NT Apocrypha*, I 374–88, 392–99. For *De Nativitate* see Michel NICOLAS, *Études sur les Évangiles apocryphes* (Paris, 1866). See also E. AMANN, ed., *Le Protévangile de Jacques et ses remaniements latins* (Paris, 1910).

8. *PL* CXCVIII.

9. HAENISCH, *CM*, pp. 3*–13*.

In ll. 9229–12712, the poet appears to have drawn only selectively from it. Such debts are difficult to prove, however, since much of the matter is common to several sources.

Legenda Aurea

Jacobus a Voragine's *Legenda Aurea* was also identified as a source by Haenisch.[10] Once again, however, the indebtedness is difficult to establish for the section edited here. Many of the details common to the *Legenda* and the *CM* appear in *De Nativitate Mariae* and Comestor's *Historia Scholastica*, from both of which the *Legenda* took much of its information, thus complicating the question of immediate debt. Whatever its exact relationship to ll. 9229–12712 of the *CM*, the widely known *Legenda* helped establish the apocryphal traditions within which the *CM* poet worked and is therefore an important guide to our general understanding of the poem and its background.

Elucidarium

Honorius Augustodunensis' *Elucidarium*,[11] not included in Haenisch's list of sources, plays a definite but minor role in this section of the poem. The poet principally drew on it for his theological discussion of the redemption (ll. 9732–94).

The Vulgate *Bible*

The Vulgate,[12] not surprisingly, furnished scant material for a narrative section dealing with the Virgin's life prior to the Annunciation and stopping on the eve of Christ's public ministry. Thus, although the poet uses the New Testament whenever he can, the opportunity does not often arise, and the Bible ends up, ironically, supplementing apocryphal writings.

---

10. Ed. Th. GRAESSE (Leipzig, 1850). See HAENISCH, *CM*, pp. 47*–56*.
11. Ed. Yves LEFÈVRE in *L'Elucidarium et les lucidaires* (Paris, 1954).
12. Unless stated otherwise, biblical quotations in Latin are based on the *Biblia Sacra juxta Vulgatam Clementinam* (Rome, 1956).

EDITORIAL PRINCIPLES

The editorial principles for this volume are the same as those outlined in Volume I, pp. 25–27.

In addition to the text of *Cursor Mundi* from MS H and variants from MSS TLB, this volume also contains, as Appendix B, a transcription of the hitherto unpublished Thornton fragment from MS Add 31042, British Library, London.

Text of
the Southern Version
of *Cursor Mundi*
(College of Arms MS Arundel LVII)

Lines 9229–12712

Blessed be she þat vs haþ sped   9229 fol. 54r col. 1
Þat we þe eldes foure han red   9230
To reherse þat lady kynne
Þe fyueþe elde we wol bigynne
Econyas ȝe herde me mone
Salatiel he had to sone
And of þi[s] ilke Salatiel   9235
Coom his sone zorobabel
Abyuth ȝit coom of him
Of abyuth eliachim
Of him azor of him sadoch
Þus was þat oon þat oþeres stok   9240
Sadoch þenne achim gat   fol. 54r col. 2
Achim eliud not forȝat
Of eliud coom eliazare
Þat leuy als to name bare
Þis leuy had sones two   9245
Matan & pantra also
Matan gat Iacob in pley
Iacob Ioseph soþ to sey
Of þat side is to telle no mo
Of pantera coom [per]pantera þo   9250
Of Perpantera coom Ioachim

9230   eldes] agis B. foure] iiij^e L.
9232   fyueþe elde] first age B.
9233   ȝe] he L.
9234   had to] was his B.
9235   þis] þi H; þat B.
9238–39   *om.* C.
9240   þat oon þat] þe ton þe TLB; oþeres] toþeres T; toþer LB.
9244   als] *om.* B.
9245   two] ij° L.
9247   pley] playn B.
9249   side is] sede B.
9250   perpantera] pantera HT; *P*erpantra, *P*er *superscript with a caret* L.
9251   *P*erpantera] Pantera B.

Oure lady Mary coom of hym
Ioseph & she may we se
Were but at þridde & ferþe kne
Þis mayden þat lord bare   9255
Þat lesed al þe world of care
Þus was þe fruyt þat bouȝt oure bote
Of þat tre þat adam was rote
Whoso wol se fro adam þe olde
How mony knees to crist are tolde   9260
Fynde wiþouten doute he shal
Sixty olde gen*er*aciou*n*s al
And neyþer tolde he ne he
Þus may þe genealogy be

Cryst was seide of p*r*ophecy   9265
Most of hym spake ysay
To þe iewes so mystrowand
He bad hem here & vndirstonde
Iesse he seide of his rotynge
Certeynly a ȝerde shulde sprynge   9270
Out of þat a flour shulde brest
Þe holy goost þeronne shulde rest   9272
Þe goost þat ȝyueþ ȝiftis sere   9275
Ȝitt þat folk was al in were
Vche to oþ*er*e seyde what may þis be
So wondir merkely spekeþ he
But ȝit he lete hit so be hid

9253   may] here may B.
9254   þridde] þe þridde TB. ferþe] iiij^{th} L. kne] degre LB.
9255   lord] þis lorde B.
9256   of] fro B.
9257   Þus] This L. fruyt] tre B. bouȝt oure] brouȝte once T; broght vs B.
9260   knees] kyndis LB.
9262   Sixty] vj L.
9263   ne] nor B.
9264   *After this line* B *adds a heading*:
       Here begynneth þe prophecy
       of þe prophetis of Isaye
9265   was] *om.* B. seide] sent L. of] of þe B.
9269–70   *reversed in* B.
9269   Iesse . . . his] þat schall come of Iesse B.
9270   shulde] sjaæ TB.
9271   þat] *om.* B. shulde] þere schall B.
9272   shulde] schall B.
9273–74   *om.* CGHTLB.
9276   þat] þe B. was] were B.
9278   merkely] derkely B.
9279   ȝit] if T.

And longe aftir to hem hit vndid   9280
Gode men he seide con ȝe not se
Of a mon þat het Iesse
A mayde of him shal brede & spryng   fol. 54v col. 1
And she shal haue a sone to kyng
I wol not hele for drede of blame   9285
Emanuel shal ben his name
Hit is to say on englisshe þus
Oure lord himself al wiþ vs
Ete hony & mylke he shal also
Þat oon to knowe þat oþer fro   9290
Fro þe wicke þe good to knawe
Þe soþe fro him shal noon wiþdrawe

// Summe Iewis seide to oþere þan
Who herde euer siche speche of man
Þat born shal be sumþing þer is   9295
He wolde not were knowen Iwis
Þenne seide ysay parfay
I shal ȝow openlyere say
I wol no lenger wiþ ȝow leyne
I shal vndo hit al pleyne   9300
I haue writen al þis þinge
Þat I shal leue to ȝoure ospringe
Þis ilke book but summe of þeim
Aȝeyn my sawe shal sett cleym
For aftir þat I am of lyue   9305
Ȝoure heires aȝeyn sooþ shul stryue
Why are ȝe of wille so wylde
A mayden shal vs bere a childe
As I tolde ȝow her biforn
To oure bihoue shal he be born   9310

9280   And] So L. vndid] kid B.
9281   men] neuer B.
9283   of . . . spryng] schall com of his ospring B.
9284   And] *om.* B.
9285   of] nor B.
9287   Hit] Þat B. on] in LB.
9290   Þat oon] Þe ton TLB. þat oþer] þe toþer TLB.
9291   wicke] whilk L.
9296   were] it were B.
9297   ysay] Isaac L.
9299   wiþ] to B.
9306   sooþ] *om.* L; þe soþe B.
9309   tolde ȝow] ȝow tolde B.
9310   oure] ȝoure H. bihoue] byhovyþ L. shal he] he schal B.

Þis childe þus ȝyuen vs tille
Shal regne at his owne wille
Men shul him calle nomes sere
Wondirful & counseilere
God of strengþe & fadir is he   9315
Cald of þe world þat is to be
Prynce of pes men shul him calle
Neuer shal his regne falle
I haue ȝow tolde how hit shal be
But I noot wheþer ȝe hit se   9320
Litil se we ȝit seide þey
Of al þat we here þe sey
Siþ we were born in werde   fol. 54v col. 2
So selcouþe sawe neuer we herde
Nor I he seide herde neuer in londe   9325
So harde men to vndirstonde
Sawe ȝe not bi goddis doome
Þe ȝerde bare leef fruyt & blome
Þat ȝerde tokeneþ a mayden clene
Shal bere þe childe þat I of mene   9330
Þat shal his folk fro baret bye
To whom men shul haue greet enuye
Ieremye hit seiþ in boke
If ȝe his prophecye wol loke
Ȝitt I shal ȝou seye a þing   9335
But holdeþ hit for no heting
Whenne þat holyest is comen
Ȝoure noyntynge shal be fro ȝow nomen
Ȝit I trowe ȝe be so blynde
Þat ȝe con not my resoun fynde   9340
Kyngis anoynt ȝe haue bifore

9311 tille] vntyll B.
9320 wheþer] ȝef B. se] schall se B.
9322 þe] seid they they, seid they *cancelled* L.
9323 Siþ] Synne L. werde] þe worlde B.
9324 sawe] þing B.
9325–11614 *om.* F, *twelve leaves missing.*
9328 ȝerde] erthe L. leef] lyf L.
9329 Þat] Þe B. ȝerde] erbe L. tokeneþ] betokenyþ B.
9330 childe] frute B.
9331 baret] bale L.
9334 his] þe B.
9336 no] non B.
9337 þat] þe B.
9338 noyntynge] anoyntyng B. be . . . ȝow] ȝow be B.
9341 anoynt] anoynted B. bifore] tofore TLB.

So shul ȝe þenne no more
Fro he be noyntide þat I say
Kyngles shul ȝe be fro þat day
Of þis telleþ ȝow Ieremye   9345
Þe prophete Ioel and helye
Ȝit is he lyuyng in hele
Þis helie þat I of mele
For noþing to hem tolde
Hit wolde not in her hertis holde   9350
Þei mystrowed & þat hem rewes
God seide hymself of þo iewes
Whenne he made of his modir mynne
Þat was comen of her kynne
He seide my lemmon is so gent   9355
Swetter smellynge þen pyement
And wel swoter hir vestiment
Þen encense þat is brent
Fair is þe mouþ of þat lady
Vche tooþ as yuory   9360
As doufes eȝe hir loke is swete
Rose on þorn to hir vnmete
Bitwene hem fairer acorde is noon   fol. 55r col. 1
Þen bitwene hir kyn & my lemmon
For as þe rose is bred of þorn   9365
So was mary of iewes born
Er we of cristis birþe neuen
Telle we howe þe fadir of heuen
Diȝte his dere sone to sende
Almoost at þe worldes ende   9370
Into erþe oure flesshe to take
To brynge monkynde out of wrake

9342 no] neuyr B.
9347 he] his B.
9348 helie] holy B.
9349 to] þat he B.
9352 þo] þe B.
9353 Whenne] Where B.
9354 was comen] were borne B.
9356 smellynge þen] þan þe B.
9357 wel] *om.* B. hir] is her B.
9358 Þen] Then eny L; Þan þe B.
9360 tooþ as] of her teth is B.
9361 eȝe] eyen B.
9362 on] ne B.
9363–66 *om.* B.
9367 cristis] þe B.
9369 dere] *om.* B. to sende] forto wende B.

How he ȝaf vs his pardoun
Shortly to telle I am boun

Now lordyngis haue ȝe herd   9375
Of þe bigynnyng of þe werd
How he þat neuer hadde bigynnyng
Made heuen erþe & alle þinge
Also to alle þinge he ȝaue
Her kyndely shap for to haue   9380
Sonne & moone þat is so briȝt
Had seuen so myche more liȝt
Alle þingis þat þo dide growe
Were myȝtyere þen þei are nowe
A greet harm bifel vs þore   9385
Þat alle shulde dyȝe lasse & more
Þat of adam & eue coom
But ȝit was hit riȝtwis doom
As ȝe shul se bi riȝtful skil
Þat here wel þis story wil   9390
Whenne þis world to ende was wrouȝt
Wantyng was þereof nouȝt
Beest gras fruyt & tre
Al was as hit shulde be
Foul & fisshe greet & smal   9395
Adam last was made of al
In ebron grene þat ilke dale
ÞerInne he dreyȝe aftir bale
Of erþe god made hym to be
Aftir þe holy trynyte   9400
His owne ymage he made him þore

9374 I am] am I B.
9375 haue ȝe] ȝe haue B.
9376 *second* þe] þis TL.
9377 neuer hadde] had neuer B.
9378 erþe] & erþe B.
9381 is] ar B.
9382 seuen] vij sithe L; sevyn tyme B.
9384 are] be B.
9385 bifel vs] fell B.
9386 shulde] schul B. dyȝe] die bothe L.
9387 eue] of Eue B.
9388 But] Yet But, Yet *cancelled* L; *om.* B. hit] þat a B.
9389 se] here B.
9390 wel] wolle L. wil] wele L.
9391 to . . . was] was to ende B.
9392 was þereof] thereof was L.
9393 &] his &, his *cancelled* L; nor B.
9395 *first* &] *om.* L.

How myȝte he loue kyþe him more
In paradys he made him rest   fol. 55r col. 2
And sleȝely sleep on him he kest
He made a felowe of his boone   9405
To Adam þat was firste his oone
Wit & skil he ȝaf him tille
Miȝte feirhede & fre wille
Ouer al þis world to be kaisere
Euerlastinge lyf for to bere   9410
In paradys as heritage
To lede her lyf wiþouten rage
In welþe wiþouten tene or tray
Bitwene and a certeyn day
Þat of his owne ospringe myȝt   9415
Fulfille þe noumbre hool & riȝt
Of þat felowshepe þat felle
Out of heuen into helle
Þenne shulde þei so blessed be
Þat þei of deeþ shulde neuer se   9420
And so swynkeles feir & briȝt
As þat tyme was þe sunne liȝt
As ȝe herde tofore neuen
Þenne shulde þei styȝe to heuen
Who herde euer of more blis   9425
Þen ordeyned was to hym & his
Lawes two were set on sise
To Adam in paradise
As in holy writt we fynde
Þe firste was þe lawe of kynde   9430
Þat is to seye kyndely to do
Al þat hym was beden to

9404 And sleȝely] A slegh B.
9406 his oone] allon B.
9409 þis] þe B.
9410 for] *om.* B.
9412 her] his B.
9413 or] & B.
9414 and] them in L.
9415 ospringe] spring B.
9416 hool &] hele in B.
9417 felowshepe] frowarde fendis B. felle] fylle *altered to* felle L.
9418 *om.* L.
9423 tofore] before B.
9424 Þenne] Þat B. to] vp to B.
9427 two] ijº L.
9428 in] being in L.
9432 was] is B.

// Þe toþ*er* haþ possitiue to nam
Þat was fully forboden Adam
Of þis fruyt god him seide   9435
I haue hit in my forbode leide
If þou so bolde be hit to byte
Þou shalt dyȝe in sorwe & site
If þou wolt my forbode holde
Þou shalt be lorde as I þe tolde   9440
Of al erþe & of paradyse
Wiþ more blisse þe*n* þou con deuyse
Þe seisine of þis adam al   fol. 55v col. 1
Alas soone he let hit fal
His greet worshepe þ*at* he had þare   9445
And brouȝte vs alle to mychel kare
Als soone as he þe appel eete
Þe lawes boþe he gon to lete
Boþe naturele & possitiue
His wyf made him to vnþryue   9450
Whenne she leued more þe fende
Þen god þat made hir so hende

// Þus was Adam for his outrage
Dryuen fro his heritage
Out of ioye and out of blis   9455
To wo & sorwe to him & his
By deþ his lyf most he tyne
Where he shal euer haue medicyne
Whe*nne* he hadde loste þ*ere* p*re*sent
His heritage by iuggement   9460
Out of þe feirest lond þat es   9473
He was put into wildernes
Þis foule synne was so vnwrast   9475
Þat of his seisyne hit gon hi*m* cast   9476

9433   toþer] oþer law L. possitiue to] breking of B.
9435   þis] þe B.
9437   so] *om.* B. hit] þerof B.
9438   & site] I hyte L.
9443   Þe . . . adam] There adam herd L. seisine] sesing B.
9446   And] *om.* B. to] in B.
9455   ioye] þe ioye T.
9456   *second* to] *om.* L.
9457   lyf] wif T. tyne] tenyd tyne, tenyd *cancelled* L.
9461–72   *om.* HTLB.
9475   vnwrast] vn vnwrest, vn *cancelled* L.
9476   of] fro B. seisyne] season L. seisyne . . . cast] sesing he was chast B.
9477–78   *om.* HTLB.

// Now is man bigyled al 9479
His owne synne made hi*m* þral 9480
Þat firste was fre as I tolde
Now haþ him sathanas to holde
To whos seruyse he hi*m* ȝelde
His þral he was to haue in welde
Whil he is þral in his seruyse 9485
He ne may be fre on no wyse
Þral may by no lawe in lede
Fre heritage aske of lordhede
Siþ he is þus þral bicomen
His heritage þus bynomen 9490
In no court owe þral be herde
Ny stonde in dome to be vnswerde
But in þe lordes þat him owe
To deme hi*m* ouþ*er* hyȝe or lowe
Þe*n*ne most him seke anoþ*er* nede 9495
To wynne his heritage to spede
Fre borne to be & not bonde fol. 55v col. 2
Þat shulde in courte shewe his eronde
His heritage aȝeyn to wynne
He most be of his owne kynne 9500
So þat he soþfaste mon shulde be
And ete not of þis forseyde tre
He most be born out of synne
And holden hadde þese lawes twy*n*ne 9504
He þ*at* neu*er* dud synne ne pliȝt 9509
What mon myȝt se so briȝt 9510

9479 al] þan B.
9480 made] haþe made B.
9482 sathanas] to sathanas, to *cancelled* T. to] in B.
9483 hi*m*] did hy*m* B.
9484 was] is B.
9485 is] his L.
9486 on no] in non B.
9487 by] be L.
9489 Siþ] Synne LB.
9490 þus] him TL; is hym B.
9491 no] non B. þral] no þrall to B.
9493–94 *om.* CG.
9495 him] he T; hem L.
9496 *second* to] and B.
9498 shulde . . . courte] in courte schuld B.
9500 He] Hym B.
9503 He] Hym B. out of] w*ith*oute B.
9504 hadde . . . lawes] haþe þis lawe B.
9505–08 *om.* HTLB.
9509 synne ne] nor B.

Þat suche a mon couþe þenke in þou3t
Þat do þat myracle mou3t
Rest a litel here whil I
A saumpel telle 3ow herby
Ensaumple cordynge þat I toke   9515
Out of seynt Robardes boke

Hit was a kyng of mychel prys
Ri3tful worþi & eke wys
Þis ilke kyng þat I of mone
He had no childe but a sone   9520
Þat wiþ his fadir was so wele
He wiste his wisdome euerydele
In al wisdome was he ryche
And algate his fadir lyche
Wiþ him of o wille & my3t   9525
His fadir wrou3te wiþ his insi3t
Al þat his fadir wolde haue wrou3te
By him to ende shulde be brou3te

// Dou3teres foure had þis kyng
To whiche vchone he 3af sumþing   9530
Of his my3te & his bounte
As fel to haue sistren Fre
To vchone dyuerse 3iftis he 3aue
Party wiþ himsel[f] to haue
Boþe of his wisdome & his my3t   9535
Þat vchone fel to haue wiþ ri3t
Of his substaunce he 3af vchon
Vchon 3af he substaunce oon
As to her fadir hit au3te to fere
Wiþoute whiche on no manere   9540
My3te he in pees his kyngdome 3eme fol. 56r col. 1

9513 here whil] here wol T; while her will L; while will B.
9514 A] And a L. saumpel] sampe to B. herby] þerby B.
9516 boke] koke T.
9518 Ri3tful] Riche B.
9520 He] *om.* B.
9525 o] oon L; all B.
9528 to] þe B.
9529 foure] iiij^e L. þis] þe B.
9533 vchone] eche B.
9534 himself] himsel H.
9536 wiþ] be B.
9540 no] non B.
9541 he] be T. in pees] *om.* B.

Ne riȝtwis domes þerynne deme
Her names shul ȝe here forþi
Þe firste of hem was called mercy
Soþfastnes þat oþer was   9545
Þe þridde riȝtwisnesse in plas
Pees þe fourþe sister hiȝt
Wiþouten pese kyng haþ no myȝt
For to reule his kynghede
Þis ilke kyng þat I of rede   9550
A seruaunt hadde in his baily
Aȝeyn his lord had done foly
And bi doom him loked was
To go to peyne for his trespas
To his moste fo feloun   9555
Was he bitauȝte into prisoun
For he hadde neuer so greet enuye
As him to haue in his baylye
Whil he was in prisoun þo
His enemye him wrouȝte ful wo   9560

// Whenne mercy him say so to be
On him she gan to haue pite
Forbere myȝte she þo no þinge
But soone coom byfore þe kynge
For to shewe him hir orisoun   9565
To delyuer þat prisoun
She seide fadir þi douȝter am I
As þiself woost witturly
Fulfilled I am of buxomnes
Of myche pite & of swetnes   9570
Þi ȝifte is me leof fadir dere
Þerfore here now my preyere
Of þis wrecche prisoun þat es
Þat he may haue forȝyuenes

9542   Ne] Be B.
9543   names] name L.
9545   þat oþer] þe toþer TLB.
9546   þridde] þryd was B.
9547   fourþe] iiij^th L.
9548   pese] thise L. kyng haþ] þe kyng had LB.
9555   his] þe B. fo] fo & LB.
9556   he] hym B.
9560   enemye] enuy B. ful] muche L.
9561   him say] say him T; sie hym L. him . . . be] gan so to se B.
9563   þo] *om.* TB.
9564   soone] first B.
9570   Of myche] Full of B. *second* of] *om.* B.

Þat is vndir his feloun fo 9575
In peyne of prisoun & of wo
Þat feloun fo him dud bigyle
And had him lad a longe whyle
To him þat þe falshede coom fro
Aȝeyn to him let hit go 9580
Lete his falshede him ȝolden be   fol. 56r col. 2
And þat prisoun be solde to me
For þou art knowen sikurly
Kyng of pite and of mercy
Þyn eldest douȝter þou wost I ame 9585
Ouer alle þi werkis is my name
Þi douȝter owe I neuer to be
But I of him may haue pite
Mercy þou owest to haue bi riȝt
For þi greet witt & þyn insiȝt 9590
And þi pite þat is so swete
Oweþ þi prisoun of bondes bete
I wol not leue mercy to crye
Bitwixe & he haue þi mercye ·

// Whenne soþfastnesse herde þis talkynge 9595
Þat mercy þus bisouȝte þe kynge
And þat she was algate aboute
For to haue þis prisoun oute
Byfore þe kyngis foot she stode
And seide fadir feire & gode 9600
Merueiles haue I herde today
Þat I may not forbere to say
Of my swete sister þat es
Mercy wiþ hir swetnes
Wolde þis prisoun delyuered ware 9605
Þat soþfastenes wolde forfare
But mercy owe not here to spede
But if soþfastenes hit bede
If my sister saue myȝt al

9575   feloun fo] fo so B.
9576   *second* of] in B.
9577   feloun . . . bigyle] foule felon he did hym wo, wo *cancelled and* gile *superscript* B.
9578   had] haþ TLB. lad] had LB.
9581   falshede him] falsnes B.
9582   þat] þe B. be] *om.* B.
9586   my] þy B.
9587   owe I] I owe B.
9588   I] ȝe B.
9589   to] to *superscript with a caret* L.
9592   þi prisoun of] þe prisoner B. bete] to bete B.
9594   Bitwixe . . . he] He must nede L; Vnto þat he B. þi] *om.* B.

Þat she wolde forecrye & cal   9610
Þenne shuldes þou be douted nouȝt
Monnes mysdedes shulde not be bouȝt
But þou art kyng euer to last
Of riȝtwisnesse & als soþfast
Þi wille is sooþ euer and ay   9615
Þis prisoun þat I of say
Þat pite on himself had nouȝt
How shuldest þou rewe on him ouȝt
Wiþ doom he mot þole forþi
Alle his mysdedis wiþ to by   9620

// Riȝtwisnesse roos vp and seide   fol. 56v col. 1
Hir resoun as she was purueide
Sir of þi douȝteres am I oon
And þou kyng so riȝtwis noon
Þi werkis alle are of prys   9625
And þi domes are alle riȝtwis
Þis þral is fro þe flemed
Wel haþ he serued to be demed
For al þe while he was fre
Mercy euer wiþ him had he   9630
Soþfastenes & riȝt also
Til he flemed vs hym fro
Hit was his owne wilful synne
Þat dud vs alle fro him twynne
He haþ him meued aȝeyn mercy   9635
Deþ him oweþ to þole forþi
Þe whiche deeþ þou him hiȝt
In prisoun be he wel by riȝt
For doom haþ ȝyuen hit him in siȝt
To soþfastnesse haue seid þe pliȝt   9640
And so þou woldest his sorwe slake
Þat he myȝte doom bifore þe take

9610 wolde] myght B.
9614 als] alle L; of B.
9617 on] of B.
9618 ouȝt] ouȝt ought, ouȝt *cancelled* L.
9620 wiþ] þerwith L.
9623 am I] I am B.
9625 alle are] ar all B.
9626 are] *om.* B.
9627 is] þat is B.
9629 he] þat he B.
9638 be] is L. be . . . wel] most he be B.
9640 To] Til T. haue] haþe L. þe] his B.
9642 bifore] by B.

For why þat doom spareþ noon
Þat soþfastnesse haþ ouergoon
To vche man she ȝyueþ wiþ wille   9645
Riȝt to haue good and ille
For soþfastenes haþ seid his sake
Þerfore wol doom him not outake
Owe no man seye him good in werd
Siþ þat pite is not herd   9650
A þat wrecche frend wiþoute
Þat no frend gete may him aboute
He may not skape where he go
But him assaileþ euer his foo
Þat witt & myȝt haþ him reft   9655
And naked his wrecche body left
Not him allone but al his kyn
He haþ to þraldom brouȝt yn
He dide him mysdo comynly
Þe doom hem coom folwynge in hy   9660
And iugget hem in soþfaste treuþe   fol. 56v col. 2
Wiþouten mercy ouþer reuþe
Nor pees at home myȝte not lende
But of lond she most wende
For pees may nowhere abyde   9665
Þere hate woneþ or werre or pryde
Nor of mercy made noon mynne
Alle lafte þe lond þat þei were ynne
Was noon of þese lafte þere
But þei alle dest[r]yed were   9670
Alle deeþ dide hem to dryue
Was noon but eiȝte laft on lyue

9645 wiþ] *om.* L.
9646 and] or B.
9650 is] nys L.
9651 wrecche] is a wrecche, is a *superscript with a caret* L. frend] fre frend, fre *cancelled* L.
9652 no] non B. aboute] oute B.
9654 assaileþ] assaieþ L.
9659 comynly] comely L.
9660 hem] *om.* B.
9661 hem] hym B.
9662 ouþer] and B.
9663 Nor] Now B. myȝte not] most B.
9666 *first* or] *om.* L.
9667 made] may B.
9669 þere] ware B.
9670 þei alle] all þay B. destryed] destyed H.
9671 deeþ] ded B.
9672 eiȝte] viijᵉ L.

Noe & his sones þre
Þat in a shippe were saued fre
His wyf & his sones wyues   9675
In al þe world laft moo on lyues
Hit is myche drede to telle
Of any doom þat was so felle
And al was riȝt in soþfastenes
Wiþouten mercy or any pees   9680

// Þe ferþe sister aftir þe þridde
Spak to þe kyng þe place amydde
Pees I hette lord of astate
Bitwene my sistren is debate
Al þe stryf bitwene hem þre   9685
Þourȝe pees hit oweþ tryed to be
For wherof serueþ any assise
Of soþfastnesse or of iustise
But for to kepe pees in londe
Doom is þerfore sett to stonde   9690
Siþ alle þese þre are sett for me
How shal I þenne forsaken be
Siþ for me al good is wrouȝt
Wiþouten me tolde for nouȝt
Saue me is not in þis werd   9695
But if þat mercy may be herd
Þou owest me here wiþouten les
For fadir art þou & prynce of pees
Pees al endeþ þat wel is wrouȝt

9673 þre] iijᵉ L.
9674 a] þe B.
9675 wyues] wyue T.
9676 moo on] no mo B.
9679 And] *om.* B. in] and B.
9680 or any] and CG.
9681 ferþe] iiijᵗʰ L. þridde] iijᵈᵉ L.
9683 astate] state B.
9684 Bitwene] Among B.
9685 þre] iijᵉ L; & þe B.
9686 Þourȝe] Be B. oweþ] owid L.
9688 *second* of] *om.* B.
9689 kepe] lepe L; sett B.
9690 þerfore] þerof B.
9691 Siþ] Synne L. þre] iijᵉ L. are . . . for] be before B.
9693 Siþ] Synne L.
9694 tolde] is tolde B.
9697–98 *reversed in* B.
9699 Pees] In pees L. al endeþ] endith all B.

Whoso haþ no pees haþ as nouȝt   9700
What is richesse who con say   fol. 57r col. 1
What is wisdome be pees away
Whoso wol for pees trauail spende
In pees forsoþe shal he ende
Þus owe pees be herde in hy   9705
For þis prisoun cryinge mercy
And of vs foure at þis assyse
Riȝtwisly to do Iustise
Wiþouten oure alle comune assent
Owe to be no Iuggement   9710
To haue recorde no doom owe
Ar we assenten alle on rowe
To oon mot we alle consent
And siþen shape þe iuggement
Or ellis owe doom be calde aȝeyn   9715
Þerfore þou wrecche þat art in peyn
Owe now to fynde sum pite
Now hastou herde my sistren þre
Here my fadir now forþi
For mercy fyneþ not to cry   9720

// Whenne þat þe kyngis sone had sene   9723
Þis stryf þo sistres bitwene
Wiþouten him myȝte þei not ende   9725
Pees bitwene hem myȝte [not] lende
Fadir he seide þi sone am I
Of þi strengþe witterly
So wel am I loued wiþ þe
Þat þi wisdome men callen me   9730
Þis world brood & longe to sene

9700   Whoso] Who B. as] *om*. B.
9701   who] whoso L.
9702   What is] And B. be pees] ȝeff pees be B.
9703   Whoso] Who B. trauail] his trauayle B.
9707   of] for B. foure] iiijᵉ L.
9710   be] be ȝeffe B.
9712   on] a L; be B.
9713   consent] assent B.
9714   þe] our B.
9718   þre] iijᵉ L.
9719   my] me B.
9720   fyneþ] sesith B. cry] d cry, d *cancelled* B.
9721-22 *om*. HTLB.
9724   Þis] The LB. þo] þe B.
9726   not] *om*. H.
9729   loued] belouyd B.
9731   brood] bl brode, bl *cancelled* L.

Hast þou made fadir þourȝe me to bene
Al þou wrouȝtest by myn insiȝt
We are boþe o strengþe & o myȝt
Of oon worshepe & of o wille 9735
Þi wille I shal euer fulfille
Fadir riȝtwis demestere
Mercy me meueþ bi hir preyere
Þat she made skilful bifore þe
For of þat wrecche I haue pite 9740
Mercy firste bigon to calle
She owȝe be herde firste of alle
For soþfastnesse algate shal I fol. 57r col. 2
At oon acorde make wiþ mercy
Þerfore fadir I wol and shal 9745
Take on me cloþing of þral
And suffere I shal þe doom on me
Þat ȝoure þral shulde vndir be
I shal crye pees in londe Iwis
And doom & pees make hem kys 9750
Þis werre to ende brynge shal I so
And saue þi folk from endeles wo

// Whoso vndirstondeþ þis saumple here
He may vndirstonde al clere
Þat þer is in oure lord riȝt 9755
Pre persones & o god of myȝt
Of god þe fadir al þing is
Of god þe sone al douȝtynys
In god þe holy goost al þing
Fulfilleþ & haþ endyng 9760
Oon in godhede vndelt is he

9732 fadir] fayre B.
9734 *first* o] oon LB. *second* o] oon LB.
9735 o] oon LB.
9738 preyere] here B.
9739 made] make B.
9742 owȝe] oght to B.
9743 algate] forsothe B.
9746 Take] Taky Take, Taky *cancelled* L.
9747 suffere] sustir L.
9748 ȝoure] oure B.
9751 werre] ward B.
9754 He] *om.* B.
9755 lord riȝt] lordes siȝt T.
9756 of myȝt] almyght B.
9759 In] Off B.
9760 &] þat B.

And oon substaunce wiþ persones þre
He hem ȝif his benesoun
Þat gladly hereþ þis sermoun
Lordyngis ȝe haue herd now   9765
Of þis world wherfore & how
Hit was wrouȝt & of þe gilt
Adam oure forme fadir spilt
And how of þraldome by no chaunce
Of his foos myȝte he haue keueraunce   9770
Aungel myȝte wiþ no resoun
Make for adam þe raunsoun
For þenne shulde noon wiþouten doute
Haue ben to aungel vndirloute
But mannes raunsonere most bi riȝt   9775
Þat make him like to aungel myȝt
Anoþer skil also we fynde
If aungel had taken monnes kynde
Þenne were he leþiere þen he was ere
For to haue powere þere   9780
And semeliere for to doun falle
As dude þe prynce firste of alle
And if god had made anoþer man   fol. 57v col. 1
For to raunsoun þat ilke adam
Hit myȝt not haue performed riȝt   9785
Þe raunsoun of adames pliȝt
For al þe bale of him gon brede
Þe bote most ben of his sede
No patriarke ny no prophete
Miȝt be sent þe synne to bete   9790
For þey geten were in synne

9762   þre] iijᵉ LB.
9767   of þe] for B.
9768   forme] first B.
9770   he] *om.* B. keueraunce] no keueraunce H; curans L; receueraunce B.
9771   Aungel] Al Angill, Al *cancelled* L. no] all B.
9773   noon] man CGB.
9775   bi] be T.
9776   make] made B. him] hem L.
9777   also] ȝett B.
9779   leþiere] logher B. was] wer L.
9781   semeliere for] lightlyer B.
9784   For to] To bye & B. þat ilke] þilk B.
9785   haue] be B.
9786   pliȝt] wyght L.
9787   of] on L.
9789   ny no] ne B.
9790   þe] þat B.
9791   þey ... were] begetyn ar B.

As comynly is al monkynne
How myȝte þei mon of synne make clene
Certis no wey as hit is sene
Siþ aungel auȝt þen hit not do 9795
Ny man had no myȝte þerto
Who shulde make þis raunsoun þon
Must be boþe god & mon
Mon for mon to suffere wo
God to sle þe fend also 9800
Man to dyȝe god for to ryse
Miȝt ellis none take þis seruyse
Myche was his swetnes þan
Greet pite had he of man
Þat come wolde fro þat hyȝe toure 9805
To liȝte in a maydenes boure
And lafte so many shepe alone
To seche on þat mys was gone
May neuer mon here sikurly
A lord of so greet mercy 9810
Whoso on siche a lorde wolde þinke
His greet loue & myche swynke
Þat firste wold so oure liknes haue
And siþen for vs his seluen ȝaue
His hert auȝte better breke in þre 9815
Þen fro his biddyngis fle 9816

Of swete ihesu þe prophesye
Listeneþ and I shal seye on hye

Of ysay I rede biforn 9817

9792 is] ar B.
9795 Siþ] Syn L; Þe B. auȝt . . . hit] þenne hit auȝte TLB.
9796 Ny] And B. man] noon T. þerto] þerto to H.
9797 Who] Whoso T.
9798 Must] Hyt must L. be boþe] boþe be T.
9801 *first* to] for to B. ryse] aryse L.
9802 ellis none] non els LB.
9805 *second* þat] þe B.
9806 liȝte in a] a symple B.
9808 mys . . . gone] was mysgon B.
9810 A] Off B.
9811 wolde] wol TB.
9813 wold so] so wolde TLB.
9814 his seluen] himseluen TLB.
9815 His] Þe B. þre] iijᵉ L.
9816 biddyngis] bidding B. fle] to fle TL; for to fle B.
9816b on] in B.
9817 ysay] Isaak L.

He seide a childe is vs born
A sone is ȝyuen vs for oure [n]ede
Susteyne he shal his lordhede   9820
A merueilous name haue [he] shalle   fol. 57v col. 2
Counseiler m[e]n shal him calle
Stalworþe god men shal him nome
God fadir of worldis to come
His riȝt name prynce of pees   9825
Þus are þe names wiþouten les
Þat þe prophete had on him leyde
Here now why þei are seide
Selcouþe his firste name is
More selcouþ herde we neuer ar þis   9830
Ne neuer shul bi riȝtwis dome
Þat god himself a man bicome
For if þou fonde as men may fynde
A childe ouer chargide so wiþ kynde
Þat hade feet or hondis þre   9835
As ofte men sawe & ȝitt may se
And if þou aftir anoþer fonde
Þat wantide ouþer foot or honde
Were þei selcouþe þerfore I say
Certis me þinkeþ þat nay   9840
Man þat couþe any good
Wolde no selcouþe haue in mood
Ouer carke of kynde haþ hem take
Or kynde turned hem by sum wrake

9818   is vs] schuld be B.
9819   nede] rede H.
9821   name] maner B. he] I H.
9822   men] man H.
9823   Stalworþe] Strong B.
9824   worldis] worldede B. come] tame B.
9826   Þus] Thise L. þe] his B.
9827   Þat] This L.
9829   Selcouþe] Wondirfull B.
9831   riȝtwis] rightful B.
9832   a] is B.
9833   men] man B.
9834   so] *om.* B.
9835–36   *reversed in* B.
9835   Þat . . . or] Two armys & B. þre] iijᵉ L.
9836   men] man B.
9838   wantide . . . foot] lackyd afftyr fete B.
9839   I] to B.
9842   no] non B.
9843   hem] hym L.
9844   hem] *om.* B.

Siche shap to se is no ferly 9845
Al is þe wille of god myȝty
But þus myȝtes þou selcouþ calle
If þou him say & so myȝte falle
Þat in al manhede he wore
Wiþouten lesse wiþouten more 9850
So þat he were mon soþfast
And al his shap wiþouten last
And had þat shap chaunged away
Into a beestes sooþ to say
Whoso myȝte fynde suchon whare 9855
Men myȝte sey selcouþe he ware
But selcouþer a þousonde folde
Is þis childe I haue of tolde
Boþe is god & mon by riȝte
Of soþfastenes is þis þe siȝte 9860
Of mannes kynde him faileþ nouȝt fol. 58r col. 1
And al is fully þat he wrouȝt
Al þinge of him bigynnynge tooke
As is bifore tolde in þis boke
But he is a god of myȝt 9865
Þat sende him in erþe to liȝt
Þat on þis wyse as we rede
Fully took oure monhede
Siþ he bicoom wolde mon
Of wommon born most he be þon 9870

9845 no] non B.
9846 myȝty] almyghty B.
9853 þat] the LB.
9855 Whoso] Who L. suchon whare] one owhar B.
9857 þousonde] M¹ L.
9858 Is þis] Þis is þe B.
9859 Boþe] Þat boþe B.
9860 is þis] þis is TLB.
9862 fully] fullfilled B.
9864 is] *om.* B. þis] þe B.
9865 a] one B.
9866 erþe] þe erþ B.
9869 Siþ] Synne LB. bicoom wolde] wolde bicom TLB.
9870 he] hym B.
    After l. 9870, ll. 9822–70 repeated in L *with the following variants:*
9826 Þus] Thise L.
9832 a man] anon L.
9835 þre] iijᵉ L.
9842 no] *superscript with a caret* L.
9860 is þis] this is, is *superscript with a caret* L.
9865 But] And L. a] *om.* L. of myȝt] alle myȝt L.
9869 Siþ] Synne L. bicoom wolde] wold bycome L.

For to louse monkynde of wo
Þat laft was wiþ þe fend his fo
But god þat wolde so hi*m* nest
In clene stude þen most he rest
A clene stude he chees forþi   9875
For to make his herbergery   9876

// In a castel semely set   9879
Strengþed wel wiþouten let   9880
Þis castel was of loue & grace
Boþe of socour & of solace
Vpon þe marche hit stond in dede
Of en[m]ye haþ hit no drede   9884
Þis castel is so polisshed briȝte   9887
Þat hit may neyȝe no waryed wiȝt
Ny no maner gyn of were
May cast þerto hit to dere   9890
Wiþ walles foure closed of stoon
Fairer in al erþe is noon
Baylyes haþ þis castel þre
Wiþ faire wardes semely to se
As ȝe shul heraftir deuyse   9895
But hit is feirer mony wyse
Þen tonge con telle or hert þinke
Or any clerke write wiþ ynke
A deop dyche is þeraboute
Wel wrouȝte wiþouten doute   9900
Wiþ carnels is hit set ful wele
Batailed aboute al wiþ sele
Seuen barbicans are þ*ere* diȝt
Þat are made wiþ myche sleiȝt
Vchone þei haue ȝate & tour   9905 fol. 57r col. 2

9871   of] from B.
9872   laft] laste L; laght CG.
9874   he] her H; hym B.
9876   For] *om.* B. his] in his B.
9877–78   *om.* GHTLB.
9879   semely] well B.
9883   stond] stode B.
9884   enmye] enuye H; enmye G; fede C; enemyes L. haþ] had B. no] no*n* B.
9885–86   *om.* HTLB.
9887   so polisshed] polised so B.
9891   foure] iiij^e L.
9893   þre] iiij^e L.
9895   deuyse] tymes B.
9900   wiþouten doute] w*ith*in & w*ith*oute B.
9901   ful] *om.* B.
9903   Seuen] vij L.

Þat neuer shul faile socour
Wiþ disese shal he neuer be led
Þe mon þat þiderwarde is fled 9908
Þis castel is not to hyde 9911
Peynted on þe vtter side
Wiþ þre colouris of dyuerse hew
Þe groundewal next hit is so trewe
Metyng wiþ þe roche of stoon 9915
Of grenes þere wanteþ noon
For þat grenes I dar wel say
His hew holdeþ lastynge ay
Þe toþer hewe nexte to fynde
Is al blewe men callen ynde 9920
Þe myddel hew is þat I mene
To siȝte is hit selcouþe clene
Þe þridde colour þere ymeynt
Þat þo carneyles wiþ are peynt
Hit ȝyueþ leem to alle so briȝt 9925
And ȝyueþ to þe neþemast liȝt
As rose reed hit is in spryng
And semeþ as a brennyng þing
Waried wiȝt comeþ þer neuer
But swetnes is lastyng euer 9930
Amyddes þe heȝest tour to telle 9935
Þer springeþ of watir a cleer welle
Þerfro renneþ foure stremes swete
Þourȝe þat grauel & þat grete
And so þei fallen euery dyke

9906 socour] no socoure B.
9908 þiderwarde is] is þedyr B.
9909–10 *om.* GHTLB.
9911 Þis] Is þis, Is *cancelled* B.
9913 þre] iijᵉ L; þe B.
9914 next hit] *om.* B.
9916 grenes] grevis L. wanteþ] lackiþ B.
9917 grenes] grevis L; gren B.
9920 al] a B.
9922 is hit] it is B.
9923 þere] is þat B.
9924 carneyles] corners L.
9925 to . . . so] also B.
9926 And] It B.
9927 in] to B.
9928 And] It B.
9931–34 *om.* HTLB.
9935 Amyddes] In middes of B.
9936 of . . . a] a water of L; a B.
9937 Þerfro] Þerof B. renneþ] rynnyng L. foure] iiijᵉ L.
9939 And] Lord B. euery] euyr þe B.

Whoso is þere wel may lyke   9940
Whoso myȝte wiþ þat watir him wesshe
He shulde haue hele on al his flesshe
Wiþynne þis tour is set forþi
A tour faire of yuory
Þat is of gretter liȝt & leem   9945
Þen someres day is sonne beem
Craftily casten wiþ a compas
Clymbynge vp wiþ seuen pas
Vchone wiþ her mesure met
Semely þere are þei set   9950
Þe leem of liȝt euer le[m]es newe   fol. 58v col. 1
Þat mengeþ wiþ þe colouris hewe
Was kyng ne cayser neuer here
Þat euer sat in siche chayere
Ȝitt fairer was wiþouten ende   9955
Þe stide þere god himself wolde lende
Was neuer siche anoþer holde
Ne wyser man in world to wolde
Ne neuer beþ made wiþ monnes wit
For god himself deuysed hit   9960
To his bihoue sondry & sere
Þerfore owe we to holde hit dere

// Þis castel is of belde and blis
Þere myrþe is neuermore to mys
Castel to haue of hope & holde   9965
Her griþþe to haue may þei be bolde

9940 lyke] hym lyke B.
9941 him] be B.
9942 shulde] schall B. on] of B.
9944 tour faire] fayre toure B.
9946 someres . . . is] in þe day þe B.
9947 casten] craftely L. a] *om.* B.
9948 seuen] vij L.
9951 lemes] lenes H.
9952 mengeþ] men mengyþ L; lemyþ B. colouris] riche B.
9953 neuer] evir L.
9954 euer] neuer B. siche] swich a B.
9955 Ȝitt] Hyt L.
9957 Was] Þere was B.
9958 Ne] No B.
9961 sondry] sumdele B.
9962 owe we] we owe B.
9963 belde and] bled & of B.
9964 myrþe . . . neuermore] neuermore is myrþe B. is . . . to] dothe nevir L.
9965 &] in B.

Þat is þat body of þat berde
Had neuer noon so blessed werde
Ny neuer so mony maneres gode
As mayden mary mylde of mode 9970
Hit is vp sett as in þe marche
And stondeþ for shelde & targe
Aȝeynes alle oure felouns fo
Þat euer wayten vs to slo
Þe roche þat is polisshed sliȝt 9975
Þe mayden mary hert ful briȝt
Þat þouȝte neuer to wicked dede
But euer lyued in maydenhede
Þat she chees þe firste day
She kept hit in mekenes ay 9980
Þe foundement þat firste is leyde
Nexte þe roche as hit is seyde
Þat peynted is wiþ grene hewe
And lasteþ euer Iliche newe
Þat is ende of þat mayden clene 9985
Liȝtyng hir holy herte shene
Grenes lastyng euer and ay
Bitokeneþ endynge of þat may
Good endynge of al & al
Of alle vertues is groundwal 9990

// Þe myddel hew þat is of ynde fol. 58v col. 2
Is no man þat may fairer fynde
Of soþfastenes tokene hit is
Trouþe stedefaste & tendurnes
She serued oure lord of myȝt 9995

9967   *first* þat] þe B. berde] brede B.
9968   Had] Þat B.
9969   Ny] No B.
9970   mayden mary] mary mayden TL.
9972   for] boþe for B.
9974   euer . . . vs] wayteþ vs euyr for B.
9975   Þe] Þat B. sliȝt] right B.
9976   Þe] Þat B. mayden mary] mary mayden T.
9980   She] Þat sche B. hit] *om.* B.
9981   firste] next B.
9983   Þat] *om.* B. is] it is B.
9984   And] Þat B.
9987   Grenes] Grene is L; Þe grenes B.
9988   endynge] þe endyng B.
9990   is] þe B.
9992   þat] *om.* B.
9994   stedefaste] stedfastnes L.

In mekenes swete day & ny3t
Þe þridde colour of hem alle
Hit couereþ al aboute þe walle
And hit reed as any blode
Of alle þese oþere is noon so gode   10000
Þat is þe holy charite
Was kyndeled in þat lady fre
And aboute bileid þat lady shene
To goddes seruyse she 3af hir clene
Þe foure torettes þere Isett   10005
Þat castel fro harme to lett
Þat are foure vertues principales
Whiche men callen cardinales
Alle oþere vertues of hem han holde
Þerfore þei are for cheef Itolde   10010
Þat is ri3twisnesse & meeþ
Insi3te & strengþe to telle ben eeþ
At þis 3ate are foure porteris
Þat noþing may come In þat deris
Þe bayles þre of þat castel   10015
Þat so wel wrou3t is to tel
Þat is in compas wrou3te aboute
And kepeþ al þe werke fro doute
On þe ouermast stage was sett
Hir maydenhede meke of met   10020
Þat neuer wemmed ones wase
She was so filde ful of grace
Þe mydmast bayly of þo þre
Bitokeneþ wel hir chastite

9996   swete] swyþe L.
9998   couereþ al] coueryd B.
9999   hit] hit is TB.
10000   þese] this L. is] er B.
10001   þe] that B.
10005   foure] iiij^e L; fayre B. torettes] turret L.
10006   Þat] Þe B.
10007   foure] iiij L; þe foure B.
10008   Whiche] Þat B.
10009   of] on L.
10010   for] *om*. B.
10011   is] ar B.
10013   þis] eche B. foure] iiij portours, portours *cancelled* L.
10015   þre] iij^e L.
10016   is] ben B.
10017   in] þe B.
10019   On] Off B.
10021   wemmed ones] oons wemmyd L.
10023   þo] þe TLB.

Þe ouermast wiþouten faile   10025
May betokene hir spousaile
Name of baily hit haþ forþy
For hit hir helde euer in baily
Makeles is she sooþ to say
Spoused modir & clene may   10030
By oon mot he go of þese þre   fol. 59r col. 1
Þat in þis world wol saued be
Þe barbicans seue*n* þat ben aboute
Þer stonden þre bailyes wiþoute
Þat wel kepen þat castel   10035
From arwe shot & quarel
Þat are seuen v*er*tues to telle
Þe seuen synnes are set to quelle
3e shulde hem here wiþoute*n* abyde
Þe firste of hem is cleped pride   10040
And fully is ou*er*comen algate
Þere buxomnes halt hir state
Charite eu*er* fordoþ enuye
And abstinens glotenye
Þe chastite of þis lady   10045
Ouercomeþ al luste of lecchery
Gredynes of euerychone
Hir fredom fordoþ hit þon
Mi3te neu*er* of wrethe in hir bihete
Hir mekenes was so grete   10050
Goostly gladnes was hir amyd
Þat al hir heuynes fordid
Þat welle of grace spronge hir Inne
Þat fyned neu*er*more to rynne

10026   spousaile] speciale C.
10027   Name] Man L.
10028   For] Þ*at* B. hir] hit T.
10031   þre] iij^e L.
10033   seue*n*] vij L.
10034   Þer] Þey B. þre] iij^e L; þe þre B.
10037–38   *om.* B.
10037   seuen] vij L.
10038   seuen] vij L.
10039   shulde] shul TLB. abyde] byde B.
10040   of . . . cleped] is þe rote of B.
10042   Þere] Þe B. halt hir] hathe his B.
10043   eu*er* fordoþ] w*ith*stondith B.
10046   al] *om.* B. of] & L.
10047   Gredynes] Þe gredynes B.
10049   of] *om.* B. wrethe] wreche T.
10052   heuynes] enmyis B.
10054   fyned] restyd B.

God ȝaf his grace to alle his dere   10055
And dalt hit wiþ mesures sere
But to hir þat his owne wase
Al hol he ȝaf fully his grase
But þat grace of hir brestes
Ouer al þis world grace kestes   10060
Þerfore is she calde in places
Modir of pite & of graces
What may I calle þo dykes
Willeful pouert þat man lykes
No gyn may on erþe be wrouȝt   10065
May caste to dere þis castel ouȝt
By whiche þe fend waryed wiȝt
Ouercome was & lost his myȝt
Þat hadde so myche myȝte biforn
Þat was no man of modir born   10070   fol. 59r col. 2
Miȝt kepe him fro þat fende felle
But he hem hadde to pyne of helle
Þis ilke lady soþely is she
Þat god seide þe nedder to
Suche a wommon shulde sprynge   10075
Þat shulde his hede al to þringe

// Now blessed be þat byrde of grace
Þe worþiest þat euer ȝitt wase
Þe kyng of al wiþouten wene
His sete made in hir so clene   10080
To reste in hir trewe body

10055   *first and second* his] her B.
10056   mesures] mesure B.
10058   hol] holy B.
10060   þis] þe B.
10061   places] place B.
10062   of graces] well of *grace* B.
10063   þo] þe TLB.
10064   man] men B.
10065   No] Þere I ne B. on] in B. be] I B.
10066   May . . . þis] Þat mayd der þat B.
10067   waryed] þat werd B.
10070   Þat] Þere B.
10071   þat] þe B. felle] so fell B.
10072   hem] hym B. pyne] þe payn B.
10074   nedder] eddir L.
10075   shulde] schall B.
10076   shulde his] schall þyn B.
10077   byrde] birþen B.
10078   ȝitt] *om.* B.
10080   made] sett B.

To brynge vs out of oure foly
And took hem out of p*r*isou*n* strang
Þat hadde layn þerin lang
Ful lef was vs þat lady lele   10085
Þat goodnesses bar in hir so fele
More þen any shaft þat es
But hir sone of riʒtwisnes
Þat in hir louely body liʒt
Made hir so monyfolde briʒt   10090
He coom in at þe ʒate sperde
And so hit was whe*nn*e he forþferde
As þe so*nn*e gooþ þourʒe glas
He myʒt do what his wille was
Mony soule lady is comen þe to   10095
And calleþ at þe ʒate vndo
Knockyng hit fyneþ not to crye
Lady swete þou haue mercye
Vndo vndo lady þyn ore
To þi caitif biset ful sore   10100
Wiþoute þi castel I am biset
Harde wiþ þre fomen þret
Þis world my flesshe þe fend als
Þat fylen me wiþ fondyng fals
To make me falle in fulþes fele   10105
Al aʒeyn my soule hele
A greet gederynge hulde þei togider
Þe fend formast he coom þider
Wiþ þre folyes bi his syde
Þo were slouþe enuye & pryde   10110

10082   out of] all fro B.
10084   layn þerin] þerin lyen B. lang] so long L.
10086   in hir] vs B.
10087   any] ane B.
10091   sperde] spred sperd, spred *cancelled* L.
10092   forþferde] out ferde B.
10093   gooþ þourʒe] doþ þurgh þe B.
10095   Mony] Many a LB.
10096   And] Þat B. þe] þy B.
10097   fyneþ] vaylet B.
10099   lady] þi lady H.
10100   caitif] kaytevis B.
10102   Harde] Fast B. þret] grete B.
10103   Þis] Þe B.
10104   fylen] folowith B. me] men T.
10105   fulþes fele] filþe ill B.
10106   hele] will B.
10108   he] *om.* B. coom] coom to H.
10110   Þo were] Þey ben B.

Þe world haþ two to his seruyse   fol. 59v col. 1
Þat is auarise & couetise
Þe flesshe haþ redy him by
Lecchery and gloteny
Þourȝe þese am I doun dryuen   10115
And as a wrecche al to ryuen
I drede me sore longe to ly
But if þi grace helpe lady
Þat on þe trist be wont to couer
Do me to passe þes diches ouer   10120
Þere þe castel stondeþ stabel
And charite is so couenabul

Listeneþ now to my lessoun
Þat wole here of þe concepcioun

Hereþ now þat wole haue mede
& I shal ȝow þe story rede
Of þe holy maydenes birþe   10125
Þat brouȝte vs alle to ioye & myrþe
How prophecies coom to ende
Ar þe iewes wiste vnhende
Þe ȝerde þat firste bar þe flour
And als þe fruyt of swote sauour   10130
Þis book is of no iaperye
But of god & oure ladye
Þerfore I rede of hem ȝe here
Þat may ȝou helpe in ȝoure mystere
And leue ȝoure wantounshipe a while   10135
Þat lyf & soule may boþe fyle
Whoso in riȝt trouþe is blynde
Þerof siȝte shal he fynde
For hit is vncouþe & vnwone

10111 two to] ijº to L; vnto B.
10112 auarise &] þe syn of B.
10114 Lecchery] Ire lechery B.
10115 þese . . . I] þis I am B.
10119 þe trist] þy þrist B.
10120 to] *om.* B.
10121 stabel] so stabyll B.
10122b of] *om.* T.
10124 þe] a B.
10128 þe] *om.* B. wiste] wist þat were B.
10130 als] *om.* B.
10131 no] non B.
10134 may] may may, *first* may *cancelled* L.
10135 wantounshipe] vntounnship L; wantones B.
10138 Þerof] Here in L. shal] here shal TB.

Þe fadir to bicome þe sone 10140
He þat bigon alle þinge
Coom to take his bigynnynge
And so for to come to hym
We shul bigynne at ioachim
Fadir he was of þat marye 10145
Þat ȝate was of oure mercye
His wyf het dame Anna
And hir sister ismaria
Ismaria & anna were two fol. 59v col. 2
Sistres I wene wiþouten mo 10150
Þe formast bare elizabeth
An holy lady mylde of meth
Þat spoused was to Zachary
Ion þe baptist bar þat lady
His modir was she out of drede 10155
As furþer in þis book we rede
Þis oþer sister to vndirstonde
Ioachim hadde to husbonde
Of him we wol oure story rede
For worþiest hit is in dede 10160
Ioachim bryngere of bote
He was comen of dauid rote
Born he was in þat cite
Of nazareth in galile
Loued he was in þat cuntre 10165
For his mychel humilite
Dam anna had he to wyf
A blessed couple wiþouten stryf 10168
More loue myȝte noon be wiþ 10171
Þen was of hem wiþynne her kiþ
So douȝty was þis ioachim
Þat god himself was wiþ him
So holy lyf þei lyued euer 10175

10144   at] as B.
10149   two] ij° L.
10151   formast] eldest B.
10152   An] Alle L.
10156   þis] þe B.
10157   to] I B.
10158   Ioachim hadde] Had Ioachim B.
10160   hit] he B.
10167   to] to his B.
10169–70   *om.* HTLB.
10172   of] *with* LB. wiþynne] in L. kiþ] lyf L.
10173   douȝty] holy B.
10175   lyf] a lyf L.

Þat god wraþþed þei neuer
To tilþe he tent & tiþe ȝaf lele
In þre his godis dud he dele
Þat god had lant of his loue
To pore he ȝaf a party one   10180
Þe secounde party þat he walt
Was amonge þe prestis dalt
Þe þridde party wiþ him left
For her owne despense eft
Miȝte no man forsoþe be   10185
Of more loue ny charite   10186
Soþfaste man was he þan   10189
Of rote of iesse he cam   10190
Fadir of dauid gentil kyng
Ioachim coom of his ospring
Þis dam anna his wyf   fol. 60r col. 1
In trouþe ladde she hir lyf
Hir godenes & gode fame   10195
So sprong þat noon couþe hir blame
In almesdede hir lyf she ledde
As we fynde in þe story redde
Twenty ȝeer no childe she bare
Þerfore had she mychel kare   10200
Eiþer þouȝte of oþere shame
Þei wist not whom to blame
Þerfore to god avowe þei ȝaue
If þei myȝte any childe haue
Wheþer hit were she or he   10205
To god offeride shulde hit be
In þe temple to serue þore
Whil hit lyued euermore

10177   tiþe ȝaf] typed B.
10180   pore] pore men B. a party] *om.* B.
10182   Was] *om.* B. dalt] he it dalt B.
10184   despense] spens B.
10186   ny] nor B.
10187–88 *om.* HTLB, *reversed in* C.
10189   Soþfaste] A stedeffaste B.
10190   rote] þe rote B. he] *om.* B.
10191–92 *om.* B.
10195   Hir] In L. &] & in L; & her B.
10196   So] *om.* B.
10198   þe] *om.* B.
10199   Twenty] xx^{ti} L. ȝeer] wynter B.
10201   oþere] other, ot *superscript with a caret* L.
10202   Þei] Thy L. whom to] who was in B.
10205   he] she L.
10208   euermore] foreuermore B.

Chylde to haue þei preyed longe
And gode werkis duden amonge   10210
Þei halwede ay þe festis dere
Þat iewes bad in þat ȝere
Among whiche I ȝow telle
A greet feest in wyntur felle
Þat iewes helde in halewynge   10215
Of temple salomon þe kynge
Vchone to þe temple brouȝt
Dyuerse ȝiftis as þei mouȝt
Summe wiþ lesse & summe wiþ more
Offered vp her ȝiftis þore   10220
And vchone for dyuerse resoun
Coom þider to make orisoun
Þe patriarke was not away
But þere vndide hem her lay
Wiþ moyses tables in his hond   10225
Þo were men god dredond
To þis feest coom ioachim
And mony frendis also wiþ him
For to preye and to honoure
Almyȝty god her creatoure   10230
Ioachym forþ gon stonde
And made him redy to offronde
Þe patriarke het Isacar   fol. 60r col. 2
Whenne he of ioachym was war
Towarde þe auter gan he stryde   10235
Ioachim he seide abyde
Al þis pepul here bifore
I bidde ȝow come no furþer more
Ioachym here shal noon
Offeryng of þyn hond forþ goon   10240
Þou owȝe not ȝitt in no wyse

10209 Chylde] A childe B.
10211 ay] euer B.
10212 Þat ... ȝere] Þat Iuus halud þan bi ȝere G; Þe Iues war wonto halu bi yere C.
       bad] held B. þat] þe B.
10213 I] as I B.
10218 mouȝt] þoght B.
10219 *first and second* wiþ] *om.* B. &] *om.* L.
10220 her] our B.
10221 dyuerse] dyuerce dyuerce, *first* dyuerce *cancelled* L.
10224 her] þe B.
10228 frendis also] oþer frendis B. also] alle L.
10230 her] oure T.
10232 him] *om.* B. to] his B.
10236 Ioachim ... seide] He sayde Ioachim B.
10240 of] oute of B. forþ] oute B.

To make here no sacrifise
Go make to god þi preyere clene
Þyn offerynge may not here be sene
Ioachim þou3te mychel shame   10245
And sayde haue I serued siche blame
Ouþer am I so ful of synne
Þat I no chirche owe come Inne
My preyeres to god to make
Say me sir what is my sake   10250
What haue I done a3eyn þe lay
I pray 3ow sir þat 3e me say
Gladly wolde I vndirstonde
Why þou forsakes myn offronde

//   Þenne saide Isacar parfay   10255
Ioachim I shal þe say
I ne seide hit [not] forþi
Þat I haue seyn þi foly
Þi synne 3itt neuer I sawe
But god himself seiþ in þe lawe   10260
Whoso in israel haþ no sede
He is cursed as we rede
Þis seed fruyt of childe is tolde
And so ow3e vche mon hit holde
Þis is þe lawe in oure si3t   10265
He calleþ þat mon maledi3t
Þat haþ no childe mayde ny knaue
Noon say we þe neuer haue
Of þe lawe for þis resoun
Is fallen on þe [þe] malisoun   10270
For þer comeþ no childe of þe
Þin offerynge mot forsaken be
Þe tre þat bereþ no fruyt in londe   fol. 60v col. 1
Shulde not among oþere stonde

10243–44 *reversed in* HTLB.
10243 Go] To TLB.
10248 owe] may B. Inne] within B.
10249 *first* to] *om.* L.
10253 wolde] will B.
10257 ne] *om.* B. not] *om.* H.
10259 Þi] Þe B. 3itt neuer] neuer 3ett B.
10263 childe is] childre er B.
10264 ow3e] holde B. vche mon] echon L.
10266 calleþ] callid L.
10270 *second* þe] *om.* H; þis B.
10272 mot forsaken] forsake mvste B.
10273 bereþ . . . fruyt] no fruyt bereþ TLB.

Whenne þou hast childe mayde or sone   10275
Þin offeryng hidur is welcome
Whenne Ioachim þese wordis herde
Shome him þou3te & þus vnswerde
Þat I naue childe reweþ me sore
If I my3te haue leuer me wore   10280
Þat I haue no childe hidurtille
Hit is al long on goddis wille
Þou3e I wiþouten be in dede
Whenne god wol he may sende me sede
Þer is no man coude say   10285
How he shamed was þat day
For þis shame & þis vmbreyde
Þat Isacar had to him seide
Fro chirche he went for þat shome
For shame wolde he not go home   10290
But to þe herdis of his fe cattle
Þat he had of greet plente
Into a wildernes he went
Þere as his fe was present
Pages were his herdes none   10295
But stalworþe men euerychone
Þat my3t a3eynes þeues fi3t
And couþe ryse at tyme of ny3t
And loke her beestis in tyme of nede
Ioachim to hem he 3ede   10300
Among his beestis dwelt he þore
In preyere wake & wepyng sore
Fastinge he was in wille to be
Til god wolde to him se
Fastinge longe had he not bene   10305
Þat god hym sent an aungel shene

10276 hidur is] is hedir B.
10279 naue] haue no B.
10283 Þou3e] 3effe B.
10284 he] I L; *om.* B. sende me] haue L.
10285 is] was B. coude] þat couþe B.
10286 How ... shamed] So sore aschamyd he B.
10287 vmbreyde] vpbrayde B.
10290 wolde ... not] ne my3t he L.
10293 a] *om.* TLB.
10294 as] *om.* B.
10295 none] nome L.
10296 stalworþe] strong B. euerychone] wer þey echon L.
10298 And ... of] Þat com a3en hem be B.
10300 he] *om.* B.
10304 to] tylle L.
10306 Þat] But L; When B.

Þat of þe liȝte þat coom of hym
Sore aferde was Ioachim
For þat briȝtenes was he drad
And stille stood as he were mad   10310
But þat aungel þat bi hym stoode
Brouȝte to him tiþyngis gode
Ioachim he seide make good chere   fol. 60v col. 2
I am oure lordis messangere
Hidur I am to þe sende   10315
Þi mournynge chere to amende
He haþ herde þi preyere
Now he þe sendeþ þyn vnswere
For þe shame & þe vmbreyde
Þat Isacar þe prest þe seide   10320
Þouȝe þou no childe had hidirto
For noon euel is hit so
Þouȝe god oþerwhile be stille
He may al worche at his wille
Wiþouten childe ofte suffereþ he   10325
Mon & wommon longe to be
Til þei be sumdel in elde
Þenne sent he hem to welde
Þat may men se þe childe herby
Is riȝt comen [n]o[gh]t of lecchery   10330
Of abraham hast þou he[r]de say
How longe he lyued mony a day
Wiþouten childe in hope alone
Þenne sent god hym siche one
Þat in his seed shulde be blessed   10335
And monkynde toward god dressed
Iacob als & rachel his wyf
Longe ladden togider her lyf
Of hem aftir Ioseph þe gode

10311 *first* þat] þe B.
10312 tiþyngis] tyþing B.
10315 I am] am I TLB.
10318 þe] *om.* TB. þyn] þe B.
10319 vmbreyde] vpbrayde B.
10320 Isacar] Isaac L.
10321 Þouȝe] They L; ȝeff B.
10322 is hit] it is B.
10323 Þouȝe] ȝoff B.
10326 longe] for B.
10329 herby] þerby B.
10330 noght] out HTLB; noght CG.
10331 herde] hede H.
10332 mony] & mane B.
10337 &] *om.* B.

Al in her elde þat blessed fode   10340
Þat stiwarde was of egipt cuntre
And had þe londe in his pouste
Samuel als þe ful of riȝt
And sampson als þat was so wiȝt
Boþe hem bar wymmen olde   10345
Þat out of childeberyng were tolde
Children þat of siche are bred
Are born to stonde in myche sted
And ben douȝty in her dede
And ofte desseruen myche mede   10350
Leue þese tales witturly
Þou shalt haue a childe in hy
A mayden childe not þerto longe   fol. 61r col. 1
Þi wyf of þe shal vndirfonge
Maria shalt þou do hir calle   10355
Fulfilde wiþ goddis grace oueralle
She shal be al to god hende
To hym presented at þre ȝeer ende
As þou of hir hast made þi vow
She shal be flour of maydenes now   10360
Of maydenes alle she shal be flour
And she shal bere ȝoure saueour
Ihesu cryst alle mennes hele
And loke þou leue þis tale for lele
Go now home þi gate   10365
Þou shalt fynde at þe gilden ȝate
Of ierusalem anna þi wyf
Þat is for þe in mychel stryf
To seche þe she noot whider to go
Þou shalt fynde hir þere so   10370

10343   þe] *om.* B.
10344   als] *om.* TLB.
10348   myche] eche L.
10350   ofte desseruen] ben worþy B.
10351   þese . . . witturly] þis tale witterly herof þou haue no drede B.
10353   þerto] herto B.
10355   shalt þou] þou schalt B.
10356   wiþ] of B. oueralle] withall B.
10357   al] *om.* B. hende] all hende B.
10358   þre] iijᵉ L.
10361   alle] *om.* B. be] bere þe B.
10362   And] *om.* B. ȝoure] oure B.
10364   tale] *om.* B.
10365   Go now] To now faste B. þi] aȝeyn þi T; ayen the L.
10366   þe] *om.* B.
10369   noot] woot not T. whider] wheþer B.
10370   fynde hir] her fynde B.

Certeynly þenne þat þou trowe
Al þat I haue þe tolde nowe
Whenne þe aungel þus had seide
He went aȝeyn at a breyde
But ar he wente he bad him make   10375
Sacrifise for goddes sake

Ioachim þo was glad & blyþe
Vp he sett an autere swiþe
Sacrifise he made on þis manere
Of ten lombis þat whyte were   10380
Þat han tokenyng bi hemselue
Siþen aftir of bolis twelue
And at þe laste an hundride sheepe
How he hem dalt take now kepe
To god he lett þo lambren falle   10385
To pore men þo boles alle
Þe hundride sheep þat I of ment
To alle þe comyn were Isent
On þis manere offered he
And dalt þus þese þingis þre   10390
Þese lombes that I of spake
Bitokeneþ ihesu crist was take
And done on cros for oure wyte   fol. 61r col. 2
And for vs sufferide greet despite
Þe twelue boles offeride also   10395
Twelue apostlis bitokenen þo
Þat for crist þoled sorwe & care

10371   þenne] *om.* B.
10372   þe tolde] tolde þe TLB.
10373   þus] þei L.
10377   þo . . . &] was þo ful B.
10380   ten] x L.
10381   han] gave L.
10382   bolis twelue] bokys xij L.
10383   at . . . laste] aftyrwarde B. hundride] C L.
10384   now] gode B.
10385   þo] þe B.
10386   þo] þe B.
10387   hundride] C L.
10388   Isent] þay sent B.
10390   þre] iijᵉ L.
10391   Þese] Þe B.
10392   crist] þat B. was take] without lak L.
10393   And] That was L. on] on þe L.
10395   twelue boles] xij bokys L. offeride also] betokenith þo B.
10396   Twelue] The xij L; Þe twelffe B. bitokenen þo] also B.
10397   for . . . þoled] þoled for crist TLB. sorwe &] mochell B.

And martired for his loue ware
Þes hundride sheep þat were þere
And dalt to þe comyne were 10400
Bitokeneþ þe felowshipis Iwis
Of seyntis hyȝe in heuene blis
Þe tokenynge of a hundride tolde
Al fulnes hit is to byholde
Fro þo þat stad are in þat blis 10405
Noþing may hem wante nor mys
Wiþouten seke or any sore
Is no nede founden þore

Of ioachim now be we stille
Of dam anna to speke oure wille 10410
Of hir sikyng & hir care
How she hir for hir husbonde bare
Whenne he him helde from home
For his dispite þouȝte hir shome
Þis lady was of myche prys 10415
Loued & le[r]ned war and wys
Whenne she herde þis tiþonde
Of ysacar & hir husbonde
Cloþes of deol she dud on þore
She sperde hir dores & wept sore 10420
Mournynge she was nyȝt & day
Hir lyf in langur lastynge lay
Gladshipe had she alþerleest
Whenne her day was comen of feest
Þat men shulde holden hem to be bliþe 10425
Vche mon goodnesse kyþe
Fair cloþing on hem to take

10398 his loue] crist þay B.
10401 þe] þo TL; þat B. felowshipis] feleship LB.
10402 Of seyntis] Þat sitten B.
10403 a] þe B.
10404 hit] *om.* B.
10405 Fro þo] For þey B. stad are] ar þere B.
10406 hem] þay B. nor mys] Iwis B.
10408 Is no] In non L.
10410 Of dam] And of B. to] *om.* B. oure] we B.
10414 For] Of B. his] þis T. hir] sche B.
10415 Þis] Þat B.
10416 lerned] leued H.
10417 þis] þat B.
10422 lastynge] lasted B.
10425 holden . . . to] most B.
10426 kyþe] siþ B.
10427 to] þey B.

For her hyȝe feestis sake
Þenne sat anna menyng hir mone
Bitwene hirself & god alone   10430
She had a mayden het vteyne
Was hir pryue chaumburleyne
Lady she seide for god dere   fol. 61v col. 1
Mende þi mood & chaunge þi chere
On þiself bettur þou þinke   10435
Þou wolt nouþer ete ny drynke
How longe wolt þou be wroþ
Cloþe þe wiþ a bettur clooþ
Biþenke þe now lady lele
Þou art of kynde of israele   10440
Woost þou not I trowe nay
Whiche an hiȝe feest is today
Sore hit greueþ me þi fare
Þat I þe se make siche care
I þe se wepe alweys   10445
Whenne þou shuldest be best at eis
Anna lady leue þi bere
Cloþe þe feire & make good chere
Goddis owne day hit es
Alle shulde be glad more & les   10450
Þus seide þat da[mi]sele þere
Anna ȝaf hir þis vnswere
She seide why seistou to me so
Be stille or ellis go me fro
Þou me blamest for my dole   10455
Wenestou I be a fole
Wherof shulde I haue ioye or blis
Whenne I my wedded lord mys
Shulde I be myry or in solace

10428   feestis] fest B.
10429   Þenne] That L. menyng] her menyng, her *cancelled* T; mevyng L; mournyng B.
10434   chaunge þi] þy gode, gode *cancelled* B.
10435   On] Off B. þou] þou s, s *cancelled* L; *om.* B.
10436   ny] nor B.
10438   a] *om.* B.
10439   now] how B.
10440   of kynde] com of þe king B.
10441   I trowe] in trewþe B.
10442   Whiche . . . hiȝe] How hye a B. today] þis day B.
10444   þe se] se þe B.
10445   þe se] se þe B. se] *om.* L. wepe] wepynge TLB.
10450   be] we B.
10451   þat] þe B. damisele] daunsele H.
10456   be] were B.

But I him say tofore my face 10460
To merþe me þar þe not wene
Vtayne þerwiþ gon to tene
And of bollyng of hir herte
She keste hir wordis ouerthwerte
Lady she seide for what þing 10465
Wites þou me þi myslikyng
Þouȝe þou may no childe brede
Whom witestou þin vnspede
Dam anna was sory þo
Whenne vtayne had hir greued so 10470
Vp she roos & wente awey
Forþ she went in tene & trey
Into hir orcharde she ȝeode anoone fol. 61v col. 2
To wepe bi hirself allone
Þere she myȝte sorwe hir fille 10475
By hir one at hir wille
Whenne she was comen into þat place
Away was al hir solace
She heef hir hondis vp to þe skye
And to preye bigon on hye 10480
Lord þou here myn orisoun
And blesse me wiþ þi benisoun
Dere god here preyere myne
As þou didest dame sarra sumtyme
Þat siche a worþi sone hir ȝaue 10485
As she desired for to haue
Whenne she had endide hir preyere
She pleyned efte on þis manere
Ofte she seide allaas allas
Þat euer I born or geten was 10490
Wheþen haue I þis malisoun

10460 tofore] before B.
10461 þar þe] dar the L; me þar B. wene] men B.
10463 hir] her B.
10466 me] me me, *first* me *cancelled* B.
10467 Þouȝe] ȝeffe B.
10471 awey] her way B.
10477 into] to B.
10480 And] *om.* B. bigon] to god þat sitt B.
10481 þou] *om.* B.
10484 dame sarra] Sarras B.
10485 ȝaue] haue, h *cancelled*, y *superscript with a caret* L.
10486 for] of þe B.
10488 pleyned] prayed B.
10491 Wheþen] Whens B.

Þat I out of chirche am comoun
I am don & for cursed holde
Why was I born of modir bolde

// Whil she mened þus hir mone   10495
Wiþ wepe & sorwes mony one
She say þe aungel tofore hir stonde
Þat had ben at hir husbonde
He seide anna herde is þi bone
Þou shalt haue a childe ful sone   10500
Þis tiþing made hir liȝt
She seide to þat aungel briȝt
Wheþer so hit be mayde or knaue
God himself shal hit haue
For to serue him nyȝt and day   10505
He woot I haue þis ȝerned ay
Anna he seide make good chere
Whatsoeuer þou se or here
I am goddis owne aungel
Trewe tiþing þe to tel   10510
Þe greet almesdede of þe
Is present bifore goddes kne
Þi desire and þi preyere   fol. 62r col. 1
Is comen to goddis ere ful dere
Blisful may þou þe welde   10515
Drede þe nouȝt for noon elde
Four score ȝeer had dam sare
Whenne she hir sone ysaac bare
Rachel þat was Iacobes wyf
Ladde longe wiþouten childe hir lyf   10520
Aftir she bare a frely fode
A greet lordynge Ioseph þe gode
Þat stiwarde was & wel wiþstode

_____

10492   am] & LB.
10493–96   *om.* B.
10495   mened] mevid L.
10496   wepe &] wepyng L.
10497   þe] an T. tofore] afore B.
10498   at] with B.
10499   is þi] this by *cancelled,* is thy *superscript with a caret* L.
10500   ful] *om.* B.
10502   þat] þe B.
10503   so] *om.* B.
10506   I] þat I B. þis] *om.* B. ȝerned] ernyd L.
10510   þe to] I þe B.
10515   Blisful] Blissid B. þe] be L; ȝe B.
10521   frely] ferly B.

Þe hongur þat egipte ouerȝode
A douȝtir shal þou haue in hyȝe   10525
Þou shal calle hir name marye
Alle shul hir worshepe wiþ resoun
Ouer alle wymmen to bere croun
Filde wiþ grace shal she be
And fostred litil childe wiþ þe   10530
Fro þre ȝere to þe temple to go
Fourtene ȝeer to dwelle þere so
Þere to serue day and nyȝt
To god as ȝe tofore him hiȝt
Shal no man by no resoun   10535
Aȝeyn hir haue no wik chesoun
Was neuer noon ȝitt forsoþe to say
So blessed born as þat may
Þis ilke mayden good & mylde
Modir shal ben of a childe   10540
Of hir shal come monnes sauere
Þe douȝter shal þe fadir bere
Of al þis shalt þou leue me
Whenne þou art comen to þe cite
Of ierusalem at þe gulden ȝate   10545
An entre is þere þat so hate
Þou shalt fynde þi husbonde þore
Þat þou hast longed aftir sore
Þou shalt se soone þat I þe tolde
Of blessed birþe þou maist be bolde   10550

// Whenne þe aungel away was quyt
Two men þer coom clad in whyt
Anna þei seide make þe bliþe   fol. 62r col. 2

10525   shal þou] þou schalt B.
10526   calle hir] it B.
10528   croun] þe croun B.
10529   wiþ] of B.
10530   fostred] festrid B.
10532   Fourtene] xiiij L; Fourten & elleuyn B.
10534   tofore . . . hiȝt] here behight B.
10535   no man] non haue B; na womman G. *second* no] non B. by no resoun] wit right resun C;
         wid right resun G.
10536   hir . . . chesoun] hym non euill encheson B.
10537   noon ȝitt] ȝitt noon TL. forsoþe] sothe B.
10541   sauere] sauyour *cancelled*, savere *superscript with a caret* L.
10544   þe cite] þat contre B.
10545   Of] Att B.
10551   away] of her B.
10552   Two] ij° L. clad] cloþid B.
10553   make þe] makeþ B.

Þi lord is comyng also swiþe
Him to mete þou þe spede   10555
Anna busked hir and ȝede
Dwelled she no lenger þere
But as þe aungel bad hir ere
To Ierusalem she is goon
Wiþ Ioachim she met anoon   10560
Þe same stide þat hem was set
At þe gulden ȝate þei met
Whenne þei boþe met samen
Þei gret wiþ gladnes of gamen
For to aske þar no man   10565
If þei were glad & ioyeful þan
Whenne þei had made her orisoun
Þei wente þenne into þe toun
Siþen þei abode & þouȝte
Of þat þe aungel bodeworde brouȝt   10570
Soone aftir togider þei lay
Anna wiþ childe was wiþ a may
Of decembre þe eiȝteþe day
Was she geten þat I of say

Whenne anne coom to tyme of birþe   10575
She bar a mayde myche of myrþe
Marie to name on hir þei leide
As þe aungel tofore had seide
Whenne þei þre ȝeer had hir fed
To þe temple whas she led   10580
Of hir þei made her offronde
To him þat is god al weldonde
At þis temple þat I of mene

10555   mete] me L.
10558   ere] þere T.
10563   met] sett in B.
10564   of] & B. gladnes of gamen] gastli game CG.
10565   þar] it nede B.
10568   toun] tone tonn *cancelled*, toun *superscript with a caret* L.
10569   Siþen] Syttyn L.
10570   þat . . . bodeworde] þe bodworde þe aungell B.
10572   wiþ . . . was] was wiþ childe B.
10573   eiȝteþe] viijᵉ L; ix B.
10575   tyme] þe tym B.
10576   mayde] child of B. of] *om.* B.
10578   tofore] before B.
10579   þre] iijᵉ L.
10582   god] *om.* B.

stair

A greece þer was of steppes fiftene
Casten hit was wiþ compas sly   10585
For to go hit was ful hy
Þis may but of þre ʒeer olde
Wente on þe greeces I eer of tolde   10588
Whil þei loked hem bisyde   10591
She to þe hyʒest ʒeode þat tyde
Wiþouten helpe of mon of welde
As she were wommon of elde
Þis bitokened sikerly   10595 fol. 62v col. 1
God wolde she grew & clombe on hy
Þourʒe gode þewis & lif clene
As siþ was on þat lady sene
Whenne her frendis gan hir se
Vpon þe alþerhyʒest degre   10600
Þei wondride how she þider wan
Þai ʒaf hir to þe temple þan
As þei made avowe biforn
Ar she were of modir born
Whenne þei had made her sacrifise   10605
And ʒyuen hir to þe chirche seruyse
Among oþere maydenes þore
Boþe to fosterynge & to lore
To god himself þei hir bitauʒt
And vchone homwarde strauʒt   10610

// Þere þei lafte þat mirþful may
God hir ledde in hir way
As she of body wexe & name
So sprange hir goodnes & hir fame

10584   greece] steiar L. fiftene] xv^{ne} L.
10587   but] *om.* B. þre] iij^e L.
10588   greeces] grees T; grees þat B. I eer] þat I B.
10589–90   *om.* HTLB.
10592   ʒeode] went B.
10593   mon of] ane B.
10595   bitokened] betokenith B.
10597   þewis &] þe Iewis of B.
10598   on] of B.
10600   Vpon] On B.
10603   avowe] her vow B.
10604   were of] was of her B.
10608   fosterynge] fostren B.
10609   þei] þat B.
10610   vchone] þey B. strauʒt] wente straght B.
10611   mirþful] medefull B.
10612   ledde] taght B.
10613   &] of L.

Witt & bounte to ouerpas   10615
Al þat in þe temple was
Þer was no mayde of noon ospryng
So hooly of lyf olde nor ȝing
Aungels ofte coom and ȝede
To coumforte hir in al hir dede   10620
To whom þis mayden knowen was
Had greet wondir of hir gras
Þat she was ȝynge & so wyse
So holy & of so greet seruyse
Þe witt þe vertu to hir ioynt   10625
May no mon wryte wiþ penne poynt
No mon couþe so myche rede
But more was hir douȝtyhede
How mylde meke how chaste & clene
Hit was þerby kyd and sene   10630
Þat god into hir wolde liȝt
And in hir dude his wonynge diȝt
Soþely may men herby se
Þat lady was of greet bounte
For hit is founden as we rede   10635 fol. 62v col. 2
Oure lorde wolde him neuer bede
To soule þat fouled was in synne
To make his wonynge stide ynne
Þus most þis may be clene & briȝt
Wiþouten pleynt of any pliȝt   10640
Of whom þe kyng þat al dud make
Sende his monhede to take
In temple was hir wonynge þo
To serue god nyȝt & day also

10615–16   *om.* B.
10618   nor] ne B.
10620   dede] nede C.
10623   ȝynge] so ȝong B.
10625   *second* þe] & B. to] of T; þat to B.
10626   penne] penne ne LB.
10627   No mon] ne non B.
10629   meke] how meke B.
10630   Hit] Hid L. *MS* Add *begins here. See Appendix B.*
10631   into] in B.
10632   dude] wolde B.
10637   To] The L. fouled] solewid C; solpede Add. in] with B.
10638   stide] *om.* B.
10639   Þus] Þan CAddG.
10640   pleynt] weme B. of any] & withowtten Add.
10641   Of] To B; In Add.
10642   Sende] Semed C; Semyd G. his] lighte Add. to] wel to C; for to B.

Wiþ al hir myȝte & al hir tent   10645
To goddis seruyse was she went
So longe had she þere bene
Þat she coom to ȝeris fourtene
Þenne commaunded þe bisshop þere
Þat alle þe maydenes þat þer were   10650
Þat coom to fourtene ȝeer were þo
Shulde go to hir frendes so
For to mare & for to spouse
Vchone to her owne house

// Many of hem þat þere were stad   10655
Dud gladly as þe bisshop bad
But mary wolde no maryinge
But mayden lyue to hir endynge
Whenne men to hir of spousyng spake
She seide mon noon wolde she take   10660
To god haue I ȝyuen me
May I to no mon maryed be
Oþer husbonde wole I noon
But god þat is my lemmon
My maydenhede to hym I hiȝt   10665
I shal hit holde at my myȝt
Þe wille þat I haue het him to
Shal I neuermore vndo
To god was I ȝyuen ere
My modir me of body bere   10670
In his seruyse most I lende
Euer to my lyues ende

10645   *second* al] *om.* B. tent] intent B.
10646   goddis seruyse] serue god B.
10647   she] þis maiden CAddG.
10648   fourtene] xiiij^{ne} L.
10649   Þenne commaunded] Þen did . . . command CAddG.
10650   þe] þo TL. þer were] were þere B.
10651   to . . . were] were to fourten B. fourtene] xiiij L.
10652   go] *om.* B; Be send CAddG. so] go B.
10655   were] was B.
10656   Dud] Bote Add. bisshop bad] Bischoppe þam bedd Add.
10658   lyue] be Add.
10659   spousyng] husband CAdd.
10660   noon . . . she] wolde sche non B; scho wolde nane Add.
10662   May I] I ne maye Add.
10663   wole I] mai i haf CG; I may ha Add.
10664   But god þat is] Of him haf i made CG; For my lemmane I hafe hym tane Add.
10667   him to] vnto B. to] ij° L.
10669   ere] here B.

// Þe bisshop nuste what to speke
He durste not hir vow to breke
Hit was bifore mony a day   10675 fol. 63r col. 1
Commaundide in þe olde lay
Þe avow þat god was made
Shulde be holden wiþouten abade
On oþere side he was dredonde
To brynge a custom newe in honde   10680
Þe maydenes frendes for to let
In mariage hem for to set
For hit was in her lede
In mariage þe folke to brede
Þe bisshop sent aftir grete   10685
Þe wysest folke he myȝte gete
Of alle þe men in þat cuntre
At þe temple to make semble
Whenne þei were comen ȝonge & olde
Þe bisshop hem þis tale tolde   10690
Whi he dide hem sembled to be
For þis avowe of chastite
For to aske at hem her rede
Ȝif she shulde holde hit to hir dede
If þei durst make hir hit to breke   10695
Herof in counseil dud þei speke
Þe bisshop bad hem loke how
She myȝte be maryed [and] holde þat vow
For vow þat is made bi riȝt
Owe no mon to breke by myȝt   10700
Þer vow is made hit comeþ of wille
Nedely most men hit fulfille
But þer was noon at þis gederynge
Þat couþe counsel of þis tiþinge

10673   nuste] must L.
10674   to] *om.* B.
10677   avow þat] vow þat to B.
10677–78   *reversed in* Add.
10679   oþere] þe toþer B.
10680   in] on B.
10681   for] hem B.
10687   in] of B.
10688   At] Alle L.
10691   Whi] For B.
10692   avowe] vow B.
10693   *om.* L. at] of B. her] *om.* B.
10695   If] Or if L. hit] vp L.
10698   and] & B; and CG; to HTLB. þat] her B. vow] a vow, a *cancelled* L.
10704   couþe] couþe ȝeve B. tiþinge] þing B.

Counsel oþere ӡaf þei nouӡt 10705
But cryed & called on god oloft
Þat he wolde sende hem grace tille
To do hem witen of his wille
What þei shulde do of þat may
To make hir breke hir vow or nay 10710
Þenne fel þei [alle] on knees doun
And made to god her orisoun
Whil þei in her preyeres were
Þei herde a voys seye riӡt þere
Lokeþ he seide þe prophecye 10715 fol. 63r col. 2
What seide ӡow ӡore ysaye
Þourӡe þat prophete may ӡe se
To whom þe mayde shal spoused be
Isay þe olde prophete
Ful longe siþen he ӡow bihete 10720
Of rote of iesse shulde sprynge
A ӡerde þat shulde a flour forþ brynge
Boþe flour & fruyt shulde þerof brest
Þe holy goost shulde þeronne rest
Þourӡe þe voys þei þere herde 10725
Þei hadde knowyng of þat ӡerde
Of rote of iesse hit shulde springe
Þere went þei into knowlechynge
Þei biþouӡte hem þenne to calle
Þe kynde of dauid kyn alle 10730
Whos fadir was iesse
Þere þei were spred in þat cuntre
Vchone of hem shulde in her honde
Be beden to bere a wonde

10705 Counsel oþere] Oþer consaile B.
10707 he] *om.* B.
10709 þat may] th L.
10710 *second* hir] þat L.
10711 on] alle on TLB.
10714 seye riӡt] þat sayde B.
10716 seide . . . ӡore] sayth þerto B.
10717 prophete] prophecy B. ӡe] you L.
10718 shal] schuld B.
10721 Of] Of the LB. sprynge] forþe sprinӡ B.
10723 þerof] þeron B.
10724 shulde þeronne] þeron schuld B.
10725 þei þere] þere þei T; þat þey B.
10726 þat] þe B.
10727 Of] Of the LB.
10730 kyn] kynrede B.
10732 Þere] Where B.
10733 shulde] *om.* B.

Whiche of hem þat blossum bere   10735
Shulde spouse þat mayden þere
Anoon þei senden vp and doun
And bad hem at a day be boun
Alle þat had no spouse to bedde
And of kyng dauid were bredde   10740
And þo þat þider come wolde
A ȝerde were made in honde to holde
And what mannes ȝerde þat did blome
Shulde marye wedde bi dome

// Þe day coom of þis assemble   10745
Laft þer noon in þat cuntre
But þei alle at þe temple were
But if he spoused were of ere
Ioseph coom to Ierusalem
A mon þat woned in bedleem   10750
His wyf was deed & he ful olde
Among þo men bifore tolde
He coom þat day to bere his wonde
As couenaunt was al þat londe .
Children had he sikerly   10755 fol. 63v col. 1
Elder and more þen mary
He was ferforþ goon in lyf
He ȝerned not to haue no wyf
Hir to haue had he not mynt
If he hit any wey myȝt stynt   10760
Leue he myȝte þat no wey
But he most nede come to þat day
Vchone wiþ ȝerde forþ gon step
On bak him drouȝe þenne Iosep
Alle her ȝerdis dud vp holde   10765

10739–40   *reversed in* Add.
10739   no] non B.
10741   þo] all B.
10742   A ȝerde] ȝerdis B.
10743   þat] *om.* B.
10745   assemble] semble B.
10747   þei alle] þo B.
10751   wyf] wyf *superscript with a caret* L.
10757   ferforþ] fertherest B.
10758   ȝerned] thoght L. no] a TL.
10760   hit] *om.* B.
10761   myȝte . . . no] ne most on non B.
10762   to] *om.* LB.
10764   On . . . him] Abak then LB. On . . . þenne] Abak þenne drowȝe him T. þenne] hym L; hym ser B.
10765   dud] þey did B.

Bihynde hi*m* drou3e Ioseph vnbolde
Þe*n*ne bad þe p*r*est hem to calle
To offere vp her 3erdis alle
Þe prest hem tolde & soone fonde
Byhynde holden was a wonde 10770
Whe*n*ne Ioseph say hit was nou3t
But nede hit most forþ be brou3t
Also soone as hit was sene
Wiþ leef & flour þei fonde hit grene
A dowfe was fro heuen sent 10775
Li3t doun & þeronne lent
Þe*n*ne was mary Ioseph bitau3t
And he hir in spousaile lau3t
Wheþ*er* he wolde ouþ*er* nay
He most hir spouse & lede away 10780

Why ih*es*u cryst borne wold be
Of spoused mayden telle we

Þer ben resou*n*s writen sere 10783
Þ*at* god wolde she spoused were
Oon for þe fend ful of wylis 10785
Shulde not p*er*ceyue bi his gilis
Þ*at* a mayde wiþouten mon
Shulde childe conceyue þon
For had he knowen hit biforn
A childe of a mayden born 10790
Wolde he neu*er* haue 3yuen to rede
Þ*at* ih*es*u cryst shulde haue ben dede
Wel he wolde haue wiste þan
Þ*at* he wolde haue saued man

10766   hi*m*] he*m* LB. vnbolde] þe olde B.
10767   Þe*n*ne] Þ*at* B. hem] hym L.
10771   say] sey sie, sey *cancelled* L.
10772   nede] nedis B. hit] his TL.
10774   leef & flour] leuys & flouris B.
10775   was . . . heuen] fro hevyn was sent B.
10778   he] Ioseph B.
10779   ouþ*er*] or ellis B.
10780   spouse] wedde B. lede] wende B.
10781–82   *om.* AddGHTLB.
10782a   Add *has a different heading.* ih*es*u cryst] þat Ih*es*u B.
10782b   Of] Of a LB, a *superscript with a caret* L. telle we] fre B.
10785   for] is B.
10786   Shulde] Schul B.
10788   childe] a childe B. þon] one B.
10789–90   *om.* CAddG.
10790   born] be borne B.
10792   haue ben] be B.

Oure lorde wolde for resoun þylke   10795 fol. 63v col. 2
Be fed of a maydenes mylke
So hir maydenhede to be hid
And hir husbonde wyde kid

// Anoþer skil we reden ryf
Was for þe iewis ful of stryf   10800
Wolde haue stoned mary þat stounde
If she wiþ childe had be founde
And she no husbonde had Ihad
Hir to haue g[o]uerned & lad
For lawe was þat tyme in londe   10805
Womman þat hadde no husbonde
And she founde were wiþ childe
Fro stonynge shulde noon her shilde

// Þe þridde skile of hir spousaile
For monnes help shulde hir not faile   10810
Hir to socoure in hir nede
Whider so she rood or ȝede
Þus kept hir þat lord Iwis
To be queen of heuen blis
Alle cristen men þat be   10815
Owe to serue þat lady fre   10816

How hir grett gabrielle
Now is good ȝou to telle

Ioseph spoused þat lady fre   10817
And ladde hir into galile
Wiþ hir she led maydenes seuen
Her names herde I neuer neuen   10820
Þei were alle of hir owen kyn
And of þe elde hirselue was In

10795   resoun þylke] resons swilk B.
10797   hid] kyd hid, kyd *cancelled* B.
10799   ryf] of ryf, of *cancelled* L.
10801–04   *om.* CAddG.
10803   no] non B.
10804   gouerned] guerned H; gouernyd L; governed T.
10806   no] non B.
10807   founde were] wer found L.
10808   noon] no man B. shilde] hild B.
10810   shulde . . . faile] schull her avayle B.
10816–17   *om.* Add.
10816   serue] worschip B.
10816b   good] good is, is *cancelled* H. ȝou] for T; here L.
10819   Wiþ . . . led] Sche led with her B. seuen] vij LB.

Þo seuen þe bisshop hir tauȝt
Whenne she fro him leue lauȝt
Wiþynne þe lond of galile   10825
Is nazareth a faire cite
Þere lafte Ioseph mary his spouse
Whil he went hoom to his house
Vnto bedleem þo went he
To make his brydale redy to be   10830
He wolde ordeyne al his þing
Ar he wyf to house wolde bring
But ar he þo to house hir fet   fol. 64r col. 1
Was she wiþ þe aungel gret

// God himself sende þe aungel   A 1
Whos name was calde gabriel
Þis aungel sende þe trinite
As messangere to a cite
Þat hiȝte galile þe londe   A 5
Nazareth þe toun to fonde
Þere woned a man þat Ioseph hiȝt
Of dauid kynde he coom ful riȝt
And had a mayde wiþ him in house
Þat hiȝte mary & was his spouse   A 10
To Ioseph house þis aungel went
For to þat mayden he was sent
And whenne he wiþ þat mayden mette
Wiþ swete wordis he hir grette
Heyl be þou mary to hir seyde he   A 15
Ful of grace & god wiþ þe
Whenne he þese wordis to hir brouȝt
She was aferde & hir biþouȝt

10823   seuen] vij LB. tauȝt] betaght B.
10824   fro] of B.
10826   Is] Was B. a] þat B.
10832   wyf] is wyffe B.
10833   þo to] to þe LB.
10835–10906   HTLB *here substitute sixty lines translated from Luc. 1:26–38.*
A 1   þe] oon TLB.
A 2   calde] *om.* B.
A 4   As] A T. a] þat B.
A 5   þe] þat B.
A 7   woned] woniþ B.
A 8   kynde . . . coom] hous & sede B.
A 9   And had] He haþe B.
A 10   was] is B.
A 11   þis] þe B.
A 16   & god] god is B.
A 18   & . . . biþouȝt] in her þoght LB; in *cancelled,* and *and by* superscript with carets L.

What þis gretynge myȝte bimene
And she hirself mayden clene   A 20
And gabriel to hir in hyȝe
Seyde drede þe not marye
For þou hast founden grace Iwis
Bifore god kyng of blis
Þou shalt conceyue a childe & bere   A 25
In þi wombe þe fende to fere
And his name shal þou ihesu calle
Sone of god þat weldeþ alle
In Iacobes hous regne shal he
And of his regne noon ende shal be   A 30
Iacobes hous here calleþ he
Iacob kyng and his meyne
Þat is to say al folk þat is
Chosen to haue heuene blis
Siche wordis were seide to marye   A 35
And þerof hir þouȝte ferlye
She seide aungel how may þis be
Siþen man is vnknowen to me
Þe aungel vnswered wiþouten boost   fol. 64r col. 2
In þe shal come þe holy goost   A 40
And goddes owne vertue now
Shal þe bishadewe for monnes prow
Forþi of þe beþ born a burþe
Synful men to ioye & murþe
Þat goddis sone calde shal bene   A 45
I shewe þe redy tokene to sene
Þin olde nees elizabeth
Haþ gon wiþ childe sixe moneþ
Al hir lyf sooþ to seyn

A 19 bimene] ben B.
A 20 mayden] a mayde B.
A 21 And gabriel] Þe aungell B. hir] her þo B.
A 27 shal þou] þou schall B.
A 28 Sone] Þe son B.
A 31 hous] *om.* B. here] þere T; hir L. calleþ] callid L.
A 32 kyng] kyn B.
A 33 al] þat B.
A 34 to] for to B.
A 38 Siþen] Sen B.
A 39 vnswered] sayde B.
A 41 goddes] þyn B.
A 42 Shal . . . bishadewe] Shalbe thy shadow L; Shalbe schadow B.
A 43 Forþi] For B. beþ] schall be B. a] þat B.
A 46 redy tokene] tokyn redy B.
A 48 sixe] vj L.
A 49 to seyn] certayne B.

She haþ lyued here bareyn A 50
Þis wommon olde & vnwelde
A sone haþ conceyued in elde
And herby may þou se ful riȝt
Þat nouȝt passeþ goddes myȝt
He þat made kynde may fulfille A 55
Aȝeyn kynde what is his wille
Whenne oure lady þese wordis herde
To gabriel þus she vnswerde
Lo me here goddis mayde
To me be done as þou hast sayde A 60
As þou hast seide me biforn 10907
Þe saueour of me be born
Þat al wrouȝte & haþ in honde
Sunne & moone see and sonde 10910
Þat ay shal be and euer haþ bene
Is loken wiþynne þat mayden clene 10912
He þat firste no deþ myȝte dyȝe 10917
Now is mon bicome to dryȝe
God bicome mon dedly þus
Not for nede he had to vs 10920
But of his grace witterlye
To suffere deþ vs to bye
To þat deþ wolde he wende
Vs to bye from þe fende
Þis sonde was sende to oure lady 10925
Of marche þe day fuye & twenty
Fro fyue þousande ȝeer were ronne

A 53   ful] be B.
A 54   nouȝt] nothyng L.
A 56   is his] he B.
A 58   gabriel . . . she] þe aungell sche þus B.
10902–03   *om.* LT.
10909   Þat . . . &] All þat is wroght he B.
10912   þat] þis B. *After this line Add copies ll. 10903–04.*
10913–16   *om.* HTLB.
10917   deþ] dede B. dyȝe] do B.
10918   mon . . . dryȝe] he come man to dye B.
10919   God] God is B. dedly þus] for vs B.
10920   nede] no nede B. had] haþe B.
10921   But] Not L.
10923–24   *reversed in* Add.
10923   wolde] will B.
10924   Vs . . . bye] To bye vs B. fende] foule fende B.
10925   Þis] Þe B.
10926   Of] In B. marche] mercy *cancelled,* march *superscript with a caret* L; mare Add.
       fuye . . . twenty] xxv L.
10927   *om.* L. were] *om.* B.

Aftir þe world was bigonne
Nynty & nyne & moneþes sexe   fol. 64v col. 1
Þat oure elde in þis mayden wexe   10930
Leue we now of þis lady
And speke we of sir zakary   10932
How þe aungel him coom to warne
He shulde haue Ion þat cely barne

Þis zacharye þat we of rede   10935
Comen was of leuy sede
Elizabeth his wyf was olde
Anna sister toforn tolde
Holy lyf togider þei led
Wiþouten childe bytwene hem bred   10940
Myche þerfore þei mournyng were
Þei hit abated wiþ good chere
Almost to her lyues ende
God at þe last hem sende
A greet feest fel in her lede   10945
Þat zachary to temple ȝede
To do þe folk her seruyse
As lawe was in her yse
He reuestide him on his manere
And so went to þe autere   10950
He bad þe folk go out vchone
Whil he preyed in þe chirche alone
As was þe vse of her lawe
Had he dwelt but a þrawe

10928   was] were B.
10929   Nynty] Nynten B. nyne &] ix L.
10932   sir] *om.* B.
10933–34   *om.* B.
10934a   Add *adds a heading.*
10937   his] þis B.
10938   toforn] before of B.
10939–40   *reversed in* B.
10941   þerfore ... mournyng] mournyng þerfore þay B.
10942   For þat sche was barayn & bare B.
10944   God] Gode God B. þe] *om.* B.
10945   her] þat B.
10946   to] to þe B.
10948   was] wolde B. yse] vse L; gyse B.
10950   so] so he B.
10951   vchone] anon B.
10952   þe] *om.* B.
10953   of her] in þat B.
10954   Had] Ne had B.

He loked to his riȝt honde   10955
And say an aungel by him stonde
Wherfore in mood he wex al mad
Þe aungel bad him be not drad
He seide he þat al may mende   10960
Zakary to þe me sende   10959
Þe to counforte & make liȝt
Þou shalt haue a childe ful riȝt
On siche a childe þou may be bliþe
For gode dedis shal he kiþe
His name shal þou Ion calle   10965
God haþ so ordeyned in his halle
Zachary seide wiþouten greue
Þis tiþinge may I not leue
I & my wyf of pure elde   fol. 64v col. 2
Are past tyme childe to welde   10970
Þou shalt haue he seide a childe parfay
And fynde al sooþ þat I þe say
Mony shul glade of his burþ
He shal be mon of myche murþe
But for þou woldest not hit trowe   10975
Þou shalt be doumb soþely fro nowe
Til þat he be born þat ȝonge
And he shal do þe haue þi tunge
Byfore almyȝty god he shal
Bicomen a greet mon wiþal   10980
Miche for riȝt shal he swynke
And nouþer wyn ne siþer drynke
But in his modir wombe shal he
Of þe holy goost fulfilde be   10984
Sir zakary haue good day   10987
Al shal þou fynde as I þe say

10955   to] on B.
10956   by] before B.
10959-60   *reversed in* HTLB.
10959   me] he me B.
10963   On] Of TLB.
10964   For] For of L. shal he] he shalle L.
10966   so] *om.* B. in . . . halle] it schall so fall B. halle] alle T.
10968   Þis tiþinge] Thise tydynggis L.
10969   pure] pore B.
10971   he . . . childe] a child he seid L. he seide] *om.* B.
10973   of] in B.
10977   ȝonge] þong B.
10979   Byfore] Afore B.
10982   siþer] ȝicer B.
10985-86   *om.* HTLB.

Þe folke þat were þe chirche wiþoute
Wondride what he was aboute 10990
Whenne þei hadde longe beden so
Into þe chirche wente þei þo
Al mad zachary þei fonde
To hem couþe telle no tiþond
Ne seruyse do so was he stedde 10995
Doumbe to his house so þei him ledde

Þenne bere she childe elizabeth
In septembre [m]oneþ
Þe foure & twenty ny3t
Was he comen bi grace & my3t 11000
Forþ wiþ þe anunciacioun
Of cryst þat brou3te vs alle pardoun
For ri3t was þat þe purueoure
Shulde come bifore þe saueoure
He þat coom vs for to bye 11005
Sende biforne his bailye
Þus sent ihesu Ion biforn
Ar he were of modir born
Her boþe modris þat were mylde
Went boþe at onys wiþ childe 11010
But elizabeth was forþer gone fol. 65r col. 1
Bi sixe moneþes & wike one
Fro seynt Ion þe concepcioun
Was til þe annunciacioun
Soone as oure lady had met 11015
Wiþ þe aungel þat hir gret
She went out of nazareth
For to speke wiþ elizabeth

10989 were þe] was in B.
10991 beden] habiden B.
10992 þe] *om.* L.
10994 hem] *om.* LB.
10996 Doumbe] Home B. so] *om.* LB.
10996a Add *adds a heading.*
10998 moneþ] noneþ H; þe moneth B.
10999 foure . . . twenty] xxiiij L.
11001 anunciacioun] nunciacioun L.
11005 for] *om.* L; bedele CAddG.
11006 biforne] vs before B.
11008 were . . . born] wolde be hedir bore B.
11012 sixe] vj L.
11013 Ion þe] Iohnis B.
11014 til] to B.
11017–18 *om.* B.

She þat bareyn was olde wyf
Þo she was wiþ childe in lyf   11020
Not fer fro hir childyng
At maryes coome mayden ȝing
Þo þei mett þis ladyes twyn
Boþe cosynes of o kyn
First seynt marye spake   11025
And hir gretyng bigon to make
To elizabeth wel forþ goon
Hir childe in wombe was glad anoon
And for þe ioye hit set vpriȝt
For to worshepe god of myȝt   11030
Aȝeyn him made he myrþes newe
Þei he not sey he him knewe
His lord knew he wel biforn
Þat he was of his modir born   11034
Elizabeth in þat place   11037
She was filled wiþ goostly grace
She bigan þis prophecye
Blessed þou be she seide marie   11040
And blessed be þe fruyt of þe
Þat þou wolde visite me
Þe modir of my god so dere
In my wombe þe childe gon here
Wiþ þe heilsyng þat þou me made   11045
Hit made ioye & was glade
Blessed art þou þat mystrowed nouȝt
Þe holy bodeworde þe was brouȝt
Þou may be triste & redy byde
Al þat is þe het shal bityde   11050

11019 bareyn] geld CAddG. bareyn was] was barayn & B.
11021 hir] þe B. childyng] childing þat si-quar CG; childynge *in* a syquare Add.
11022 At] Þat B. mayden] þat mayden B.
11026 bigon to] to her gan B.
11029 þe] *om.* TLB.
11030 of myȝt] almyght B.
11031 he] *om.* B.
11032 Þei] Þough B. not sey] not sie yet L; ne sawe hy*m* B.
11034 Þat] Or B.
11035–36 *om.* HTLB.
11038 She] *om.* B. goostly] goddis B.
11040 þou be] be þ*o*u B.
11043 god] lorde B.
11044 þe] my B.
11047 art] be B. mystrowed] mystrowist B.
11048 holy] *om.* B. bodeworde] word L. þe was] þat was to þe B.
11050 þe] *om.* B. bityde] abyde B.

// Þes ladyes loued hem so wel
Eiþer to oþer her wille did tel
But þe menskyng hem bitwene   fol. 65r col. 2
Was dyuerse as I hit wene
Þe ton was ȝong mayden þon   11055
Þe toþer had knowleched wiþ mon
Oure lady dwelt þere wiþ hir nese
[Til] Ion were born þat good pece
And at hir childynge was helpande
And as in summe bokis we fande   11060
I may hit leue ful sikurlye
Þat wiþ hir owne honde marye
Was hirself þe firste wommon
Þat lifted fro þe erþe Ion

// Whenne Ion was born also swiþe   11065
His frendes were glad & bliþe
And hadden of hir myche myrþe
Þat was so longe wiþouten birþe
Not only of ierusalem bourȝe
But also al þe cuntre þourȝe   11070
His feest is in someres tyme
Hit holdeþ boþe iewe & sarazine
Þourȝe al þe heþen lede
As fer as ani pepul sprede
Þerfore of him witnesseþ hit þus   11075
Oure lord oure saueour Ihesus
Of wommon was neuer born none
Gretter childe þen seynt Ione

11051   hem] eyþer B.
11052   Eiþer] Þat eyþer B.
11053   menskyng] mensyng B.
11055   ȝong] a B.
11056   had ... wiþ] was knowing of B. knowleched] knowleche T.
11058   Til] Þat H. good] blissid B.
11059   hir] þe TB.
11061–62 *om.* Add.
11061   I] It B. ful] *om.* B.
11064   fro ... Ion] it fro þe erþe þan B.
11067   hir] hym B.
11070   also] all B. þourȝe] þorough & þorough B.
11071   His] Þis B. tyme] tide tyme, tide *cancelled* L.
11072   boþe iewe] Iewis B.
11073   Þourȝe] Þoroughoute B.
11075   hit] *om.* B.
11077   was neuer] nevir was L.
11078   Gretter] Bettyr B.

Alle made myrþe of þat beryng
Fadir & modir olde & ȝing   11080
Togider gedered þei hem alle
Þe[i] wist not what hit to calle
Zakary þei dude forþ take
But no speche ȝit myȝte he make
Byfore ȝe herde þe resoun why   11085
Þenne loked aftir sir zakary
Tables & poyntel tyte
He bigon þe name to write
And wroot as þe aungel bad
Ion his name shulde be rad   11090
His frendis þouȝte þerof selcouþ
How þis name coom in mouþ
Þei seide þat in al her kynde   fol. 65v col. 1
Noon siche name couþe þei fynde
Whenne þei had circumcised Ion   11095
His fadir had his speche anoon
And þus wiþ mouþ anoon gon melle
Blessed be þou god of israelle
Þat visitynge þi folke hast sent
And raunsonynge to hem lent   11100

Þis childe was fostered ful dere
Whenne he of elde was seuen ȝere
He laft his kyndely kiþþe & fode
And to wildernes he ȝode
For he wolde fle fro synne   11105
He lafte kiþþe & al his kynne
In wildernes longe abode
And lad þere harde lyflode
He lyued wiþ rotis & wiþ gresse
Wiþ hony of þe wildernesse   11110
Breed ne wyn coom him noon Inne
He wered nouþer wollen ny lynne

11082 Þei] Þe H. wist not] nist B.
11086 sir] *om.* B.
11093 þat] *om.* B.
11094 Noon] No TL. þei] men L.
11097 And] *om.* B.
11098 þou] *om.* B.
11101 was] is B.
11102 of . . . seuen] was olde vij B. seuen] vij L.
11104 to] into L. he] hym L.
11107 abode] & brode B.
11108 And] He B.

Þis was Ioon þe good baptist
Þat baptized aftir ih*esu* crist

W he*n*ne Ion of his modir war born   11115
Oure lady as I seide biforn
Bitauȝte to god elizabeth
And went hoom to nazareth
Oure blessed lady on þis wise
Bi þis hir wombe bigon to ryse   11120
Aftir þ*at* Ioseph þis may   11123
Hadde spoused as ȝe herde say
Þre moneþes & more dwelled he   11125
At home in his owne cuntre
Ioseph þe*n*ne soone wente
To nazareth wiþ ful entente
Þe lady whe*n*ne he coom nerehonde
Wiþ hir to speke as husbonde   11130
To speke of nedis of her house
As men mot þat ben in spouse
He fonde wiþoute*n* more warn
Þat þis lady was wiþ barn
Whe*n*ne he knewe hir in siche state   11135 fol. 65v col. 2
Was [t]he[re] neu*er* mon so mate
So sory was he neu*er* his lyf
As to fynde wiþ childe his wyf
Þat he neu*er* touchid tille
He wex þouȝtful & loked ille   11140
Wondir was hit noon for he
Wiste not of hir pryuete
But whateu*er* he had in þouȝt

11113   þe good] *om.* B.
11114   Þat] Which L.
11115   war] was LB.
11117   Bitauȝte] Broght C; Bot taght G. to god] on leue B.
11118   hoom] her home B.
11120   Bi . . . hir] Her blessid B.
11121–22   *om.* HTLB.
11124   as . . . herde] þe soþe to B.
11127   þe*n*ne soone] þo forþe B.
11128   ful] good LB. entente] ent T.
11130   *om.* L. as] as her B.
11132   mot] most B.
11134   þis] his TB.
11136   there] he CGHT; ther*e* L.
11137   his] in his B.
11140   þouȝtful] soroufull B.
11143   whateu*er*] what that eu*er* L.

Mislikyng chere made he nou3t
In his hert he helde him stille 11145
But forsoþe he was in wille
Awey sodeynly to stele
From þat lady þat was so lele
His hert nolde for no þing
Let him discouer his mystrowyng 11150
But was in wille for to fle
Pryuely and let hir be
Wiþ wille he wolde fle hir fro
Þat ny3te he þou3te to haue don so
An aungel þere he slepyng lay 11155
To hym coom þus gon he say

// Ioseph dauid sone forwhy
Wol þou leue þi spouse mary
Þe childe she haþ in body bred
Þat þou art so of adred 11160
Be triste & in no drewerynes
Þe holy goostis werk hit es
Hit is þe holy goostis my3t
Wiþouten part of any pli3t
Þat childe þat she goþ wiþalle 11165
His name shal men ihesu calle
Hir fadir & sone shal boþe bene
To saue his folk fro endeles tene
Fro þis tyme had Ioseph noone
Mistrowyng to þat mayden one 11170
Into his kepyng hir toke he
And lyued wiþ hir in chastite
Wiþ menske & worshepe hir to 3ime
And for to socoure & to queme

11144   chere] ther L. made] had T.
11149   nolde] wolde T; wolde lete hym B.
11150   discouer] discare B.
11151   was] he was B.
11152   Pryuely and] And so previly to L; And preuely to B.
11153   fle] haue stole B.
11154   þou3te . . . so] was in will þerto B.
11156   coom] *om.* T.
11160   so of] of so sore B.
11161   drewerynes] deberynes L; drednes C; deewrynes T; sekirnes Add.
11167   boþe] euer B.
11170   to] of BCG.
11172   chastite] charite B.
11173   menske &] mochell B. hir for B. 3ime] 3eue B.
11174   for] *om.* B.

On þis man*ere* wiþouten faile   11175 fol. 66r col. 1
Helde þei togider her spousaile

Þe tyme þ*at* brou3te al to fyne
Was bi þis at moneþes nyne
Ioseph di3te him for to go
To bedleem wiþ mary þo   11180
Lenger þ*ere* nolde he dwelle
For wordis of þe iewes felle
For to fle her false fame
To bedleem went þei same
In þat tyme þ*at* þei went þus   11185
Was emp*er*oure sir augustus
A mon men had of myche doute
And drad was al þe world aboute
Al þe world ordeyned he
Þat þei shulde vndir him be   11190
And vche kyn[d] shulde make hi*m* bou*n*
To come to hir kyndely tou*n*
To make knowleche wiþ su*m*þing
To augustus her aller kyng
A baily toke þis werke on honde   11195
Was calde cyrinus in þat londe
He dud alle me*n*nes names wryte
Þat of þis 3elde shulde he*m* not quyte
Ioseph coom þat tyme þere
To bedleem as I tolde 3ow ere   11200
To his owne hoome & house
And brou3te wiþ hi*m* mary his spouse
So fer was þo gon þat mylde
Þat she was at þe tyme of childe
What shulde I telle 3ow more   11205

11177   Þe] To B.
11178   at] a L. nyne] ix L.
11181   Lenger] No lengg*er* L. nolde] wold L.
11182   wordis of] wondir on L. þe] þo T.
11183   For] And for L.
11184   same] in same LB.
11185   þat] *om.* B. went] was B.
11186   Was] Was þe B. sir] *om.* B.
11187   A mon] Þat mone B.
11191   vche] eche a B. kynd] kyng GHTLB; kynd C.
11194   aller] alder B.
11195   þis] þat B. on] in L.
11196   cyrinus] tyrinus B.
11198   he*m*] hym B. he*m* not] non he*m* L.
11204   þe] *om.* B.
11205   What] Wherto B. 3ow] *om.* B.

THE SOUTHERN VERSION OF *CURSOR MUNDI*

Ihesu hir childe bar she þore
Hir childe bar she neuerþeles
Mayden wiþouten wem of flesshe
Whoso knewe his myȝte witterly
Þerof wolde he haue no ferly   11210
Mary bere childe in chastite
Siþ god wolde hit most so be
He þat þe dryȝe ȝerde made ere
In oon nyȝt fruyt to bere
Wiþouten erþe aboute to fode   11215 fol. 66r col. 2
Leof & blossomes also gode
He þat dide as I haue seide
Miȝte he not þat al purueyde
Be borne of a mayden eþe
At þe ende of nyne moneþe   11220
He wrouȝte al in litil stounde
To speke also he made þe doumbe
He dude þe see to cleue in two
His enemyes alle to slo
He myȝte make a mayden þenne   11225
Childe to bere wiþouten wemme
But as þe sunne gooþ þourȝe þe glas
And leueþ hit hool as hit was
So coom þe sonne of riȝtwisnesse
Into oure lady clene flesshe   11230
Kyndely he coom & ȝeode
And saued his modir maydenhede
Þus bar she þat barnteem
Þat blisful birþe in bedleem
Siche cloþes as she hadde to honde   11235

11206 childe] son B.
11208 Withouten wem mayden sche was B.
11209 knewe] knowe B. myȝte] wy myght, wy *cancelled* L.
11210 wolde he] he wold L.
11211 childe] her childe B.
11212 most] schuld B.
11214 fruyt] forto B.
11217 haue] þe B.
11220 nyne] ix L.
11221 in] in a B.
11222 Hevyn & erþe and þe worlde round B. þe doumbe] þe dumb asse CG.
11223 to] *om.* B. two] ij° L.
11224 His] And his B. alle] for L.
11226 Childe] A child B.
11227 *second* þe] *om.* TL.
11233 þat] her B.
11235 to] *in* B.

Wiþ siche she swaþed hi*m* & bonde
Bitwene two cracches she hi*m* leide
Þ*ere* was noon oþ*ere* greyþe greyde
Was þ*ere* no pryde of couerlite
Curteynes ridelles ne tapite   11240
Þo herdes þ*at* were wonte to be
On felde was þo wiþ her fe
Þere li3ten au*n*gels bri3te of heuen
And brou3t word wiþ syngi*n*ge steue*n*
I brynge 3ow word of ioye & blisse   11245
Borne tony3te 3oure saueour isse
Bi þis tokene þat I 3ow say
Gooþ tomorwe whe*n*ne hit is day
To bedleem & fynde 3e shalle
Þe saueoure borne of alle   11250
Þere is þe kyng of alle kyngis
Born tony3te bi þese tokenyngis
In a cracche he shal be fou*n*den
Liggynge þ*er* an asse is bounden
Honoureþ hi*m* forwhy he shal   11255 fol. 66v col. 1
Be set in dauid kyngis stal
Whil þis aungel tiþinge tolde
Oþer li3ten doun monyfolde
Seyinge þus men to knowe
On hy3e be ioye & pees on lowe   11260
Whe*n*ne þei had seide þ*at* þei wolde sey
Þe aungels went soone her wey
Þe herdis dredden of þat li3t
Þat coom of þo au*n*gels bri3t
Suche a li3t say þei neu*er* ere   11265
As þei sey þat ny3te þere
Þei seide to bedleem go we

11236 Wiþ] *om.* B. &] in & B.
11237 two] ij° L.
11238 greyþe] gere TLB.
11240 Curteynes] Off corteyne B. ridelles] ridell B.
11241 Þo] Þe B.
11242 was þo] were þay B.
11243 au*n*gels] þe au*n*gels B.
11246 Borne ... saueour] 3our Sauyour þ*is* night born B. tony3te 3oure] this nyght our L.
11251 alle] *om.* B.
11252 tony3te] this nyght L. þese] alle L; þis B. tokenyngis] tokeny*n*gg B.
        After l. 11254 Add *has two extra lines.*
11257 Whil] Wl T. þis aungel] þes au*n*gels B.
11258 Oþer] Þere B. li3ten] lyghtynd L.
11264 þo au*n*gels] þat au*n*gell B.

Of þis typing sooþ to se
Whenne þei coom mary þei fond
And wiþ hir Ioseph hir husbonde   11270
And þe childe þat swaþe[d] was
In cracche bytwene ox & as
What þei had herde & sene þei tolde
Alle merueiled þeron ȝonge & olde
Marye helde in herte stille   11275
And þonked god al his wille

// In augustus tyme [þe] emperoure
Was vs born oure saueoure   11278
Þe eiȝteþe day fro he was born   11283
Circumcised he was & shorn
Ihesus to name on him þei leide   11285
As þe aungel had hem seyde

Aftir þe terme of fourty dayes
Aftir þat þe gospel sayes
Þei bar þe childe fro bedleem
Into þe temple of Ierusalem   11290
For to do of him þat day
Þat ordynaunce was of þe lay
Þe lawe of moyses þenne was
A womon þat knawe childe had bi graas
At þe firste birþe shulde sho   11295
Hit offere þe holy temple to
Aftir þat she shulde haue lyn
Fourty dayes in Iesyn
For mayden childe als longe also   fol. 66v col. 2

11268   þis ... sooþ] thise tydynggis for L. sooþ] þe soþe B.
11271   þe] a B. swaþed] swaþe H.
11272   In] In a B.
11274   þeron] on L; þerof B.
11275   helde] all helde B.
11276   al] of B.
11277   þe] *om.* HT.
11278   vs] he B.
11279–82   *om.* HTLB.
11283–84   *om.* B.
11283   eiȝteþe] viij L.
11285   on ... þei] þey on hym B.
11286   had] to B.
11287   fourty] xl L.
11292   Þat] As B. of] on L.
11294   A] *om.* TL; Þat B.
11298   Fourty] xl L.

Ar she shulde to þe temple go   11300
Wiþ hir childe shulde she offere þere
A lomb if she so ryche were
And ellis who þat myȝte not so
Shulde offere turtur doufes two
Ouþer of oþere doufis double brid   11305
Þis lay mary wiþ ihesu did
Pore ȝifte gon she [for] him ȝyue
Þat coom in pouerte to lyue
Of pouerte no disdeyn had he
Þat biddeþ vs loue wel pouerte   11310
Pouerte þar no man myslyke
If he trowe in god so ryche

// Þer was a good holy man
In þe temple wonyng þan
Of six score ȝeer & symeon hiȝt   11315
Þat mony a bone had beden riȝt
Þat he myȝte in lyf & hele
Se þe coumforte of israele
Þat mannes raunsoun shulde bere
And god him had ȝyuen vnswere   11320
By þe holy goost hym sent
Þat þus seide to him present
Þat he in deeþ shulde not dyȝe
Ar he cryst had seen wiþ eȝe
Þerfore whenne þat mary mylde   11325
Into þe tempel brouȝte hir chylde

11300   she] þay B.
11301   shulde she] sche schuld B.
11302   so] *om.* B.
11303   who] þo B.
11304   two] ijº L.
11305   Ouþer] Or B.
11307–08   *om.* Add.
11307   ȝifte] ȝefftys B. for] wiþ H.
11308   pouerte] porte B. to] *superscript with a caret* B.
11309   he] she L.
11311   þar] that L.
11314   In] Þat in B. wonyng] wonyd B.
11315   six] vj L. &] *om.* B. symeon] vij L. hiȝt] he hight B.
11316   bone] shour L. had] haþe B.
11317   Þat] T He praide that, T *cancelled* L.
11320   him . . . ȝyuen] had ȝeffe hym B.
11321–22   *om.* CAddG.
11321   hym] to hym B.
11322   to] *om.* B.
11323   in deeþ] ne B. not] neuer B.
11326   þe] thy L.

Þis symeon þat had sauour
In þat lorde of al socour
Of his come was he ful fayn
And soone wente him aȝayn 11330
And for ioye he made a cry
Þat alle herde þat stode him by
God haþ seen his folk ful riȝt
And sent hem þat he hem hiȝt
Anoon he ran to ihesu swete 11335
And fel doun bifore his fete
Þus honoured him symeon
And toke him in his armes þon
He kuste his feet & pre[y]ed of grace fol. 67r col. 1
Þat he myȝte reste in place 11340
Now haue myne yȝen seen þi hele
Þat þou hast het to israele
Also þer was an olde wyf
Þat fe[r] in elde was goon hir lyf
Lyued she hadde foure score ȝere 11345
In widewehode & daye[s] sere
Trewe she was in al hir dede
Out of þe temple she not ȝede
But euer was she þerynne boun
In almesdede & orisoun 11350
Whenne þat she ihesu gon se
She honoured him on hir kne
Þis is he she seide to sene
In whom þe world shal saued bene
Of prophecye sooþ þis word wes 11355
Þerfore anna was prophetesse

// Þat same day a prophecye
Symeon seide of oure ladye
Of hir & of hir sone ihesu

11328 þat] all our B. al] *om.* B.
11329 was he] he was B.
11335 swete] schete C; skete G.
11336 bifore] toffore B.
11339 He] And B. preyed] preed H.
11340 in] in his B.
11341 þi] þe B.
11345 Lyued] Þat lyuid B. foure score] iiij^{xx} L.
11346 &] *om.* B. dayes] dayed H. sere] thre C.
11351 ihesu] þat childe B.
11354 In] Þurgh B. shal saued] sauid schall B.
11355 sooþ] *om.* B.
11357 Þat] Þe B.

Whiche I shal telle new   11360
Þis childe he seide biforn alle
Shal be to fele men in dounfalle
And to fele in vprysyng
In tokene also of ȝeynseying
Þis dounfal shal we vndirstonde   11365
Shul be alle þe mystrowonde
Þis vprisyng of oþere fele
Þat in trouþe were trewe & lele
Mary he seide to þyn hert
A swerd of sorwe shal stryke ouerthwert   11370
Þat swerd þourȝe hir hert stoode
Whenne she hir sone say honge on rode
F[ro] he was born þe day þrettende
Offeride to him þo kyngis hende
Riche ȝiftis þat þei brouȝt   11375
But in þe firste ȝeer was hit nouȝt
Sum men seyn þe nexte ȝeere
Folewynge & somme wiþ resouns sere
Seyn two ȝere aftir þei coome   fol. 67r col. 2
Ion gildenmouþ seiþ his dome   11380
Þat he fonde in oon olde boke
Þese kyngis þre her weye toke
A twelfmoneþ er þe natiuite
For ellis myȝte not þo þre
Haue rauȝte to ryde so fer way   11385
And comen to cryst þilke day
He seide in þat boke he fond

11360   new] ȝow now B.
11362   in] *om*. B.
11363   in] *om*. B.
11364   also] *om*. B.
11365   dounfal] domefulle L.
11368   & lele] to tell B.
11370   stryke] stik TL. ouerthwert] outwerd L.
11372   she] *om*. B. sone say] *om*. B. on] on þe B.
11373   Fro] For HT; *om*. L.
11374   Offeride] And offird L. þo kyngis] þe kyng B.
11377   men] *om*. B.
11378   Folewynge] *om*. B.
11379   two] ijᵒ L.
11380   gildenmouþ] w*ith* gildenmouþ B. his] þis B.
11381   Þat] *om*. B. in] it in B.
11384   For] Or B. not . . . þre] it not so be B.
11385   Haue . . . ryde] To haue raght B.
11386   þilke] þat ilk B.
11387   þat] a B. he] I it B.

Of a prophecye of estern lond
Þat balam hett crafty & olde
And mychel of a sterre he tolde   11390
A sterre he seide shulde be sene
Was neuer noon bifore so shene
Ion telleþ vs als gyldenmouþ
Of a ferren folke vncouþ
Wonynge by eest occione   11395
Byȝonde hem is pepul none
Among whiche was brouȝt a writ
Of seth þe name spake of hit
Of siche a sterne þe writ spake
And of þese offeryngis to make   11400
Þis writt was kept fro kyn to kyn
Þat þei wolde þeronne myn
At þe laste þei ordeyned twelue
Þe wysest among hemselue
And dude hem in a mounteyne derne   11405
Bisily to waite þat sterne
Whenne any dyȝed of þat doseyn
His sone was sett for him certeyn
Or his nexte frende or fere
So þat eueryche a ȝere   11410
Whenne her cornes were In done
Þei went into þe mounteyne soone
Þere þei offered preyed & swank
Þre dayes nouþer eet ne drank
Þus vche osprynge þere dyde   11415
Til þe sterre was to hem kide

11388   prophecye] prophete LB. estern] þe estrenest B.
11390   And] Þat B. he] om. B.
11392   bifore] tofor L. shene] clen B.
11393   als] of B.
11394   ferren] sterre L.
11395   Wonynge] Wonid B. eest] þe est B.
11397   whiche] hem B.
11398   seth þe] swich a B. name] man G.
11400   And] om. B. þese offeryngis] þis offring B.
11403   twelue] xij L.
11405   dude] bid L.
11406   þat] þis B.
11408   His] Þe B.
11409   Or] Of B.
11411   were] was B.
11412   mounteyne] nounteyn T.
11415   vche . . . þere] þey hauntyd & B. dyde] *altered from* dude H.
11416   was . . . hem] to hem was B.

Þulke sterre hem coom to warn
Vpon þe mounte in fourme of barn
And bare on hit likenes of crois   fol. 67v col. 1
And seide to hem wiþ monnes vois   11420
Þat þei shulde go to iewis londe
Þei went & were two ȝere walkonde
Þe sterre bifore hem euer led
And wondirly were þei fed
Her scrippes wheþer þei rood or ȝode   11425
Hem failed neuer drynke nor fode
Þes kyngis riden forþ her rode
Þe sterre euer bifore hem glode
Þei seide go we to þat kynge
Þat shal in erþe haue noon euenynge   11430
We wole him bere offerynge newe
And honoure him wiþ trouþis trewe
Alle þe kyngis of þis werd
For him shulde quake & be ferd
Þei folwed on þe sterre beme   11435
Til þei come to Ierusaleme
But fro þei coom þere at þat tyme
Þe sterre him hidde & wolde not shyne
Þourȝe þe myȝte of god aboue
Þat was for fals heroudis loue   11440
Ȝit wiste þe kynges hit nouȝt
But wende to fynde þere þat þei souȝt
Þei took her Innes in þe tounne
And asked aftir him vp & dounne
But þe burgeis of þat cite   11445

11417 Þulke] Þis ilk B. hem coom] com hem B.
11418 Vpon] Vp B. fourme] from L. of] of a B.
11419 hit] his B. of] a B.
11421 Þat ... shulde] And bade hem B. to] to þe B. shulde] shul T.
11422 two] ij° L. walkonde] wakand C.
11423 hem euer] euer hem B.
11424 And] *om.* B.
11425 scrippes] schippes B.
11426–27 *om.* B.
11429 þat] þe B.
11430 euenynge] ending B.
11431 newe] now B.
11432 wiþ] in B.
11433 þis werd] þe worlde B.
11434 shulde] shulle LB.
11437 at] *om.* B.
11438 wolde] nold L.
11441 þe] þo TL. hit] *om.* B.
11444 aftir] for B.

Had wondir what hit myȝte be
Þei asked hem what seche ȝe
A blisful childe þei seide parde
He shal be kyng of kyngis alle
To honde & foot we shul him falle 11450
Say ȝe no sterre þat lad vs hider
Þo þei gedered hem togider
And spak þerof wiþ greet wondringe
And word coom to heroude þe kinge
Þat siche kyngis þer were comen 11455
And had her In in toun nomen
Whenne he þis tale vndirstood
Him þouȝte hit nouþer faire ny good
For he wende he shulde come fol. 67v col. 2
And put him out of his kyngdome 11460
Swiþe togider let he calle
Þe maistris of his clerkis alle
And asked of hem him biforn
Where þat crist shulde be born
Þat kyng of iewis shulde be 11465
Þei seide in bedleem Iude
Þe prophetis han hit writen ȝore
In bedleem Iuda he to be bore
Þei hit be not þe moost cite
Of dig[ni]te leest shulde hit not be 11470
Of þe shal he be born & brede
My folke of israel shal lede

// Heroude asked þo kynges in derne
Whenne þei sey þat ilke sterne

11446 hit] þat B.
11447 Þei] He B.
11448 blisful] blissid B.
11450 To] On B. him] to hym B.
11455 kyngis] þre kyngis B.
11456 In in] In in þe T; innys in þe B.
11457 þis tale] þes talis B.
11458 hit] that L; hem B.
11460 And] To B.
11461 let] gan B.
11462 his] þe B.
11465 *om.* B.
11469 Þei] ȝef B. not] not not, *first* not *cancelled* L.
11470 dignite] diginte H. not] *om.* B.
11471 shal he] schuld B.
11472 shal] to B.
11473 kynges] kyinges H. in derne] dere B.

Gooþ he seide & fast enquere 11475
How he is born & where
Comeþ aʒeyn & telleþ me
Wiþ worshepe wol I hym se
Sir þei seide hit shal be done
On her weye went þei sone 11480
Whenne þei & heroude were atwynne
Þe sterre to shyne dud bigynne
Herby hit semeþ to me
Say noon hit but þe kyngis þre
Bitwene eyr & erþe hit shone 11485
A fairer was þer neuer none
Þe toun of ierusalem fro
Into bedleem hit lad hem þo
Ouer þe hous stood þe sterne
Þere ihesu & his modir werne 11490
Þei kneld doun & brouʒte in honde
Vchone ʒaf worþi offronde
Þe firste of hem Iasper hiʒt
He ʒaf hym golde wiþ resoun riʒt
He ʒaf hit hym in tokenyngis 11495
Þat he was kynge of alle kyngis

// Melchior coom alþer neest
And kid he was boþe god & preest
Wiþ cense bifore hym he felle fol. 68r col. 1
Þat shulde in chirche brenne & smelle 11500
Hit is a gumme þat comeþ of firre
Baltizor he offered myrre
A baum of wondir bitturnes
Þat dede men wiþ anoynt es
For rotyng is no bettur rede 11505

11475 & fast] faste & B.
11480 went þei] þey went B.
11482 dud] gan B.
11483 to] by B.
11484 þre] iijᵉ L.
11485 eyr &] þe ayre & þe B. hit] *om.* B.
11487 Þe . . . ierusalem] When Ierusalem þey went B.
11488 lad] left L.
11492 worþi] full riche B.
11493 hem] hem þat TLB.
11494 He] *om.* B.
11495 hit hym] him it B.
11498 And] He B. he] þat he B. boþe] *om.* B.
11499 Wiþ] And with L. cense] encens B. he] *om.* B.
11502 he] *om.* B.

In tokene he was mon to be dede
Þes þre ȝiftis seiþ som boke
At ones alle he hem toke
Ful swetly wiþ smylyng chere
Byhelde þo ȝiftis ryche & dere   11510
Ioseph & mary his spouse
Feire called hem to house
And faire arayed þei hem diȝte
Wiþ þe childe þei were þat nyȝte
Wiþouten pride to telle ȝow alle   11515
Had þei no bed sprad wiþ palle
But riȝt as þei þere fonde
Þei toke & þonked god his sonde
Fayn þei were þat þei had sped
Þe kyngis þre were brouȝte in bed   11520
Thre wery kyngis of her wey
Þis chylde souȝte wiþ þis aray
He knew hem wel & kyd in dede
Wel he quyt hem her mede
Þei were in wille þilke nyȝt   11525
To turne to heroude as þei hiȝt
But as þei into slepe were lad
An aungel coom & hem forbad
To wende by hym any way
For he was traytour fals of fay   11530
Anoþer weye shulde þei fare
On morwe whenne þei risen ware
Whenne þei þus hade do to þe childe
Þei toke her leue at mary mylde
And þonked Ioseph curteysely   11535
Of her nobel herbergery

11506 to] & schuld B.
11507 þre] iij⁰ L. ȝiftis] þingis B. som] þe B.
11509 wiþ] with a B.
11510 þo] þe B.
11513 And] In L. arayed] aray LB. þei] with B.
11514 þat] all B.
11516 no] non B.
11518 god his] godis B.
11520 Þe . . . þre] Tho kynggis iij⁰ L; Þes þre kynggis B. in bed] abed B.
11525 þilke] þat ilk B.
11527 into] in her B.
11530 fay] lay B.
11532 On morwe] On morn L; Amorn B.
11533 þus . . . do] had don þus B. to] to *superscript with a caret* L. þe] þat TLB.
11534 at] of B.

// Þo kyngis ȝeoden anoþ*er* wey
Whe*nn*e heroude herde þerof sey
Wrooþ wex þ*at* wrongful kyng   fol. 68r col. 2
And helde hym dryuen to scornyng   11540
Þei sett aspyes bi þe strete
If þei myȝte þo kynges mete
He bad sle hem for his sake
If þei myȝte hem ouertake
But god wolde not he met hem wiþ   11545
Saaf þei went into her kiþ
Whe*nn*e heroudes say he myȝte not spede
Wrooþ he was as he wolde wede
For his wille myȝte not ryse
He þouȝte to venge hi*m* on oþ*er* wyse   11550
He made oon ordynau*n*ce in hyȝe
Þat mony gulteles shulde dyȝe
For he myȝte not fynde Ihesus
Awreke wolde he hym þus   11554
For þe chesoun of o barn   11557
Mony wolde he haue forfarn
He co*mm*au*n*dide his knyȝtis kene
To sle þo children alle bidene   11560
WiþInne þe tou*n* of bedleem
And wiþouten mony barnteem
He dide hem sakles of lyue
Ful sory made he mony a wyue
Wiþynne þe londe laft he none   11565
Of two ȝeer elde but let hem slone

11537 Þo] Þe B.
11538 þerof] þ*at* B.
11539 wex] was LB.
11540 And] He B.
11541 Þei] He B. aspyes] alle spies L; spyes B.
11542 þo] þe B.
11543 sle hem] he*m* sle hy*m* B.
11545 he] þey B. hem] w*ith* hem, w*ith* cancelled L.
11547 heroudes] heraud B.
11548 wolde] wold wold, *first* wold *cancelled* L; were B. wede] wode B.
11550 on] *om.* B.
     After l. 11551 Add has an extra line.
11555–56 *om.* HTLB.
11557 chesoun] encheson B. o] þat B.
11560 þo] þe B.
11562 mony] eny LB.
11563 hem] hem alle L. of] on B.
11565 þe londe] þ*at* contre B.
11566 two] ij° L. elde] old LB. let] did B.

Of two ʒeer or wiþynne þus
So he wende to sle Ihesus
Al for nouʒte gon he stryue
Myʒt he not ihesu brynge of lyue 11570
He þat oure aller lyf may ʒyue
Wiþouten hym may no man lyue
Ar he wolde þat myʒty kyng
Miʒt noon him to deþe bryng
And ʒit not þenne but he shulde ryse 11575
Riʒt at his owne deuyse
Þis was þe somme in certeyn
Of þe childre þat were slayn
An hundride fourty & foure þousande
Þourʒe ihesu coom to lyf lastande 11580

But seuen dayes bifore we rede fol. 68v col. 1
Ar heroudis made do þis dede
Þer Ioseph on slepe lay
An aungel to hym gon say
Ryse vp Ioseph do þe to go 11585
Wiþ marye & hir childe also
ʒe mot nedis alle þre
Into egipte londe fle
Riseþ vp er hit be day
And folweþ euer þe wete way 11590
Heroude þat is þe childes fo
Now awayteþ him to slo
Þere shul ʒe dwelle wiþ þat barn
Til I come efte ʒow to warne
Soone was Ioseph redy boun 11595

11567   two] ijᵒ L. ʒeer] ʒere olde B.
11568   So] Þus B.
11570   of] on B.
11571–72   *om.* C.
11571   aller] alder B.
11574   noon him] hym no man B.
11575   shulde] schul B.
11579   fourty ... þousande] xl and iiij M¹ L.
11580   Þourʒe] To L.
11581   seuen] vij L. bifore] afore B. we] wer H.
11582   Ar ... made] Þat heraude schuld B.
11586   hir] þe B.
11587   ʒe] ʒow B.
11590   folweþ] wendith B.
11592   awayteþ] waiteþ B. to] for to B.
11593   þat] þe B.
11594   efte ʒow] you efte TL.

By ny3te he went out of þe toun
Wiþ mary mylde & her meyne
A mayden also & knaues þre
Þat þenne were in her seruyse
Alle were þei war and wyse   11600
Forþ she rood þe mayden mylde
And in hir armes lad hir childe
Til þei coom by a caue depe
Þere þei þou3te to reste & slepe
Þei dide marye þere to li3t   11605
Soone þei sawe an vgly sy3t
As þei loked hem bisyde
Out of þis caue þei sawe glyde
Mony dragouns sodeynly
Þe gromes þo bigon to cry   11610
Whenne Ihesus say hem drad so be
He went doun of his modir kne
And stood vpon þe beestis grym
And þei louted doun to hym
Þus coom þe prophecye al clere   11615
To dede as seiþ þe sautere
3e dragouns wonynge aboute
Þat lord owe 3e loue & loute
Ihesu went biforn hem þon
Forbede harm to any mon   11620
Mary & Ioseph not forþi   fol. 68v col. 2
For þat childe were dredy
Ihesu seide to hem vchone
For me drede haue 3e none
Lete no sorwe into 3ou bite   11625

11596   he] þay B. þe] *om.* TLB.
11598   also &] & also TL.
11601   þe] þat TLB.
11602   armes] arme T. lad] bare B.
11603   by] to B.
11604   *repeated in* Add.
11606   Soone] Þere B. vgly] hidous B.
11607   As] *om.* B.
11608   þis] a B.
11610   þo] þere B.
11611   be] *om.* B.
11612   of] on B.
11613   þe] þo T.
11615   al] *om.* B.
11617–18   *om.* F.
11618   loue &] for to B.
11622   þat] þe B. dredy] drery B.
11625   into] to B.

For I am mon al parfite
Alle þo beestis þat are wylde
To me shul be tame & mylde
Lyouns ȝeode hem amydde
And lebardes as þe dragouns didde 11630
Bifore mary & Ioseph þei ȝede
In riȝt wey hem to lede
Whenne mary say þe beestis route
Firste she was greetly in doute
Til ihesu loked on hir bliþe 11635
And bad hir no drede kiþe
Modir he seide haue þou no warde
Nouþer of lyoun ny libarde
Þei come not vs harm to do
But only to serue vs to 11640
Boþe asse & ox þat wiþ hem were
And beestis þat her harneys bere
Out of ierusalem her kiþ
Þe lyouns mekely went hem wiþ
Wiþouten harm of ox or asse 11645
Or any beest þat wiþ hem wasse
Þenne was fulfilde þe prophecye
Þat seide was of Ieremye
Wolf weþer lyoun and ox
Shal come togider lomb & fox 11650
Wiþouten harm or any tene
Þat þenne shal be hem bitwene
A wayn þei hadde & oxen two
Þat her gere was lad in þo

11629–30 *reversed in* B.
11629 Þe lions & þe dragons did B.
11630 And] Þe B.
11631 mary & Ioseph] hem mekely B.
11632 In] Þe B. to] for to B.
11634 greetly in] in grete B.
11638 ny] nor T.
11640 *first* to] for to L. *second* to] ij° L.
11643 her] þat B.
11645 or] & B.
11649 weþer] were þere B. and] or L. ox] foxe B.
11650 &] or *cancelled*, & *superscript with a caret* L. fox] ox B.
11651–52 *om.* CAddG.
11651 or] of L.
11652 shal] sche B.
11653–56 *om.* F.
11653 two] ij° L.

Forþ went þei her wey þon   11655
Wiþouten techyng of any mon

Mary folwede rydynge good pas
Greet hete in wildernesse hit was
Of greet trauaile she was wery
A palme tre she say hir by   11660
Ioseph she seide now wolde I rest   fol. 69r col. 1
Vndir þis tre me þinke best
Gladly [he said] þat wol resoun
Anoon he went & toke hir doun
Whenne she was set sikerly   11665
She bihelde þis tre so hy
She say a fruyt þeron hongonde
Men clepe palmes in þat londe
Ioseph she seide fayn wolde I ete
Of þis fruyt if I myȝte gete   11670
Mary he seide me merueileþ þe
Þat seest þe heȝenes of þis tre
To haue þat fruyt how shulde we do
Monnes honde may noon com to
But I syke for anoþer þinge   11675
Þat we haue of watir wantynge
Oure watir purueaunce is gone
In þis wildernes is none
Nouþer for vs ny for oure fe
Ny for none of oure meyne   11680

// Ihesu sat on his modir kne
Wiþ a bliþe chere seide he
Bowe þe doun anoon þou tre
Of þi fruyt ȝyue vs plente

11655–56 *om.* Add.
11659   greet trauaile] her iorney B.
11660   she say] stode B.
11661   wolde] will B.
11663   he said] *om.* HT.
11667   a] þe B.
11668   clepe] clepid L.
11670   if I] who B. gete] it gete B.
11672   þis] þe B.
11673   þat] þe B.
11674   noon] not B. to] þerto B.
11676   of] *om.* B.
11678   In] And in B.
11679   Nouþer] None B.
11680   *om.* Add.
11683   anoon] he sayde B.

Vnneþes had he seide þat sowne   11685
Þat þe tre ne bowed downe
Riȝt to mary his modir fote
Þe crop nyȝe euen wiþ þe rote
Whenne alle had eten fruyt ynouȝe
Hit bowed stille vche a bouȝe   11690
Til he commaundid hit to ryse
Þat dud hit bowe to his seruyse
To þat tre he spake wiþ myȝt
Ryse vp he seide þat þou þe riȝt
Þou shalt fro nowe forþwarde   11695
Be plauntide in myn orcharde
Among þe trees in paradys
Þat þou & þei ben of prys
Vndir þi rote þer is a sprynge
I wol þat out þe watir wrynge   11700
To be wellyng for my sake   fol. 69r col. 2
Þat we may plente of watir take
Anoon þe tre stert vp stidefast
Vndir þe rote a welle out brast
Wiþ stremes clere fresshe & colde   11705
Alle to drinke ynouȝe þat wolde
Mon & beest in þat place
Vchone þonked god his grace
Vpon þe morwe þo hit was day
And þei were redy to her way   11710
Ihesu turned to þat tre
And seide palme I bid þe
Þat of þi braunchis oon be shorn
And wiþ myn aungel heþen born

11685 þat] þe B.
11687 to mary] evyn to B.
11688 nyȝe . . . wiþ] nere to B.
11691 to] vp L.
11692 Þat] Hit L. hit] *om.* L. to] tille L.
11694 Ryse vp] Arise B. þat . . . riȝt] & stonde vpright B.
11695 fro] he sayde fro B. forþwarde] forward L.
11696 plauntide] blantid L.
11697 in] of B.
11698 of] of o T; one off B.
11700 out . . . watir] þe water oute B.
11703 stidefast] faste B.
11704 out] vp B.
11708 his] of his TLB.
11709 Vpon] On B. morwe] morn LB. þo] when B.
11710 redy to] ridyng on B.
11711 þat] a B.
11714 heþen] hennes TB.

In paradys plaunted to be   11715
Þere is my fadir murþes to se
Vnneþe was þis word spoken
An aungel coom a bowe was broken
And born away also soone
His commaundement was done   11720
Þe bouȝe to heuen wiþ him he bere
Þei fel in swowne þat þere were
Þe siȝte of aungel made hem mad
Ihesu seide why are ȝe drad
Wheþer þat ȝe wite hit nouȝt   11725
Þat hondes myne þis tre wrouȝt
I wol now þat of þis tre
Stonde in paradis to be
To my seyntis in stide of fode
As hit in þis wey stille ȝit stode   11730
Þenne ȝeode þei forth her way
Ioseph gan to ihesu say
Lord þis is a mychel hete
Hit greueþ vs hit is so grete
If þou rede þerto we wolde   11735
Þe weye bi þe see to holde
Þere be townes in to rest
Þat wey to go me þinke best

//   Ioseph drede þe not I say
     I shal make short þi way   11740
     Of þritty dayes iourney þro   fol. 69v col. 1
     Þou shalt haue but a day to go
     As þei togider talkyng were
     Þei loked aboute fer & nere
     Soone bigon þei þo to se   11745
     Of egipte lond a good cite

11716   murþes] mirthe B.
11717   þis] þe B.
11721   he] a B.
11722   Þei fel] Þan fill þey B. þere were] were þere B.
11723   Þe] Þis B. of] of þe B. mad] drad B.
11724   why] what B. drad] mad B.
11730   stille ȝit] ȝit stille T; till vs B. ȝit] yt L.
11733   a] *om.* B.
11736   to] *om.* B.
11741   þritty] xxx L. þro] so B.
11742   a day] one B.
11744   fer] boþe fer B.
11745   þo] for B.
11746   a] þe B. cite] contre B.

Þen wex þei glad & bliþe
And coom to þat cite swiþe
Fonde þei þere no knowyng
To aske any gestenyng   11750
Þat tyme þat þei coom to towne
Were prestis at her temple bowne
To make þe folk as þei were set
Do sacrifise to her maumet
Mary ny3e was Inned þere   11755
To se þe chirche hir sone she bere
Whenne he was þe chirche comen In
Men my3te a selcouþe se to myn
Alle þo deueles in a stounde
Grouelynge fel to þe grounde   11760
Doun to þe erþe were þei leide   11763
Þenne coom þe prophecie was seide
Whenne he seide þe lord shalle   11765
Come to egipte ydoles alle
Shul falle & wax to nou3t
Whiche þei wiþ her hondis wrou3t

// Of þat toun was a lordyng
Whenne him was tolde þis tiþing   11770
He gedered folk & dwelt nou3t
And to þe temple he hem brou3t
For to wreke hem was he boun
Þat þus cast his goddis doun
Whenne he say in þe tempel lye   11775
His goddis & his maumetrye
He coom to mary wiþouten harme

11747   wex] were B.
11748   þat] a B.
11749   no] non B.
11752   at] to L. her] þe B.
11754   Do] To make L; To B.
11755   ny3e] dere B.
11757   was ... chirche] þe chirch was B.
11758   a selcouþe] haue mervayle B.
11759   a] þat B.
11760   Grouelynge] Develing þay B. to] vnto B.
11761–62   *om.* CAddGHTLB.
11764   was] þat B.
11766   ydoles] & þe ydols L.
11767   & wax] & was T; awey L.
11768   Whiche] Swich B.
11769–72   *om.* B.
11773   wreke] worke B.

As she hir childe bar in barme
Wiþ honour bifore him he felle
And to þe folk þus gan telle 11780
But þis childe were god of myȝt
Oure goddis had stonde[n] vpriȝt
But for he is almyȝty sene fol. 69v col. 2
Oure are fallen doun bidene 11784
Þe wreke of him sore may we drede 11787
As witnesseþ oure elderes dede
How hit bitidde of pharaone
Wiþ alle his folke was fordone 11790
For þei wolde not on god leue
Þerfore had þei þat greue
Alle þei drowned in þe see
I trowe by him so do now ȝe
Was no temple in al þat toun 11795
Þat þerof ne fel sumdel doun

// In egipte leue we Iesus þus
To telle sumwhat of heroudus
Heroude had regned þritty ȝere
Whenne þat mary ihesu bere 11800
Siþen he regned [yer]es seuen
Fer he brouȝte himself fro heuen
Þat false feloun goddis fo
Souȝte his lord for to slo
How had he hert to shede her blood 11805
Þat neuer dide but good
Þat wilful wolf þat ferde so fals

11778 As] And B. hir childe] hym B. in] in her B.
11781 of myȝt] allmight LB.
11782 Oure] Þes B. had stonden] hadden stonde H.
11784 fallen] fals & B.
11785–86 *om.* HTLB.
11787 wreke] werk B.
11788 As] Þat B.
11789 of] on B.
11791 leue] beleue B.
11792 had . . . þat] all had þey B.
11793 drowned] drenchid B.
11794 so . . . now] now so do L. ȝe] non B.
11795 Was] Ther was L. no] non B.
11796 Þat . . . sumdel] But som thereof fyllyn L; Bote þat þere fell som þerof B.
11799 þritty] xxx L.
11801 yeres] þryes GHTLB. seuen] vij L.
11805 her] his B.
11806 Þat . . . dide] Off hym þat did neuer B.

Aȝeynes fremde & frendis als
His deolful dedis most be knowen
Monqueller was he to his owen   11810
Þat gredy gerarde as a gripe
Now his wrongis bigon to ripe
And for his seruyse mony a day
Þenne coom tyme to take his pay
Þat cursed caitif so vnmeke   11815
Þo bigan to waxe seke
Þe palesy smoot his oon syde
Þat dud him faste abate pryde
On his hede þer wex a skalle
Þe scabbe ouergooþ his body alle   11820
Þus at ones coom þis þ[r]ing
Þe folk say sorwe on her kyng
Þe ȝicche toke him sikerly
Þe fester smoot þourȝe his body
Þe goute potager euel to bete   11825 fol. 70r col. 1
Hit fel doun into his fete
Ouer al was he mesel pleyne
Þerwiþ he had þe feuer quarteyne
Þe dropesy so togider him prest
Þat he wende his body wolde brest   11830
Þe fallyng euel had he to melle
His teeþ out of his heed felle
On vche syde him souȝte his sore
Miȝte no mon wiþ lyf haue more
Ouer al wrong out þe wore   11835
Maþes cruled in him þore

11808   fremde] his frend L.
11811   gripe] crip B.
11812   Now] Anon L.
11813   And] Now B. a] *om.* B.
11818   faste] *om.* B. pryde] his pryde B.
11820   ouergooþ] ouerwent B.
11821   þring] þing HT.
11822   on] of B.
11825–26   *om.* L.
11825   potager] patagre B.
11827   was he] he was B.
11828   þe] *om.* B. feuer] fyre L.
11829   prest] threst L.
11830   Þat] *om.* B. brest] tobrest B.
11831   had] had had, *first* had *cancelled* B.
11833   him] it B. his] hym B.
11834   wiþ . . . haue] lyffe wiþ B.
11835–36   *om.* L.
11835   þe] þere B.

Þis caitif so vnmeke
Doþ him leches for to seke
Þei comen boþe fro fer & neer
Þe sliȝest of þat ilke mister   11840
And for þei myȝte not leche his wo
Alle he dude hem for to slo
Fro him fledde his owne meyne
Boþe sone & seruauntis to se
Þus his frendis fro him fledde   11845
Miȝt noon for stynke come to his bedde
Alle fled fro him away
And preyed aftir his endynge day

// Whenne þat archelayus his sone
Say þus his sory fadir wone   11850
To þe baronage soone he sent
To make a pryue parlement
Gode men he seide what is ȝoure siȝt
Of my fadir þat þus is diȝt
Ȝe seen he haþ no monnes taile   11855
Þerfore say me ȝoure counsaile
He is so stad in his wo
Sawe we neuer noon oþer so
Þe rotyng of him þat renneþ oute
And þe stynke him aboute   11860
May no lyuying mon hit þole
He sleeþ his leches deed as cole
Wood is he þus in þis debate
He is in a sorweful state
For wo he is out of his wit   11865 fol. 70r col. 2
I rede if ȝe assente to hit
Þat we gete vs leches tweyne
In whiche he may triste certeyne

11838 Doþ] Did B.
11840 ilke] *om.* B.
11846 to his] ner his, his *superscript with a caret* B.
11848 aftir] for L.
11850 þus] *om.* B.
11854 þus is] is þus TB.
11855–56 *copied after ll. 11863–64 in* Add; *om.* L.
11855 taile] entaile B.
11860 aboute] all aboute B.
11863–64 *reversed in* Add.
11863 þis] his B.
11864 in] *om.* L. state] estate L.
11866 assente] sent B.
11868 he] we TL.; me B.

A newe baþ to make & proue
Of picche & brymston for his loue   11870
And whenne hit welleþ in þat hete
Caste him In & lete hym swete
Þe baronage seide good is þis rede
For almes were þat he were dede

// Þo leches soone dud þei brynge   11875
Whenne þei coom bifore þe kynge
He lift vp his lodly chyn
Lokyng felounly and grym
Horesones he seide what are ȝe
Leches þei seide to leche þe   11880
Medicyne shal þou of vs take
A nobul baþ we shul þe make
By þat þou come þerof oute
Þou shalt be hool as any troute
Þei filled a leed of picche & oyle   11885
And faste diden hit to boyle
Whenne hit was at her wille diȝt
Þei liften vp þat cursed wiȝt
Traitours he seide ȝe shul goon
To honge but I be hool anoon   11890
Nay certis þei seide sir kynge
Shal þou neuer no man hynge
By þat we ones fro þe part
But if we failen of oure art
Herwiþ þei let þe heed doun   11895
And vp þe feet of þat feloun
Soone helde þei him her hete

11872 In] þerin B. lete] make B.
11873 baronage] barons B. þis] thy LB.
11874 he] sche *cancelled*, he *superscript* B.
11875 Þo] Þe B.
11876 Whenne] And when B.
11877 lodly chyn] body schen B.
11878 And lokid loþely as I wen B.
11879 Horesones] Here sonnys L.
11880 leche] hele B.
11885 of] with B.
11886 to] for to B.
11887 at] alle L. diȝt] wroght B.
11888 liften] lyftyd L. vp] hym vp B.
11893–94 *reversed in* B.
11895 let . . . heed] held hym B.
11896 of . . . feloun] & doun þe croun B.
11897 helde] shovid L. þei] *om.* T. him her] in his L.

Þ*er*Inne þei honged hi*m* bi þe fete
In þat baþþe of picche & tarre
And sende hi*m* þere he fareþ werre   11900
Wors þen he ferde euer are
For neu*er* comeþ ende of his care
He was lefte wiþ sathonas
And wiþ þe traitour fals Iudas

//   Whenne he was deed gerarde grym   11905 fol. 70v col. 1
Archelaus was kyng aftir him   11906

//   Whe*n*ne heroude was of lyf farn   11911
An au*n*gel coom Ioseph to warn
And seide tyme is þat ȝe go
Ih*esu* wiþ þe mary also
In goddis name into ȝoure kiþ   11915
I bidde ȝow ȝe wende in griþ
For þei þat souȝte þat childe to quelle
Are alle dede I þe telle
Ioseph was of þe tiþing fayn
And hyȝed him to wende aȝayn   ·   11920
But not to þat syde of þe lond
Þere archilaus was reynond
Into þe lond þat het Iude
Þidur turne shulde he

11898 Þ*er*Inne ... hi*m*] And lete hym hang L.
11900 þere ... werre] vnto lucifer B. fareþ] farid L.
11901–04 *om.* B.
11901 he ... euer] euyr he farid L.
11903 lefte wiþ] sent to L.
11904 And ... traitour] There to wonne w*ith* L.
11905 gerarde] þat fals so B.
11907–10 *om.* CGHTLB.
11909–10 *om.* Add.
      After l. 11912, ll. 12077–78 copied and cancelled L.
11913 And] He B. is] it is B.
11914 þe] þe & B.
11915–16 *om.* L.
11916 ȝe wende] þat ȝe go B.
11917–20 *illegible in* F.
11917 *second* þat] þe B.
11918 I þe] as I ȝow B.
11919 þe] þis TB; that L.
11921–24 *om.* L.
11921 þat] þe B. þe] þat T.
11922 Þere] Þat B.

Into galile he went 11925
In wille & also good entent

How ih*e*su dude in childehede
Som*þ***ing I wol ʒow rede**

Hit fel vpon an haliday
Þat sabat het in Iewes lay 11930
Ih*e*su & oþ*er*e childre samen
Wente hem bi þe ryuer to gamen
Ih*e*su sat dou*n* on his play
And de*m*myngis seue*n* made of clay 11934
Þat watir myʒte re*n*ne fro & tille 11937
Out of þe flou*m* al at wille
Among þo childre oon þ*er* was
Þat sibbe was to satanas 11940
Wiþ [ni]þe & wiþ euel wit
Þe watir re*n*nyng gon he dit
Þat watir to þe lakes brouʒt
And shende þe werke þat ih*e*su wrouʒt
Þe*n*ne seide ih*e*su þou goddis fo 11945
Son of losse & of deþ also
Þat I haue done þou hast spilt
Þou shalt abye þat ilke gilt
Was þ*er* þe*n*ne no lenger mote
But dede he fel dou*n* at his fote 11950
His frendis þo bigu*n*ne to crye fol. 70v col. 2
Aʒeyn Ioseph and marye
Þei seide ʒoure sone wantou*n* & wylde
Wiþ his cursyng haþ slayn oure childe
Whe*n*ne mary & Ioseph herden þis 11955
Soore dredde þei tresoun Iwis

11925–34 *illegible in* F.
11926 also] in B.
11926a in] in his T.
11929 vpon] on B.
11931 samen] in samyn L; in same B.
11932 to] for to B.
11933 sat] sett hym B.
11934 de*m*myngis] da*m*mes B. seue*n*] vij L.
11935–36 *om.* HTLB.
11937–54 *illegible in* F.
11938 al at] att his B.
11941 niþe] erþe HTLB.
11943 Þat] Þe B.
11944 ih*e*su] crist haþe B.
11946 losse . . . deþ] deþe and los B. deþ] dett L.
11950 dou*n*] *om.* B.
11955–58 *om.* L.

Of þe frendis of þis barne
Soone wente þei ihesu to warne
Penne seide Ioseph to marye
Speke þou wiþ him priuelye   11960
And aske him why he makeþ vs
For his maneres be hated þus
Oure neyȝebores wol hem on vs wreke
Speke þou for I dar not speke
Mary souȝte & fonde him soone   11965
My lord she seide what haþ he done
Pis body ded worþi to be
Ihesu seide worþi is he
Wh[e]nne he wolde not suffer to stonde
Pe werke made of my honde   11970
She seide sone worche not þis wyse
Lest alle wol vpon vs ryse
Ihes[u] þat was so curteyse
His modir algate wolde he pleise
On þe dede cors þere he lay   11975
Wiþ foot he smoot & þus gon say
Ryse vp þou ful of felony
Pou wast neuer ny art worþi
In my fadir riche to be set
For þou hast my dedis let   11980
Pis cors vp ros whenne he seide so
And on his wey did him to go
Ihesu soone in þat tyde
Let þe watir renne & slyde

the sparrons of clay

11957   þis] þe B.
11960   þou] *om.* B.
11962   For] With B.
11963–64   *om.* L.
11964   þou] ȝe B.
11965   Mary . . . &] She sowght hym & L. him] *om.* L.
11966   haþ he] haue ȝe B.
11967–68   *reversed in* L.
11967   Pis . . . worþi] Is he worþy dede B. Pis] His L. worþi] for L.
11969   Whenne] Whonne H; For L. to] *om.* LB.
11970   made of] þat I made with B.
11971   þis] on þis B.
11973   Ihesu] Ihesc H.
11974   algate] all way B. pleise] prays B.
11975   cors] body L.
11978   wast] were B.
11979   to] *om.* B.
11980   dedis] werkis B.
11981   Pis cors] The body L.
11983   soone] right sone L.

And of cley of þo lakes selue   11985
Wiþ hondis made he sparwes twelue
On her sabot þus he dide
Mony childre were in þat stide
Whenne iewes þis gon se & here
Þei spak to Ioseph in þis manere   11990
Seest þou not Ioseph bi þi fay   fol. 71r col. 1
How ihesus brekeþ oure haliday   11992
Ioseph þenne to ihesu spake   11995
Why dost þou men þus pleynt to make
For þi werkis on oure sabot
Ihesu togider his hondis smoot
And seide in her aller siȝt
Ryse vp briddes & make ȝoure fliȝt   12000
Fleeþ & lyueþ ouer al þis werd
Þei toke her fliȝte & forþ ferd
Whenne þei þis say þat bi him stood
Summe seide him euel & summe good
Somme him loued & helde of pris   12005
Somme him blamed þat were not wys
Somme þat þis wondir sawe
Wente to prestis of þe lawe
And seide how Ioseph sone
To do siche maystryes was wone   12010
Bifore þe folke of israelle
Þat hit was sooþ for to telle
At þe last coom þis tiþonde
To twelue kynredes of þe londe

A prestis sone þo stood þere   12015
And in honde a ȝerde he bere

11985–86   *reversed in* B.
11985   And of] Of L; Off þe B. *second* of] and of L. þo] þe B.
11986   twelue] xij LB.
11990   in] on B.
11992   How] Oure L.
11993–94   *om.* CGHTLB.
12000   make] take TLB.
12002   ferd] þay ferde B.
12003   *om.* B.
12004   him] *om.* B. good] sayde gode B.
12005   & helde] þat were B.
12006   Somme] And som B.
12014   twelue] xij L.
12015–28   *partly illegible in* F.
12015   þo] *om.* B.
12016   in] in his B.

Þourʒe enuye wraþþe & tene
He brake þo lakis alle bidene
Boþe he ditted þe watir lade
And temed þe lakes þat he made   12020
Þenne seide ihesu in hiʒe
Þow wrecche seed of felonye
Werk of deeþ sone of satone
Of þi fruyt shal be seed none
For þi rotis are alle drye   12025
Shal neuer þi braunchis multiplie
Wiþ þis he drouʒe away for drede
And siþen fel he doun dede
Þenne took ioseph ihesu to lede
Mary & þei homwarde ʒede   12030
Comeþ a childe malediʒt
Aʒeyn ihesu to ryse he tiʒt
Wiþ childer coom he him aʒeyn   fol. 71r col. 2
And wolde haue felde ihesu certeyn
Ihesus seide to þat feloun   12035
Shal þou neuer com sounde to toun
Þat þou didest were resoun none
Wiþ þat he fel doun dede as stone
Þe childes frendis þat deed him say
Cryed & sayden waileway   12040
Þei seiden what childe is þis
Þat þus may do þat his wille is
And þat he biddeþ also soone
Wiþouten lettyng hit is done
To Ioseph on pleynt ʒeode þei   12045
And þus gon þei to him say
Do way fro vs ihesus þi sone
For in no toun may he wone
Or ellis teche him þan
Blessing to vse & not to ban   12050

12018   brake þo] brast þe B.
12019–20 *reversed in* B.
12022   wrecche] workest B. felonye] folye B.
12023   *second* of] *om.* B.
12026   Shal . . . braunchis] Þy branchis schall neuer B.
12031–32 *om.* F.
12037   were] was B.
12039   deed] did L.
12042   þus] *om.* B. *second* þat] what B.
12045   on . . . ʒeode] to playne did B.
12048   no] non B.
12050   Blessing . . . vse] Vs to blisse B.

Þenne seide Ioseph wiþ mylde chere
Why dostou sone on þis manere
Seestou not how mony wedis
Of þis folk for þi dedis
Þei hate vs alle & han in leþ   12055
And we may not þole her wreþ
Ihesu ȝaf Ioseph vnswere
Is no wyues sone nowhere
But he mot bi his fadir be lerd
Aftir þe wisdom of þis werd   12060
Of þe fadir þe waryinge dereþ nouȝt
But to þat sone þat mys haþ wrouȝt

//   Þe grete lordyngis were ful tene
On ihesu roos þei alle bidene
And pleynt on him made comunely   12065
Boþe to Ioseph & to mary
Þen gon Ioseph sore to drede
Þe tresoun of þe Iewis dede
Þat him & mary þus gon blame
And ihesus hent vp þat licame   12070
Þat lay deed bifore þe þrong
Ihesu bi þe heer him vp hong
Þat alle myȝt se him speke him to   fol. 71v col. 1
As childe shulde to fadir do
And þe spirit awey fled   12075
Come aȝeyn in þat sted
Þe dede cors wex hool & fere
Alle had selcouþe þat þere were

12055   leþ] wreþ B.
12058   sone] son w, w *cancelled* B.
12059   be lerd] lerd L; lere B.
        After l. 12060, B *inserts an extra line:* Þat he is euer afferde
12061   dereþ] dredith B.
12062   *first* þat] þe B.
12063   ful] full of B.
12065   comunely] comely L.
12069   &] on L. þus gon] gan to B.
12070   licame] lykid hame L.
12071   deed] day L.
12072   heer] arme F. him] *om.* B.
12073   Þat alle] And alle L; All þat B. him . . . to] speke or go B.
12075   þe] his L.
12076   Come] And come L.
12077   &] in L.
12078   selcouþe] marvayle LB.

A maister þat was wondir kene
At ihesu was he ful tene 12080
For he spak so skilfuly
To him had he greet enuy
Þourʒe swellyng of his herte
To Ioseph spak he wordis smerte
Þo wordis were ful of despite 12085
As he wolde wiþ Ioseph flite
If þou he seide loue þi sone
To bettur þewis þou him wone
But if þou wolt him haue a fole
Þou most do set him to þe skole 12090
For to lerne & stonde in awe
And to his eldre worshepe drawe
But hit is sene wel þerby
Leuer þe is þou & mary
Þat he loue ʒow þen londis lawe 12095
For ʒe him done in noon awe
Þe firste þat men shulde him ken
To menske prest & elder men
Wiþ oþere childre suche as he
To holde fast loue & charite 12100
And wiþ hem louesumly to dwelle
Boþe þe lawe to here & telle

// Ioseph seide on what manere
Miʒt men holde him to lere
If þou wenest him to lerne 12105
Þat to do wol we not werne
Þing þat falleþ to monnes lore
Ihesu vnswered þe maistir þore
Þou art commaundur of lay

12079 þat] þer TB.
12080 he ful] full of B.
12082 had he] he had B.
12086 Ioseph] hym a B.
12090 þe] *om.* B.
12094 þou &] and þou B.
12097 shulde] shulle L.
12098 To men myspeke & to preistes he sen, he *cancelled, then this line cancelled and l. 12098 copied correctly* L. menske prest] worschip prestis B. elder] old B.
12102 þe] in B.
12103 on] in B.
12104 to] forto B.
12105 wenest] couettis L.
12107 Þing] Þat B.
12109 Þou art] Now art þou B. lay] þe lay B.

As I now here þe say   12110
Þou & oþer are holden þerto
But I am not holden þat to do
For I am departide sooþ to say   fol. 71v col. 2
To be bounden to erþely lay
Of [ʒ]oure lawes outaken am I   12115
I haue no fadir erþely
Þou art vndir lawe bounden
And I am ar þe lawe was founden
And ʒit þou wenest makeles to be
Þat noon in lore shulde teche þe   12120
I con þe teche þat þou not can
Þinge I lerned neuer of man
Þou woost not whenne þou was born
I woot wel & þer biforn
Not ʒit allone þat tyme past   12125
But als how longe þi lyf shal last
For to be lyuynge in þis werd
Alle wondride þat þis word herd
Anoon alle gan þei crye
Who herde euer siche ferlye   12130
Of any man bi norþ or souþ
Who herde euer siche selcouþ
We witen alle wel of þe now
Where þou were born & what art þow
Þin elde is not to vs in were   12135
Vnneþis art þou ʒ[i]t of fyue ʒere
Wheþen coom þou þat art so ʒing
For to brynge forþ siche talkyng

12110   now] *om.* B. say] here saye B.
12111   are] be B.
12112   holden þat] beholden so B.
12114   erþely] ethir L.
12115   Of] To B. ʒoure] oure HL. outaken] vntaken B.
12116   haue no] ne have L. no] non B.
12117   lawe] þe lawe B.
12123   was] wer B.
12125   þat] þe B.
12126   als] *om.* AddB; ellis CFG.
12128   þis word] þes wordis B.
12131   Of] Be B. bi] of B.
12133   wel] *om.* B.
12135   elde is] eldris L.
12136   ʒit] ʒt H. of fyue] of v L; fifften B.
12137   Wheþen] Whens B.

Alle seide so mot we þryue
We herde neuer siche a child on lyue   12140

// Ihesu ʒaf to hem vnswere
To alle þe iewis þat þere were
Alle he seide ʒe haue selcouþ
To here siche speche of childes mouþ
Wherfore wole ʒe not trowe   12145
Soþer þingis þat I telle ʒowe
ʒe wondir on þat I seide ore
Þat I knowe þe tyme bifore
Whenne ʒoure modris ʒow bere
ʒit I say more forsoþe here   12150
Of Abraham whiche ʒe calle
For to be ʒoure fadir alle
I say hym & wiþ him spake als   fol. 72r col. 1
And ʒitt ʒe wene þat I am fals
Whenne ihesu þus had seide his wille   12155
As a stoon þo wex þei stille
Alle þat weren þore olde & ʒonge
A word durst not speke wiþ tonge
To þat folk spak ihesu shene
As childe wiþ ʒow haue I bene   12160
Among childre as childe I spake
To me no knowleche wolde ʒe take
Wiþ wyse spake I wisdome wiþ
But wolde ʒe no þing wiþ me kiþ
ʒe vndirstode me not forþi   12165
Lasse I woot are ʒe þan I
Hit is sene ʒe are of litil faye
Þen gan a maistir for to saye   *Levi*

12139   we] I B.
12140   siche . . . child] non swich B.
12143   Alle] Alle they, they *cancelled* L.
12146   þingis] þing B.
12147–48   *copied as one line in* Add.
12147   on] *om*. B. ore] of oþer B.
12148   knowe] knew L.
12149   Whenne] When þat B. ʒow] ye L.
12150   I . . . here] se I ferþermore B. I say] say I TL.
12154   am] sey L; be B.
12155   þus had] had þus B. his] his wa, wa *cancelled* L.
12156   wex] stode B.
12164   kiþ] kt kyth, kt *cancelled* L; liþ B.
12167   sene . . . are] sevyn yer L.
12168   a] þe B.

Þus to Ioseph & to marye
We haue a maistir het leuye   12170
Him to teche wol he not warn
To him biteche ӡe ӡoure barn
Þo ӡeode Ioseph & mary meke
Wiþ cherysshynge to ihesu speke
To þe scole him to tille   12175
But in þat scole he sat so stille
Þat euel ny good spake he nouӡt
Þenne þei him to sir leuy brouӡt
Maistir leuy þe olde mon
Tauӡte him a lettre þon   12180
And bad him ӡyue vnswere
And ihesu helde him stille þere
Leuy for wrooþ a ӡerde hint
And smot him on þe hede a dynt
Ihesu seide þo to leuy   12185
Wherfore smytest þou me & why
I say forsoþe if þou wolt trow
Þou smytest him co[n] more þen þow
For þat þou techest to oþer men
Þyn owne word I con þe ken   12190
Þei are blynde þat oþere leres
[And] woot [not] what þei teche her feres
As a chymbe or a brasen belle   fol. 72r col. 2
Þat nouþer con vndirstonde ny telle
What tokeneþ her owne soun   12195
Þei wante witt and resoun
Ihesu folwede on his speche
And of þis resoun vnswere to seche
Þe lettres fro alpha to tayu
Wiþ dyuerse siӡte may men sew   12200
What is tayu seye firste to me

12169–70   *reversed in* Add.
12171   he] we B.
12176   *om.* Add. þat] þe B.
12177–78   *reversed in* Add, *and an extra line added.*
12178   him to] to hym B.
12179   þe] an B.
12185–12383   *om.* L, *one leaf missing.*
12187   þou] ӡe B.
12188   con] com H.
12192   And] I H; þat B. not] *om.* H.
12194   nouþer con] can not B.
12198   And] *om.* T. resoun] wite B.
12199   fro] of B. tayu] trowe B.
12201   What] Þat B.

And I shal vndo alpha to þe
He þat alpha con not seen
How shulde he knowe tayu to ben
Ipocritis ȝe are Iwis   12205
Telle me firste what alpha is
And I shal þenne leue ȝow trew
Whenne ȝe telle me what is tayu
Ihesu ȝaf him þenne his taske
Of vche lettre for to aske   12210
Questioun of vchone bi name
Whenne leuy herde he þouȝte shame
Acombred was he for to here
Aske of so mony lettris sere
Þenne he bigon þis cry to ȝyue   12215
Þis chylde oweþ not to lyue
Abouen erþe he lyueþ longe
Worþi he were on gibet honge
Fuyr I woot may him not brynne
An[d] oþer peyne he mot bigynne   12220
I trowe þat þis ilke fode
Was longe tofore noes flode
What wombe him bar & bredde
Wiþ whoos pappis was he fedde
Fle fro him now wol I   12225
His wordis may I not vndirly
Myn hert clyngeþ him to here
But god himself wiþ him were
Is noon may his wordes bere
I wende I hadde ben of mistere   12230
But I caytif al in skorn
I wende my maistir were not born
As prentis wende I him ouercomen   fol. 72v col. 1

12207 trew] *om.* B.
12208 is tayu] it is B.
12210 Of] An B.
12211 vchone] eche B.
12214 Aske . . . so] Þe asking of B.
12215 he . . . þis] began he a B.
12216 to] forto B.
12217 longe] to lone B.
12218 honge] to hong B.
12220 And oþer] Anoþer HT. mot] bot B.
12222 tofore] before B.
12223 What] Whos B.
12227 clyngeþ] cleneth B.
12231 al] *om.* C. in skorn] bi-scorn CG; borne F.
12232 were not] had not be B.
12233 As] A T. wende I him] I wolde hym haue B.

But in his resouns I am nomen
Alas he seide fro þis day   12235
I am ouercomen for euer and ay
Bi a childe of litil belde
Ouercomen I am in myn elde
For he argueþ of siche a þinge
Þat I ne knowe ende ny bigynnynge   12240
In his witt is he so bolde
Þat I may not on him byholde
Me þinkeþ bi my resoun
Mani may not wiþ him comoun
Noþing can I him discryue   12245
Say I neuer sich on my lyue
Ouþer a tregettour he most be
Or ellis god himself is he
Or ellis sum aungel wiþ him dwelleþ
To teche þe wordis þat he telleþ   12250
Wheþen he coom what he shal be
Not woot I by my lewte

// Whenne ihesu had him herde a whyle
He seide & þerwiþ gon to smyle
A commaundement make I here   12255
Þat ȝe alle may se and lere
Þe bareyn shal hir fruyt fynde
And oþer sene þat ȝitt are blynde
The pore also to gete sum bote
And cripul to go riȝt on fote   12260
Þe dede to rise & oþere vchone
Be set into her state anone
To be lastyng in him þat is

12234 resouns] respons B. I am] am I TB.
12237 Bi] With B.
12238 I am] am I B.
12239 a] *om.* B.
12240 ne] *om.* B. ende ny] endyng nor B.
12241 is he] he is B.
12246 on my] one on B.
12250 teche] teche hym B.
12251 what] ne what B.
12253 ihesu] Crist B.
12254 to] he B.
12256 ȝe alle] all ȝe B. lere] here B.
12257 Þe] Her B.
12258 ȝitt are] ere were B.
12260 And] Þe B.
12262 into] vnto B.

Rote of lyf lastynge swetnes
Whenne þat ihesu had seide so   12265
Alle had bote þat were in wo
No more durste þes oþere say
But pryuely þei stale away

Penne went ioseph & mary boun
Wiþ ihesu to anoþer toun   12270
Alle þat meyne mylde & meþ
Wente hem into nazareth
In þat toun mary was   fol. 72r col. 2
Whenne þe aungel brouȝte hir gras
Ihesu went him forþ to play   12275
Wiþ childre on an haly day
In a solere was in þat toun
A childe cast anoþer doun
Out of þat lofte he fel to grounde
So þat he diȝed in a stounde   12280
His frendis herde þis in hyȝe
Þei ron to I[o]seph & to marye
Loude on hem gon þei calle
Wherfore haue ȝe leten þis falle
Ȝoure sone haþ ouris feld wiþ stryf   12285
And felounly brouȝte him of lyf
Þus þei seide on him her wille
Ihes[u] alwey helde him stille
Þat noon vnswere ȝyue wolde he
Til mary & Ioseph were þere fre   12290
Mary seide sone me say
Wheþer put þou þis childe or nay
He seide nouþer euel ny goode
But doun of þat solere he ȝeode
Til he coom þere þat licam lay   12295
Þus to him dide he say

12265   þat ihesu] Ihesu þat B. seide] s sayde, *first* s *cancelled* B.
12268   þei] *om.* B.
12271   Alle] With all, With *cancelled* B. þat] his B. &] of B.
12273   In] Into B.
12282   Ioseph] Ieseph H. *second* to] *om.* B.
12283   hem] hym B.
12284   falle] all B.
12285   sone] s son, *first* s *cancelled* B. feld] slayn B.
12286   of] of his B.
12288   Ihesu] Ihesc HT.
12290   Til . . . Ioseph] To Ioseph & Mary B.
12295   Til] To B. þat licam] þe cors B.

Zeno he seide how farestow
Wel he seide fare I now
If I putt þe soþ þou say
He vnswered lord nay   12300
Þe childes frendis fro þat hour
Helde ihesu wiþ honour

To Iericho whenne þis was done
Ioseph went also soone
Wiþ him mary þat byrde bolde   12305
Ihesu þenne was six ȝeer olde
He bowed to al þat [þei] wolde bidde
Her biddynge bleþely he didde
His modir him bitoke a pot
Watir fro þe welle to fot   12310
Wiþ oþere childre of þe toun
Whenne he had his watir boun   12312
[A childe þat wiþ hem was þare   MS T fol. 76v col. 2
Brake þe pot þat ihesu bare
Wiþ wille or wiþ recheles dynt   12315 MS T fol. 77r col. 1
And ihesu vp þe watir hint
And bare hit hoom as a balle
And presented his modir wiþalle
Whenne mary say þis maistry
In herte she hidde hit priuely   12320
She was trusty & douted nouȝt
But goddes wille wolde be wrouȝt
To his modir berne he ȝede
And toke of whete a litil sede
Vpon þe felde himself hit sewe   12325
And þat same day hit grewe
So þicke þat wondir was to se
Hit mu[l]teplied so greet plente
Hit ȝalde whenne hit was shorn

12302 wiþ] worþe TB.
12303–04 *reversed in* Add.
12306 þenne . . . six] was þo sexten B.
12307 þei] he H.
12309 bitoke] toke B.
12310 fro] at B.
12313–474 *om.* H, *one leaf missing. The text here is printed from* T.
12313 hem] hym B.
12315 Wiþ] *om.* B.
12316 And] *om.* B.
12325 felde] erþe B.
12328 multeplied] muteplied HT. so] *om.* B.
12329 whenne] when þat B.

An hundride fold þat ilke corn   12330
Ihesu toke þis corn in walde
And wondirly aboute him dalt

// From Ierico to flum iurdone
Among þo weyes þere is one
Þat lay riȝt bi þe watris syde   12335
Þere lay a leones þat tide
Norisshinge hir whelpes so
Þat nomon durst bi hir go
Towarde þe flum on a day
Ihesu goynge coom þat way   12340
To þe leones caue he ȝode
Þere he þe whelpes vndirstode
But whenne þe leonesse him sawe
Anoon she dud hir lorde knawe
Alle aȝein him gan rise   12345
And honoured him on her wise
Ihesu sat bitwene hem þon
Aboute his feet þe whelpes ron
Pleyinge wiþ him on her manere
Wiþ her fawnyng made him chere   12350
Þese oþere leouns þat were olde
Stoden afer as bestis wolde
Wiþ hedes bare þei lowe sail
Honoured him wiþ faunnyng tail
Þe folke stood fer & loked tille   12355 MS T fol. 77r col. 2
We say neuer beestis of þis wille
And seide but he or his kynne
Had wrouȝt er som greet synne
Ȝit wolde not leouns on þis wise

12331 þis] his B.
12334 þo] þe B.
12335–36 *reversed in* Add.
12336 leones] lion B.
12340 þat] his B.
12342 whelpes] lions B.
12343 leonesse] lions B.
12345 rise] þey ris B.
12348 His whelpis aboute his fete ran B.
12349 him] hem B.
12350 her] his B. him] hem B.
12351 Þese oþere] Þis olde B.
12352 wolde] bolde B.
12354 Honoured] And honouryd B. faunnyng] hede & B.
12356 þis] swich B.
12358 er] here B.
12359 not leouns] þe lions not B.

Bede to him her seruyse 12360
Whenne ihesus of þe caue coom oute
Þe liouns coomen him aboute
Þe whelpes ran aboute his fete
Wiþ him to pley þouȝte hem swete
Þe folke bihelde & stood on ferre 12365
For leouns durst þei com no nerre

// Ihesu seide now may ȝe se
How beestis are bettur þen ȝe
Þat con our lord honoure & ken
And ȝe þat he haþ made to men 12370
And þat aftir his owne ymage
To him take ȝe no knowlage
Þese beestis in mekenes knowe me
And men knowe not þat þei se
Þenne he ȝede þe flum to passe 12375
Wiþ alle þe leouns þat þere wasse
Þe watir ȝaf him wey ful gode
On eiþer side as wal vp stode
Whenne þei had companyed him so
Forþ in pees he bad hem go 12380
To noye no mon ny no mon þaym
Til þei had her erde aȝayn
Her leue þei toke wiþ her entent
Ihesu hoom to his modir went
Ihesu was þat tyme þore 12385
Of eiȝte yeer olde & more
Ioseph was a parti wriȝt
Plowȝe & harwe coude he diȝt
Treen beddes was he wont to make
And þerfore his seruyse take 12390

12361 þe] þis B.
12362 aboute] all aboute B.
12365 &] þat B.
12366 leouns] drede B.
12368 How ... are] Þat best is B. ȝe] ar ȝe B. Þat] Þey B.
12369 our] her B.
12371 þat] om. B.
12372 no] non B.
12378 vp] it B.
12379 þei] he B. companyed him] convayde hem B.
12381 mon þaym] þing þan B.
12382 her] þe B.
12386 eiȝte] viij L; eygten B.
12388 Plowȝe] Plowes B. harwe] harowes B.
12390 seruyse] labour L.

A mon coom to him in þat sted
To haue made a treen bed
Þat shulde in lengþe þre ellen haue
And Ioseph bad þo to his knaue
Þat he shulde him tymber felle   12395 MS T fol. 77v col. 1
And he þe mesure gon him telle
Þe knaue þat þis tymber fet
Helde not redily his met
Ouershort he brouȝt a tre
Whenne Ioseph coom him for to se   12400
For short miȝt hit not geyne
Doun he hit leide & toke aȝeyne
Whenne ihesu him sey so bisy to be
Aboute þat ilke forseide tre
Ioseph he seide to me þou shawe   12405
Þe on ende þerof for to drawe
Take þou þe oþere for I hete þe
We wol hit lengþe a quantite
Þis tre drowȝe þei hem bitwene
Soone was þere a maistry sene   12410
Þat furst was short & wolde not be
Þo was hit longe ynouȝe to se
Þenne fond Ioseph of lettyng nouȝt
But at his wille his werke he wrouȝt

// Ȝitt souȝte þe folke as tofore   12415
To sette ihesu to lore
Þerof bisouȝte þei marye
Ioseph hem grauntide sikurlye

12391 A mon] Anon one B.
12392 To . . . made] That wold have made L; For to make B.
12393 þre] iij^e L.
12394 And] *om.* B. bad] had L.
12395 him] to hym L.
12397 Þe . . . tymber] Þe tymbir þat þe knaue B.
12400 him] it B.
12402 Doun he] Oft laid dun C; Oft laide he F; Oft he laid G. toke] toke up F.
12403 him sey] se hym B.
12406 on] tone B.
12407 oþere] tothir LB. for] *om.* B. hete] bid B.
12408 a quantite] quarters þre B.
12409 drowȝe þei] þey drowe B.
12410 a] *om.* B.
12411 Þat] *om.* B. was] was it B.
12413 Þenne] They *altered to* Then L. fond] had B.
12414 he] *om.* B.
12415 souȝte] þoght B.
12416 sette] Iohn sett, Iohn *cancelled* B. *second* to] vnto B.

To þe scole was he brouȝt
Þe maistir foly on him souȝt   12420
He bigon him for to lere
Wiþ wicked wille & euel manere
He bad him alpha for to say
Ihesu vnswered & seide parfay
Telle me furst what is betha   12425
And þenne shal I saye of alpha
Þe maistir wrooþ wiþ him wase
And smot ihesu in þat plase
For he him smoot wiþ no resoun
Deed in place he fel adoun   12430
And ihesu þat had þoled shome
To his modir went home
Ioseph anoon þenne sikurlye
For þat childe called marye
Marie he seide myn hert is sare   12435 MS T fol. 77v col. 2
I drede men wol þis childe forfare
Þe folke to him haþ euel wille
I drede lest þei wol him spille   12438
Nay she seide hit is no nede   12441
Of goddes son for to drede
Þat any mon shal do him wronge
For he þat sent him vs amonge
To be born he wol him seme   12445
F[ra] wicked men him to ȝeme
He þat sent him in his name
Shal him kepe fro al shame

// Þe þridde tyme was ihesu þore
Beden to be set to lore   12450
Þe iewes wolde algate þat he

12419   was he] þey hym B.
12420   Þe] His B.
12425   betha] alpha B.
12426   And] om. B.
12430   place] þat place, þat cancelled B.
12433   þenne] om. B.
12436   þis] our B.
12438   lest] me þat B.
12439–40   om. CAddGTLB.
12442   Of] On B.
12446   Fra] For HT; Fro B.
12448   Shal] He schall B.
12449   þridde] iijᵉ L. was] om. B.
12450   Beden] Þey bade B.

Of her lore shulde lered be
Ioseph & marye wolde not werne
But to þe scole lad him ȝerne
Wiþ cherisshynge & talus mylde   12455
But wel wist þei þat þis childe
Miȝt not be lered of mannes lare
Þat al wiþ-inne himself bare
Whenne ihesus coom into þat scole
If he were ȝong he was no fole   12460
Wiþ þe holy goost he was led
A book to him þe maistir bed
Þat book spake of mannes lawe
Mony þere stood herde & sawe
How he vndid þat he fonde þore   12465
And oþere þingis muchel more
Þe holy goost dud hit him telle
Riȝt as þe spring of a welle
Þat euermore out rennyng es
And þe welle neuer þe les   12470
And so verrely he tolde
Herde neuer mon ȝonge ny olde
So kyndely goddes werkes telle
Þe meister doun for wondir felle]
Honourynge him he fel him vndir   12475 fol. 73r col. 1
Þat al þe folke on him gon wondir
Whenne Ioseph herde he ran blyue
And wende þe maistir were of lyue
As oþer þer toforne were
Þat mys to ihesu hem bere   12480

12452   lore] lawe B.
12455   talus] talking CFG; speche Add.
12457   mannes] mens B.
12459   þat] þe B.
12460   was] nas L.
12461   he was] was he B.
12462   A] Þe B.
12464   stood] was B. &] þat B.
12466   þingis] þing B.
12467   hit him] hym yt L.
12470   neuer] is neuer B.
12472   mon] non B.
12473   werkes] werkys to L; wordis B.
12474   doun] did B.
12475   he fel] he no fel H.
12476   folke] scole L. on . . . gon] had grete B.
12477   blyue] swiþe B.
12478   And] He B. were] had ben B. of] on LB.
12479   toforne] before B.

Þe maister seide to Ioseph ȝerne
Þou brouȝtest not a childe to lerne
But maistir is he al ful parfite
Þerof may no man him quyte   12484

Þen flitted þei to a toun   12487
Þat called was capharnaoun
Þere woned Ioseph & marye
For to fle þe iewis enuye   12490
A burgeis woned in þat cite
Þat Ioseph hett was riche of fe
He had ben seke mony a day
And ded þo in his bed he lay
Whenne ihesu herde þat woful chere   12495
In þat cite so mychel bere
He had þerof ful greet pite
And þus to Ioseph mened he
Wherfore Ioseph seide ihesu now
To þis man þat het as þou   12500
Ne dost þou grace or bounte none
What bounte he seide haue I in wone
Ihesu seide þou hast ful gode
Take & bere to him þi hode
On his face þou hit lay   12505
And þerwiþ to him þus say
Ihesu he shal saue þe
And soone shal he saued be
Ioseph took þis commaundement
And to þe dede cors he went   12510
His hode he leide on his face
And ihesu sent him soone his grace
Vnneþis had he hit on leide
And þo forseide wordis seide

12482   a] þis B.
12483   is . . . al] he is B.
12485-86   *om.* CAddGHTLB.
12494   þo] þere B. his] *om.* B. he] *om.* B.
12495   woful] rewfull B.
12496   þat] þe B.
12501   or] nor T; ne LB.
12502   in] in my L.
12506   to . . . þus] þus to him TL. þus] *om.* B.
12509   took] takeþ B. þis] his L.
12510   þe] þis B.
12512   And] *om.* B.
12513   on] on hym B.
12514   þo] þe B.

Whenne þat cors boun to bere   12515
Roos vp al hool & fere

// Not longe dwelled þei þere so   fol. 73r col. 2
But to bedleem flitted þo
Þere wiþ ihesu woned þai
Ioseph calde him on a day   12520
His eldest sone hette Iame
And sende him to þe ȝard bi name
For to gider hem sum cale
And ihesu aftir stilly stale
Ioseph & mary vnwitonde   12525
Whil þei were þat cool gederonde
An edder sprong out of þe sond
And stong iame in his riȝt hond
He was hurt selly sore
Ruly he gan to crye & rore   12530
He swal so faste & wondirlye
Þat almest bigan he for to dye
· For bitternes doun he him leide
And ofte weylawey he seide
Myn honde is stongen bitturly   12535
Whenne ihesu herde þis reuful cry
Þat þis wrecche Iames made
To him he ȝede wiþouten abade
Dide he þere noon oþere gyn
But hent his hond & blew þerIn   12540
So he made al hool his hond
Deed byside þe worm þei fond

W henne Ioseph was wont to wende
To gestenyng wiþ any frende

12515   þat] þe B. cors] bodi F. boun] was boun L; gan B.
12516   Roos] Hyt rose L; And ros B. al] *om.* B.
12518   flitted] flite þay B.
12520   him] to hym B.
12521   hette] þat hight B.
12522   sende] sayde to B. þe] *om.* B.
12523   hem] hym B.
12526   þat] þe B.
12529   selly] felly B.
12530   Ruly . . . gan] He began B.
12532   bigan . . . for] he gan B.
12533   doun . . . him] he hym doun B.
12536   þis] his TL; þat B. reuful] dolfull B.
12539   gyn] Iynne L; þan B.
12540   hent] toke B.
12541   So] Keland CFG. he made] made he B.

His sones went wiþ him boun 12545
Iame Ioseph Iude & symeoun
Wiþ him went als his douȝteres two
Mary wiþ ihesu coom also
And wiþ hir mary cleophe
Þat oon was of þe sistres þre 12550
Two sistres had oure lady we fynde
As we shul aftir make mynde
Whenne þis meyne was gedered samen
Alle hem wantide goostly gamen
Til ihesu was comen in place 12555
To ȝyue him blessyng of his face
Ar he wiþ hem were set in sete fol. 73v col. 1
Wolde þei nouþer drynke nor ete
Ny breke her breed nor messe taste
Til he were to hem comen in haste 12560
And til he were among hem lad
And wiþ his benysoun hem bad
If he were fro hem þat tyde
Til he coom alle shulde abyde
Whenne he shulde to meteshipe go 12565
Mary Ioseph his breþere also
Iosephs sones as I seide ȝore
Alle felowshipe him bore
Þe folk him helde day & nyȝt
Bifore hem as a candel briȝt 12570
Þei him loued & doutid ay
And where he slepte nyȝt or day

12547–48 *reversed in* Add.
12547 als] *om.* B. two] ijº L.
12549 hir] hym B.
12550 þe] þo TL. þre] iijᵉ L.
12551 Two] ijº L.
12552 mynde] in myde B.
12553 was] were B.
12554 hem] þay B.
12556 him] hem B. face] *grace* B.
12558 nor] ne L.
12559 her] *om.* B. nor] ne LB.
12560 to . . . comen] com to hem B.
12562 his] *om.* T. benysoun] hye blissing B. bad] fed B.
12563 hem] home TL.
12564 coom . . . shulde] were come þey wolde B.
12565 meteshipe] mete LB.
12566 also] as also, as *cancelled* L.
12567 ȝore] ore B.
12570 hem] hym B.
12572 And] Or B.

Þe clerenesse of goddis liȝt
Shoone on him no sonne so briȝt
Þe soþe hit is as I ȝow say   12575
We fynde on slepe he lay

// Mony are his childehedes I of tolde
Done ar he were twelue ȝeer olde
Now of somme shul ȝe here
Done whenne he was of twelue ȝere   12580
As luk seiþ vs þe gospellere
Þat trewe witnes is wont to bere
In ierusalem þat hiȝe cite
At a feest was greet semble
Alle þe gode men coom þat day   12585
Mary & Ioseph were not away
Her frendis wiþ hem þider souȝt
Ȝonge ihesu wiþ hem þei brouȝt
Whil þis feest was lastonde
Euer were þei þere dwellonde   12590
Whenne hit was done hoom þei went
And forȝat ihesu wiþouten tent
At þe outcomynge of þe gate
He turned aȝeyn þei him forȝate
Vnto þe iewis folke he ȝede   12595
And loked on bokis of her lede
Disputynge among hem he sat   fol. 73v col. 2
And þei him vnswered mony what
Alle þat in þat folk were stad
For wondir of his witt were mad   12600
Of þis childe þat was so ȝonge
Aȝeyn his resoun had no man tonge

12574 no] as B. so] *om*. B.
12575–76 *om*. FAdd.
12575 hit] *om*. B.
12577 his] þe B.
12578 Done ar] Or þat B. twelue] xij L.
12579–80 *om*. F.
12579 ȝe] we B.
12580 whenne] are Add. of] *om*. B. twelue] xij L.
12581 vs] *om*. B.
12584 semble] solempnite B.
12593 *om*. B.
12595 folke] bokis B.
12596 of] on B.
12597 among hem] hem among B.
12599 in . . . folk] folke þerin B.
12601 Of] Aȝen B.
12602 no man] þay no B.

Among þese maystris þus was he ay
Til mary had made hir iournay
Þenne firste on him þouȝte sho   12605
But wist she neuer what to do
Þei hem biþouȝte in certeyne
Ioseph & mary turned aȝeyne
To seke him þere his frendis wiþ
Oueral aboute in þat kiþ   12610
So longe had mary aboute gone
Þat wery was she liþ & bone
And him she dred wondir sore
And was aferde in hert þe more

// Into þe scole she coom goonde   12615
And greet gederynge þerInne fonde
Of wyse maistris of þat lawe
Wiþ hem sittyng ihesu she sawe
Þe best maystris of þat toun
He ȝaf hem alle redy resoun   12620
His modir seide to him þus
Leue sone why hastou fered vs
Þi fadir & I mony weyes
Han þe souȝte þese þre dayes
Wiþ heuy hert & droupyng chere   12625
Whi didest þou þus leof & dere
He seide modir why souȝt ȝe me
Wherfore shulde ȝe mournyng be
Wite ȝe not þat I most do
Þing þat falleþ my fadir to   12630
What he of þese wordis ment
Þe[i] wiste not fully þe entent

12603   þese] his T; this, t *superscript* B. þus] *om.* B.
12612   she] Mary B.
12614   *om.* B.
12615   coom] gon *cancelled*, com *superscript with a caret* L.
12616   And] A B. þerInne] þere sche B.
12617   þat] þe B.
12619   best maystris] grettest mayster B.
12620   resoun] respon B.
12622   fered] gloppened CFAddG.
12624   þre] iij⁰ L.
12625   droupyng] weping B.
12626   leof &] my leff B.
12628   shulde ȝe] shull ȝe in B.
12631   *om.* Add. ment] w ment, w *cancelled* L.
12632   Þei] Þe H. fully] fulle B.

Fro þenne of ihesu sprong þe nome
Wiþ his modir he went home
And bar him as a childe in doute   12635
To fadir & modir for to loute
How þei wolde lede him was ful eeth   fol. 74r col. 1
Þei went þenne into nazareth
Al þat euer þei wolde him bidde
Wiþouten any stryf he didde   12640
In hert stille held his modir ay
Al þat she herde hym do or say
He wex in witt as was his wille
Miȝt no man him fynde wiþ ylle
Fulde was he wiþ þe holy goost   12645
In nazareth he soiourned moost
Til ihesu was comen nere
To þe elde of þritty ȝere   12648
Þenne him þouȝte tyme þat he   12653
In cristen lay wolde baptised be
Wiþ cristen lawe þe trouþe to sprede   12655
Þerof hereaftir shul we rede
But ar I þerof to telle bigyn
I shal ȝow telle more of his kyn

Whenne þat Ioachim was dede
Anna wiþ hir frendis rede   12660
Was ȝyuen to anoþer husbonde
A douȝty mon of þat londe
Cleophas was his name
Riche of good dede & fame
Soone wiþ hir a douȝtir he gat   12665
Þat mary as hir sister hat

12633–34   *reversed in* Add.
12633   Fro] *om.* B.
12637–38   *reversed in* Add.
12637   was ful] it was B.
12638   þenne] hem B.
12644   him fynde] fynde hym B.
12645   was he] he was B.
12648   elde] age B. þritty] xxxⁱ L; xxx F; twenty Add.
12649–52   *om.* CAddGHTLB.
12655   Wiþ] In B. trouþe] tretys B. sprede] spede B.
12656   hereaftir] afftir B.
12657   I] we B. to telle] *om.* B.
12658   ȝow telle] speke B.
12662   douȝty] noble B.
12664   of . . . &] & also of grete B.
12666   hir] his L.

A mon in mariage hir toke
Alpheus het as seiþ þe boke
Two sones bi hir had alpheus
Þat was Ioseph & Iacobus   12670
Þis Iacob þat I telle of now
Was cald þe broþer of Ihesu
Ihesu broþer calde was he
For sibrede worshepe & b[on]te   12674
Holy lyf he led alwayes   12677
Fro he was born þe story sayes
He dronke neuer cider ny wyne
Ne neuer wered clooþ of lyne   12680
Flesshe eet he neuer of al & alle
He fyned neuer on god to calle
Him þouȝte himself neuer wery   fol. 74r col. 2
On god on knees for to cry
His knees þerof were bollen so   12685
Þat vnneþis myȝte he go
Aftir coom þat tyme men wende
He were þat crist þat shulde be sende
Þis ilke Iacob þat I of telle
As he stood on a day to spelle   12690
In ierusalem was he slone
His soule anoon to heuen did gone

// Whenne he was deed þis cleophas
Anna was ȝyuen to salomas
She wex wiþ childe & bar in hyȝe   12695
A mayden childe hett marye

12668   Alpheus het] Hight Alpheus B.
12669   Two] ijᵒ L; Four B.
        After l. 12670, B *adds*:
        Symon & Iude were oþer two
        Þre were postils with god to go.
12673   *om.* B. broþer] brothir, *first stroke of* w *written and cancelled* L.
12674   sibrede] synbred B. worshepe] lykenes B. bonte] bewte HTLB.
        After l. 12674, B *adds*: Ihesu most lyke was he.
12675–76   *om.* FHTLB.
12678   þe] as þe B.
12680   neuer . . . clooþ] werd cloþe þat was B.
12681   he] *om.* T.
12682   fyned] sesid B.
12684   On] To LB.
12687–88   *om.* F.
12687   Aftir] Affore B.
12696   hett] þat hight B.

She was ȝyuen to zebedee
A douȝty man of galile
Of hir were born gode childre twey
Miche[l] iame þat is to sey 12700
Whiche kyng heroude dide to slo
Þe toþer broþer of þese two
Was seynt Ion þe euangelist
Þat wel was loued wiþ ih*es*u cryst
For his mychel douȝty dede 12705
And for he lyued in maydenhede
Alle þe apostlis he hem past
Þourȝe his maydenhede stidfast
In feloushipe was he ih*es*[u] nest
And lay & slept on his brest 12710
And say þe pr*i*uytees ful euen
Moo þen any man kan neuen

12698 douȝty] noble B.
12699 gode] *om*. B.
12700 Michel] Miche H. iame] Iacob B.
12701 to] *om*. B.
12702 two] ij° L.
12703 euangelist] vangelyst L.
12705 mychel douȝty] doghty & noble B.
12709 he] *om*. L. ih*es*u] ih*es*c H.
12710 And] He B. &] on L. slept] slepe LB. on] vpon B.
12711 ful euen] of hevyn B.

EXPLANATORY NOTES

The general intention behind the abbreviated references was to devise forms both brief and clear. The following list expands the contracted forms with a view to identification and location in the Bibliography, where complete publication details can be found.

LIST OF ABBREVIATIONS

Chester Plays — *The Chester Mystery Cycle*. Lumiansky, R. M., and David Mills, eds.
CM — *Cursor Mundi*. Morris, Richard, ed.
Court of Sapience — Spindler, Robert, ed.
De Nativ. Mariae — Amann, Emile, ed. *Le Protévangile de Jacques*.
Elucid. — *Elucidarium*. Honorius Augustodunensis.
Grosseteste — *Le Château d'amour de Robert Grosseteste*. Murray, J., ed.
Hennecke, *NT Apocrypha* — Hennecke, E., and W. Schneemelcher, eds. *New Testament Apocrypha*.
Herman's *Bible* — *La Bible von Herman de Valenciennes*.
Hist. Schol. — *Historia Scholastica*. Petrus Comestor.
Horrall, *SVCM* — Horrall, Sarah M., ed. *The Southern Version of Cursor Mundi*.
Leg. Aur. — *Legenda Aurea*. Jacobus a Voragine.
Lud. Cov. — *Ludus Coventriae*. Block, K. S., ed.
Lydgate, *Life of Our Lady* — Lydgate, John. *Life of Our Lady*. Lauritis, J. A., ed.
Metrical Life — *The Metrical Life of Christ*. Sauer, Walter, ed.
Mirk's Festial — Mirk, John. *Mirk's Festial*. Erbe, T., ed.
New Cath. Enc. — *New Catholic Encyclopedia* (1967 ed.).
OED — Oxford English Dictionary.
Opus Imperf. — *Opus Imperfectum in Matthaeum*. Pseudo-Chrysostom.
PG — *Patrologia Graeca*.
Piers Plowman — *The Vision of William Concerning Piers the Plowman*. Langland, William. Skeat, W. W., ed.
PL — *Patrologia Latina*.
Protevangelium — *Le Protévangile de Jacques*. Amann, Emile, ed.
Pseudo-Matt. — *Pseudo-Matthaei Evangelium*. Tischendorf, K. von, ed. *Evangelia Apocrypha*.
Sajavaara, *ME Trans.* — Sajavaara, Kari, ed., *The Middle English Translations of Robert Grosseteste's Château d'amour*.
SE Nativity — *The South-English Nativity of Mary and Christ*. Pickering, O. S., ed.
Stanzaic Life — *A Stanzaic Life of Christ*. Foster, Frances A., ed.
The Three Kings of Cologne — Horstmann, C., ed.
Traver, *Four Daughters* — Traver, Hope. *The Four Daughters of God*.
Wace — Wace. *L'Établissement de la fête de la conception Notre Dame*.

NOTES

9229–12712 The section of the *CM* edited here corresponds to the summary of contents presented in ll. 151–66.

9232 The "fyueþe elde" extended from the Babylonian captivity to the birth and early manhood of Christ.

9233–64 Except for a few minor additions, the genealogy is based on *Matt.* 1:11–17.

9244 Neither Matthew's genealogy (1:15) nor *Num.* 3:32 gives an alternate name for Eleazar. Levi comes from *Luc.* 3:24.

9246–51 *Matt.* 1:15 lists only Mathan. JACOBUS A VORAGINE, *Leg. Aur.*, Sept. 8, p. 585, citing JOHN DAMASCENE, *De Fide Orthodoxa*, IV 87 (ed. Buytaert, p. 320) identifies Panthar as Levi's son. Panthar's brother, however, is Melchi, not Mathan as in *CM*. Perpantera derives from Barpanthar, the father of Joachim in *Leg. Aur.*

9260–62 The claim of sixty generations between Adam and Christ is difficult to verify. *Matt.* 1:17 puts the total number of generations between Abraham and Christ at forty-two. *Gen.* 5:4–31 and 11:10–27 list twenty generations from Adam to Abraham inclusive. Possibly the poet felt that Abraham was counted twice in these combined reckonings and that Adam should not have been included since he was not the product of human generation. This would reduce the total to sixty.

9265–347 The immediate source is Herman's *Bible*, ll. 2685–2742a. See also the edition by Ina SPIELE, *Li Romanz de Dieu et de sa mere* (Leyden, 1975).

9269–72 *Is.* 11:1–2.

9273–74 F's "atte sulde bringe vs alle to rest" (l. 9272) radically alters the sense of the line and so requires the extra couplet.

9281–86 The ultimate debt is to *Is.* 7:14.

9287–88 The definition is not in Herman's *Bible*.

9289–91 MSS CFGT support the more familiar "milk and honey" combination as opposed to "Burre et miel" (Herman's *Bible*, l. 2703), and "Butyrum et mel" (*Is.* 7:15). Lines 9290–91 are derived from "Que ert biens et qu'est mals, n'en volra pas douter," Herman's *Bible*, l. 2704, which is based on *Is.* 7:15: "ut sciat reprobare malum, et eligere bonum."

Christ's uncanonical milk and honey diet is puzzling, however. The context is not the traditional one of prosperity, abundance, or fertility, as in *Deut.* 32:13–14; *Ex.* 3:8, 17; 13:5; *Lev.* 20:24; *Ier.* 11:5; *Ezek.* 20:6. Instead these symbolic foods are employed in connection with distinguishing "þe wicke [and] þe good," a usage for which I can find no parallel. Nor does Penna's commentary on the *Isaiah* passage shed any light on the problem: "Probably the reference is not to the awareness of ethical distinctions, but simply . . . to the child's learning to know which food he likes, after being weaned at the age of two or three" ("*Isaiah*" in *A New Catholic Commentary on Holy Scripture*, p. 576).

9294 Much closer to "Quis audivit unquam tale?" in *Is.* 66:8 than to "N'oï mais si parler,/Aucuns fors rois naistra, nel volt del tot mostrer" in Herman's *Bible*, ll. 2705–06.

9297–302 A close rendering of Herman's *Bible*, ll. 2707–11. The promise of a written legacy does not appear in *Isaiah*. In l. 9298 both the positive "openli" (F) and the comparative "opinliker" (CGHTLB) are possible.

9306 "vos fix ert contraire," Herman's *Bible*, l. 2712.

9313–17 Most of these designations are in Herman's *Bible*, ll. 2718–21. "God of strengþe" (l. 9315), however, seems less indebted to "mout par ert redoutés,"

Herman's *Bible*, l. 2721, than to "Deus, Fortis," *Is.* 9:6. Here, as in l. 9294, the *CM* poet shows a readiness to work closely with more than one source at a time.

9318   Probably a return to Herman's *Bible*, whose "empires" (l. 2723) is closer to "regne" (l. 9318) than is "pacis" (*Is.* 9:7).

9328   Herman's *Bible*, l. 2728 and *Is.* 11:1–2.

9329   Herman's *Bible*, l. 2730 identifies the maiden as "Marie." The *CM* poet does not reproduce the play on words found in Herman's *Bible*, l. 2729: "chele verge le vierge senefie."

9332   The notion of envy is from Herman's *Bible*, l. 2732: "Et avra un enfant dont tout aront envie."

9333–38   A close translation of Herman's *Bible*, ll. 2734–37, including the erroneous attribution of the prophecy to Jeremiah. See note on ll. 9341–46 below.

9339   This accusation of spiritual blindness is not found in Herman, whose tone at this point is closer to impatience than to condemnation: "Ne sés tu que j'ai dit? Escoute!" (l. 2738).

9341–46   Herman's *Bible*, ll. 2737–42. The prophecy about the end of anointed kings, here attributed to Jeremiah, was usually credited to Daniel. See *Piers Plowman* B xviii 109; the "Adoration of the Magi" in *Chester Plays*, VIII 297–301; and *The Three Kings of Cologne*, 16/1–2. Although derived from *Dan.* 9:24, the wording of the prophecy comes from PSEUDO-AUGUSTINE, *Contra Judaeos*, PL XLII 1124.

9349–51   The poet here lays particular emphasis on the Jews' unwillingness to believe. The corresponding passage in Herman's *Bible*, ll. 2746–47 is essentially transitional in character and makes no reference to disbelief or sorrow.

9353–66   The abrupt change in subject matter, from the disbelief of the Jews to Mary, is more smoothly managed in Herman's *Bible*, ll. 2744–51. Although the printed text of Herman reads "de mirre si dent" (l. 2759) and *CM* reads "yuory" (l. 9360), the latter reading is among the variants cited in Herman's *Bible*, III, p. 32n. The catalogue of Mary's attributes is taken directly from Herman's *Bible*, ll. 2753–62, with occasional minor omissions and changes in the order. Such flattering comparisons are regularly found in courtly love writings of the period. See M. S. LURIA and R. L. HOFFMAN, eds., *Middle English Lyrics*, nos. 24, 26, 27, 29, 33, 43. The influence of the *Song of Songs* is also clear. See *Cant.* 1:2, 14; 2:2; 4:1–2, 10–11; 7:4. "A Salutacioun to vre Lady," in C. HORSTMANN, ed., *Minor Poems of the Vernon Manuscript*, pp. 121–31, similarly lauds such parts of the Virgin as her thumbs, womb, back, maidenhead, knees, toes, and entrails. As Morris (*CM*, VI xlv) observes, ll. 9362–64 are unacceptable as they stand in MSS HTLB. The intended sense is surely that the rose is as different from the thorn (bush) that produced it as Mary is from her stock, the Jews. MS C is clearest:

Als rose and thron ar tua vnmete;
And tuix þam fair a-cord es nan
Sa es tuix hir kin and mi lemman.

9365–66   Closely translated from Herman's *Bible*, ll. 2755–56, but positioned after the description of Mary, not before, as in the source.

9367ff.   The preceding lines on Mary, in particular l. 9366, suggest that Mary, not Christ, will be the focus of attention. The explanation for the abrupt change to a different subject is that the *CM* poet now abandons Herman, whose course is clear — "Or dirai d'une dame et de son grant parage" (l. 2747) — in favour of Robert Grosseteste, whose *Le Château d'amour* provided the theological debate among the Four Daughters of God concerning Christ's birth. Grosseteste will be the closely-followed source for almost the next thousand lines. The edition cited will be that of J. MURRAY (Paris, 1918). The transitional passage (ll. 9367–80) appears to originate with the *CM* poet.

9381–82   The initial use of Grosseteste in this New Testament section illustrates the *CM* poet's tendency to compress if he is not translating faithfully:

> Li soleil fu a iceu tens
> Set fez plus cler ke ne est ores,
> E la lune si cler lores
> Cume li soleil ore luit
> Luseit adonke de nuit. (ll. 48–52)

These lines were used in the Old Testament portion of *CM* (ll. 701–05) but in an accurate translation. In the present passage, further compression is achieved by omitting Grosseteste's supporting reference (l. 54) to *Is*. 30:26 concerning present-day diminished brightness. Sarah HORRALL's note to ll. 701–10 (*SVCM* I) mentions both the earlier and present debt to Grosseteste and also provides excellent references to other occurrences of the theme of the loss of brightness.

9384   Grosseteste's redundant list, "En terre, en mer, a val, a munt" (l. 56), has been omitted.

9385, 9387   Grosseteste's charge that Adam and Eve forfeited Paradise "par folage" (l. 59) is not repeated by the *CM* poet who seems disinclined to censure. Cf. ll. 9415–18.

9391–94   A good example of the line-for-line translation technique often adopted by the *CM* poet. Grosseteste reads:

> Kant Deu le mund fet aveit,
> Si ke nule rien n'i failleit,
> Bestes, arbres, erbe ne fruit
> Chescun solum ceo ke il fut. (ll. 67–70)

9396   Ultimately from *Gen*. 1:24–31 but, more immediately, Grosseteste, l. 74: "Tud au derrain Adam criad."

9400   A faithful rendering of Grosseteste, l. 77, but omitting the important conclusion: "Crea sa alme" (l. 78). An early Middle English version of *Le Château d'amour*, the *Myrour of Lewed Men* (Sajavaara, *ME Trans*.), makes explicit the spiritual basis of the "imaginem nostram": "in saul make him lik to the haly trinite" (l. 36). Horrall (*SVCM*, n. to ll. 319–22) remarks that Augustine had pointed out the "threeness" of man's soul as *memoria*, *intelligentia*, and *voluntas*. The poet previously summarized this theory as

> His godhede is in trynite
> Þe soule haþ propur þinges þre. (ll. 561–62)

These are "Menyng" (l. 563), "Vndirstondynge" (l. 565), and "Wisdome . . . in wille" (l. 567).

9404   "sleȝely" is effective alliteratively and also evokes a sense of mystery not present in the matter-of-fact "Somoil en lui ad geté," Grosseteste, l. 82.

9415–18   Grosseteste, ll. 95–100, but without the censure of "par folie/. . . par orgoil" (ll. 98–99). The idea also receives expression in AUGUSTINE, *De Civitate Dei* XXII 1, *PL* XLI 752; MILTON, *Paradise Lost* II 832–35; the fourteenth-century *Stanzaic Life of Christ*, ll. 4001–12; and *Mirk's Festial*, 290/31–33.

9427–34   The account in *Gen.* 2:16–17 is not so precisely legalistic as here claimed. The relevant phrasing is "praecepitque ei dicens: 'Ex omni ligno paradisi comede; de ligno autem scientiae boni et mali ne comedas . . . .'" In Grosseteste the laws are termed "natureus" (l. 114) and "positive" (l. 118). Concerning natural law, Grosseteste explained: "Rationalis igitur creatura considerata in statu conditionis suae incorrupto non eget aliqua lege exterius scripta." Of positive law he remarked: "Ratio probandae et consummandae perfectae obedentiae consistet in observantia mandatorum indifferentium in se ipsis carentium ratione." Both opinions are cited by Murray in *Le Château d'amour*, pp. 172–73, n. to ll. 114–18, from Grosseteste's *De Cessatione Legalium*, pp. 74, 78. Natural law was regarded as discernible by human reason alone, divine positive law only through revelation. See P. K. MEAGHER, "Law, Divine Positive," *New Cath. Enc.*, and AQUINAS, *Summa Theologica*, Qu. 91, Art. 2:1–11, and Qu. 94. For a discussion of Grosseteste and law, see John A. ALFORD, "Literature and Law in Medieval England," especially pp. 943–44.

9437–38   Grosseteste, ll. 122–24, and *Gen.* 2:17.

9439–42   Grosseteste, ll. 125–28. The promise, not stated in *Genesis*, can be inferred by combining 1:26, 28, and 2:16–17.

9443   "La Saisine est la possession d'une terre, d'une chose, d'un droit"; see Grosseteste, p. 173, n. to l. 166.

9458–60   The affirmative here, and in MSS TLB, is not psychologically consistent with the enormity of Adam's transgression. The corresponding lines in Grosseteste, ll. 146–48, are interrogative, as they are in MSS CG.

9461–72   These lines, corresponding to Grosseteste, ll. 151–64, emphasize the gravity of the sinful act. They are found in MSS CG, but not in HTLB.

9477–78   The omitted lines, based on Grosseteste, ll. 166–68, round out the discussion of Adam's crime in feudal legal terms and argue for the appropriateness of the loss of Paradise, according to current feudal law.

9480–83   Whereas in Grosseteste the thraldom is to sin ("a le pechié," l. 170), in *CM* it is to "sathanas" (l. 9482).

9493–94   These lines occur only in HTLB and are probably spurious, as they do not correspond to anything in Grosseteste.

9505–08   These lines, found only in CG, include a third law, given to Moses on Mount Sinai. See Grosseteste, ll. 193–96.

9516   The poet here identifies his source. ROBERT MANNYNG OF BRUNNE also refers to "Grostet/Of Lynkolne" as "Seynt Roberd," in *Handlyng Synne* I 4740–42. Grosseteste was never canonized although his canonization was proposed in 1280, 1286, 1288, and 1307. See Sajavaara, *ME Trans.*, p. 31 n., and Grosseteste, p. 15.

9517–752   The beginning of the debate among the Four Daughters of God is signalled calligraphically by the flourished initial "H" at l. 9517.

By the tenth century A.D., "Misericordia et veritas obviaverunt sibi;/justitia et pax osculatae sunt" (*Ps.* 84:11) was developed in Midrashic writings into an allegorical debate on the creation of man. With Hugh of St. Victor (1097–1141) the argument shifted to the redemption of mankind; see *idem, Miscellanea, PL* CLXXVII 621–25. This rapidly became the more popular of the two versions. Bernard of Clairvaux (1091–1153) altered Hugh's settlement, man's confession and repentance, to the substitution of Christ for sinful man; see BERNARD OF CLAIRVAUX, "In Festo Annuntiationis Beatae Mariae Virginis: Sermo I," *PL* CLXXXIII 383–90. Bonaventure (ca. 1217–74) and Grosseteste (ca. 1175–1253) also helped to establish and popularize this form of the debate. The subject receives extensive study in Traver, *Four Daughters*. For a more recent bibliography see Tony HUNT, " 'The Four Daughters of God'."

The Four Daughters *topos* was very popular in the Middle Ages and appears variously in Lydgate, *Life of Our Lady*, II 1–350; *The Early English Versions of the Gesta Romanorum*, ed. F. MADDEN and S.J.H. HERRTAGE, ch. 34; *Vices and Virtues*, ed. F. HOLTHAUSEN, pp. 113–17; "Salutation and Conception," in *Lud. Cov.*, 99/49–103/188; *Piers Plowman*, B xviii 112ff.; *Court of Sapience*, I 176–896. The source here is Grosseteste, 205–456.

9520   MSS GHTLB make the son an only child, thereby creating an apparent contradiction of l. 9529, which states that the King also had four daughters. Grosseteste and *CM* MS C avoid the difficulty altogether through formulations that are not mutually exclusive: "un fiz aveit" (l. 207) and "Quatre filles out" (l. 217). Considered theologically, the problem is less troublesome. Both Christ and the daughters are "of" the Father, the former by way of emanation, the latter as attributes. Such theological subtleties are disregarded, however, in the allegorical representation in the interests of simplicity and immediacy. The *Court of Sapience* explains the significance of the son thus: "Hys son ys Cryst" (l. 418).

9529   "hys doughtres in degree/Byn vertues foure annexyd to hys godhede"; see *Court of Sapience*, ll. 418–19.

9533   The scribe of MS T repeated the "s" in "ʒiftis" and so produced the erroneous pronoun "she."

9544ff.   Mercy, Truth, Justice, and Peace are the customary names and number involved in the debate. Occasionally extra characters, such as the Devil and Sapience, were added. See Traver, *Four Daughters*, p. 49.

9551   "Hys seruaunt ys olde Adam," *Court of Sapience*, l. 420.

9567–94   Mercy's entire speech is closely translated from Grosseteste, ll. 255–82.

9590   This line is not in Grosseteste.

9596–97   In Grosseteste, ll. 295–96, Truth emphasizes her filial relationship to the Father, just as Mercy does earlier in ll. 255–56. *CM* omits the later instance.

9621–80   Largely a line-for-line translation of Grosseteste, ll. 311–70.

9632   *CM* omits Peace; Grosseteste, l. 322.

9655–56   In reverse order in Grosseteste, ll. 342–43.

9679–80   The rhyme words in MSS CG are "sothfastnes/reuthnes" and "sothfastnes/rightwisnes" respectively. Grosseteste has "Mes sanz Pès e sanz Pité" (l. 370). HTLB substitute "pees" for "reuthnes."

9682   *CM* omits Peace's opening remarks about her filial relationship to the Father (Grosseteste, ll. 373–74) and her complaint that Truth and Justice passed judgement without consulting Peace and Mercy (Grosseteste, ll. 376–84). The remainder of Peace's argument is a faithful translation of Grosseteste, ll. 385–424.

9728   *CM* omits "De tun sanc," Grosseteste, l. 432.

9729–30   Grosseteste, ll. 433–34, but in reverse order.

9731–33   Grosseteste, ll. 435–36. The idea is also found in *Elucid.* (*L'Elucidarium et les lucidaires*, ed. Yves LEFÈVRE, I 115–19), where the Son's role in creation is expressed thus: "Dei dicere est Verbo, id est in Filio, omnia creare ut dicitur: 'Omnia in sapientia fecisti'," *Elucid.* I 18. Cf. "Dei Filius, per quem omnia. . . ," I 118.

9753–816   Grosseteste, ll. 457–96.

9761–62   Cf. AUGUSTINE, *Quaestiones ex Novo Testamento: Appendix*, *PL* XXXV 2280.

9771–94 The explanation of why neither angel nor man could ransom mankind is not found in Grosseteste, who merely states its impossibility, ll. 475–76. Cf. the explanation offered in *Meditations on the Supper of Our Lord*, ed. J. M. Cowper, ll. 1126–28:

He [God] my3t ha sent an angel to saue vs here,
But þan of oure saluacyun we shulde nat þanke hym,
But calle þe aungel sauer of alle man kyn.

The *CM* poet's source, however, is *Elucid.*, I 115–16. On the possibility of angelic redemption, ll. 9771–79, Honorius says: "Si angelus hominem redemisset, tunc illius et servus esset; homo autem sic restitui debuit, ut aequalis angelis esset. Et aliud oberat: angelus in sui natura invalidus erat hominem redimere; si autem homo fieret, minus posset" (I 115). The argument of ll. 9783–88 is based on *Elucid.*, I 116: "de suo enim genere esse debuit, qui pro homine satisfaceret."

9807 The "Nonante e noef," Grosseteste, l. 487, is left vague. Cf. *Matt.* 18:12; *Luc.* 15:4.

9811 The original reading of "lord" was probably "hird" (Grosseteste, "Pastur," l. 489). This was corrupted to "bird" in CG. However, "lord," as in HTLB, appears in Grosseteste, l. 490, as "Seignur."

9815 "li cuer crever," Grosseteste, l. 495.

9817–76 Grosseteste, ll. 499–568.

9817ff. Of the ten prophets listed in Grosseteste, ll. 499–508, the *CM* poet retains only Isaiah.

9819 The agreement of MSS CGTL on "nede" and the occurrence of "rede" two lines earlier suggest that H's "rede," although defensible, is probably wrong.

9821–25 The designations, ultimately from *Is.* 9:6 but more immediately from Grosseteste, ll. 513–16, occurred earlier in *CM*, ll. 9314–17, where Herman's *Bible* (ll. 2718–21) was the direct source.

H's "I" (l. 9821) should read "he," as in CGTL. The scribe's eye may have caught the repeated "I" (ll. 9816–17) a few lines above where he was copying.

9846 A substitution for the statement in Grosseteste, l. 536, that such aberrations are "monstres." CG translate Grosseteste's line, "Mes monstres seient apelez," as "Bot monstres moght man call þam like." The purpose of the illustration is to enhance the mysterious nature of Christ who "Bothe is god & mon," l. 9859.

9853–54 G preserves the original reading of l. 9853: "And stedfast horis and oþer tolike"; cf. Grosseteste, l. 543: "E pus fust verrai cheval." HTLB's "beestes" is a generalization.

9858 "I haue of tolde" in HTLB replaces "Ke Ysaïe ad nuncié," Grosseteste, l. 549. The *Isaiah* reading is preserved in MSS CG.

9874 H's mistaken feminine form "her" (for "he") probably arose from anticipating the initial letter in the succeeding word "rest." Cf. l. 11581, note.

9877–78 These lines are found only in MS C and do not correspond to anything in Grosseteste.

9879–10094 The Castle of Love section closely follows Grosseteste, ll. 571–788. The suggestion for the allegory derives from *Luc.* 10:38, whose "castellum"/village was translated as "castle," and "mulier"/woman was interpreted as "virgin," thus prompting the depiction of the incarnation as an entering into a castle. See Anselm, "Quoddam, id est singulare castellum fuit virgo Maria," in "De Conceptu Virginali: Homilia ix," *PL* CLVIII 646, and Ailred of Rievaulx, "Audacter enim dico, quia nisi beata Maria hoc castellum praeparasset in se . . . ," in "In

Assumptione Beatae Mariae: Sermo xvii," *PL* CXCV 303. On the history of the castle allegory, see G. R. OWST, *Literature and Pulpit in Medieval England*, pp. 77–85, and Sajavaara, *ME Trans.*, pp. 91–99. The latter notes (p. 93): "No direct source for Grosseteste's castle has been found."

9884   Grosseteste, 1. 576 — "N'ad regard de ses enemis" — suggests that the correct reading is "enmye" (GL) rather than "enuye" (HT). The minims in "enmye" could be easily misread.

     The *CM* poet omits additional details on the military security of the castle found in Grosseteste, ll. 577–82.

9902   The poet deletes 1. 598 of Grosseteste on the brightness of the carnels.

9909–10   These lines, present only in C, do not correspond to anything in Grosseteste.

9920–21   Grosseteste, ll. 613–14, but in reverse order.

9931–34   These lines, present only in CG, stress the snow-white brightness of the castle and correspond to Grosseteste, ll. 625–28.

9942   A couplet on the health-giving properties of the water (Grosseteste, ll. 637–38) has been omitted.

9950–51   Not in Grosseteste. Conversely, the reference to "Le arc du ciel" (Grosseteste, 1. 647) does not appear in *CM*.

9953–54   A reversal of Grosseteste, ll. 649–50.

9983   A conflation of Grosseteste, ll. 679–80.

9985–89   As HAENISCH observed (*CM*, p. 29*), "end," "ende," "endynge," "Good endynge," are misreadings of "Ce est la fei de la Virgine," Grosseteste, 1. 681, and "fei est . . . /De tutes vertuz fundement," Grosseteste, ll. 685–86. The *CM* poet, or the scribe of the Old French manuscript he was using, apparently confused "fei"/faith with "fin"/end. Other Middle English translations of *Le Château d'amour* (see Sajavaara, *ME Trans.*) avoid the error. In *Myrour of Lewed Men*, for example, Green signifies "the treuth of our ladye" (1. 404), and in *Castle of Love*, "þe Maydenes bi-leeue so riht" (1. 777).

9992   Not in Grosseteste.

10006   Grosseteste, 1. 703 is omitted.

10009–10   Added by the *CM* poet.

10026   MS C reads "speciale" for "spousaile."

10039   A filler by the *CM* poet.

10045–46   A reversal of Grosseteste, ll. 739–40.

10059   "of hir brestes" is much less explicit in Grosseteste, 1. 753: "ki surunde."

10062   Grosseteste, 1. 756 has "Sur tutes autres beneuree."

10084   A substitution for "Ce est la nostre gareison," Grosseteste, 1. 778.

10091–92   An accurate translation of Grosseteste, ll. 785–86: "Par la porte close entra/A l'issir close la lessa." The door metaphor, in turn, derives from an exegetical interpretation of *Ez.* 44:2–3: "Porta haec clausa erit; non aperietur, et vir non transibit per eam, quoniam Dominus Deus Israel ingressus est per eam . . . . Princeps ipse sedebit in ea . . . ; per viam portae vestibuli ingredietur, et per viam eius egredietur." See PSEUDO-AUGUSTINE, "Sermo CXCV," *PL* XXXIX 2107, and *Elucid.* I 126. On a more popular theological level, the Expositor in the Chester "Balaam and Balak" play interprets the gate as "that way the Holy Ghost in went,/when God tooke flesh and bloode." See *Chester Plays*, 477/323–24.

10093   The analogy of sun through glass to explain the mystery of Christ's incarnation and birth is not in Grosseteste. See the discussion on ll. 11227–32 where the poet makes extended use of the analogy.

10095–10122   Grosseteste, ll. 789–820. Line 10095 is a conflation of Grosseteste, ll. 789–91.

10102–03   The standard mediaeval trio against whom the good Christian must always fight. Cf. *Piers Plowman*, B xvi 1–45; *Castle of Perseverance* in *Chief Pre-Shakespearean Dramas*, ed. J. Q. ADAMS, *passim*, and "Sayings of St. Bernard: Man's Three Foes," in *The Minor Poems of the Vernon Manuscript*, ed. F. J. FURNIVALL, II 515: "mon, þou hast þreo luþer fon, . . . þyn oune flesch, þe world, þe fend."

10108   MS H's "to þider" is perhaps defensible but "to" was probably copied from the previous line. The scribe made a similar error less than two lines earlier.

10123   Grosseteste has now been abandoned as a source. "Hereþ" is perhaps inspired by "Or entendés," Herman's *Bible*, l. 2735, and "Or escoutés," ll. 2743, 2752, 2763, which begin successive stanzas.

10131   Cf. Herman's *Bible*, l. 2744: "Ne dirai de folie, ne dirai de putage."

10144ff.   Mary's ancestry is not recorded in the Bible "quia consuetudo scripturae dicitur fuisse, ut non mulierum, sed virorum generationis series texeretur" (*Leg. Aur.* Sept. 8, p. 585). *Matt.* 1:1–16 and *Luc.* 3:23–38 trace Christ's lineage through Joseph.

The names of Mary's parents, Joachim and Anna, and legends about them and about the childhood of the Virgin began to circulate in the first century A.D., however. The main texts in the tradition are the Greek *Protevangelium Jacobi* (second century) and the Latin *Gospel of Pseudo-Matthew* and *De Nativitate Mariae* (both eighth or ninth century). For editions of these texts and discussion of their provenance, see K. VON TISCHENDORF, ed., *Evangelia Apocrypha* and Emile AMANN, ed., *Le Protévangile de Jacques*. Later writers known to the *CM* poet, such as Herman de Valenciennes and Wace, use this material in their works.

George L. Hamilton has suggested that the *CM* poet used an interpolated version of Wace, such as that found in MS Add 15606, as a source for these lines. Close comparison of *CM* with the text of Add 15606, however, shows that this interpolated MS is not the poet's source. For Hamilton's suggestion, see his review of G. H. GEROULD's *Saints' Legends*, p. 238.

The poet's genealogical interest in Mary is scarcely surprising, for he devoted his work to her (ll. 111–15). Perhaps less obvious is the polemical role of the Marian genealogy in countering the calumnious charges against the Virgin's ancestry and character (that she was ousted from home for shameful conduct and that Jesus was the illegitimate son of a soldier of fortune and a camp-following mother. See ORIGEN, *Contra Celsum*, PG XI, 720–21). Thus the natural desire to supplement the meagre details of canonical scripture went hand-in-hand with the need for an apologetic approach. See A. F. FINDLAY, *Byways in Early Christian Literature*, pp. 148–78; *Protevangelium*, pp. 12–14; and O. CULLMANN, "Infancy Gospels," in Hennecke, *NT Apocrypha*, I. 363–69.

10148–54   Anna's sister is called "Hismeria" in *Leg. Aur.*, Sept. 8, p. 586, and "Emeria" in Wace 54/3, but if the form of the name in *CM* is closer to that of *Leg. Aur.*, the content and expression incline towards Wace 54/2–7. *Luc.* 1:5 does not go beyond naming John's parents, Elizabeth and Zachary, except to describe the former as "uxor illius de filiabus Aaron."

10161–98   The poet draws selectively on both Herman's *Bible* and Wace in this section.

10169–70   The couplet, based on Herman's *Bible*, ll. 2774–75, and concerning the exemplary harmony of Anna and Joachim's marital life, is found in MSS CG but is missing in HTLB.

10178–84   Disagreement exists over what happened to the final third of Joachim's offering. Herman's *Bible*, l. 2787a, states unequivocally that it went "au temple meïsme." *Pseudo-Matt.* I.1, *De Nativ. Mariae* I.2, and *Leg. Aur.*, Sept. 8, p. 587, are equally explicit that Joachim kept it for his own needs. *Protevangelium* 1.1, in turn, specifies that Joachim's gifts were divided only two ways: to God (for personal forgiveness) and to the people. In Wace 10/17–22, almost certainly the poet's source, the third part is returned to Joachim's household.

10187–88 Present in MSS CG, missing in HTLB, the couplet corresponds to Herman's *Bible*, ll. 2790–90a, and emphasizes Joachim's great mercy and chastity. MS G preserves the order of the lines in Herman's *Bible*.

10190–91 Herman's *Bible*, ll. 2793–94, which includes Solomon as well as Jesse and David in Joachim's lineage.

10199ff. The childlessness of Joachim and Anna is variously treated. The *CM* poet clearly regards the couple as having tried, unsuccessfully, to produce offspring. In contrast, Herman's *Bible*, ll. 2799–802, emphasizes their total abstinence from sex: they do not even sleep together. In *De Nativ. Mariae* I.3, they live in chaste and childless wedlock, but their offering to God of any child He might grant them suggests something less than total abstinence. Similarly, in *Pseudo-Matt.* II.2 Anna's lamentation of her barrenness bespeaks a desire for, and presumably an attempt at having, offspring. Anna bewails her childlessness in *Protevangelium* 2.1, but nothing is said about their conjugal relations. Beginning with a paraphrase of "Vingt anz ensamble converserent" (Wace 11/1), the *CM* poet here turns to the French source which he will follow closely for most of the next seven hundred lines.

10203–08 The dedication of the child to God likewise receives varying treatment in the different accounts. The *CM* poet regards the vow as a means of attracting divine help for a problem that has defeated human solutions for twenty years. The dedication is thus presented in Wace 11/3ff. In Herman's *Bible*, ll. 2936ff., the vow is mentioned, without details as to time and motive (as in *De Nativ. Mariae* I.3), by an angel sent to tell Joachim of his impending fatherhood. In *Pseudo-Matt.* II.2, Anna's vow dates from the beginning of her marriage; the curse of sterility is thus less a factor than the love of God, to whose service the child would be dedicated. Anna's dedication in *Protevangelium* 4.1 takes the different form of a spontaneous thanksgiving in response to the angel's annunciation of the birth to Mary.

10214 The winter date is found only in Wace 11/17.

10222–29 This passage offers an interesting example of how the *CM* poet utilizes his sources. Line 10222 translates Wace's "Si faisoient lor orison," 11/24. Lines 10223–26, however, are taken from Herman's *Bible*, ll. 2808–12. In ll. 10227–29, the poet returns to Wace, 12/1–3.

10233 The patriarch is thus named in Wace 12/7, Herman's *Bible*, l. 2829, and *De Nativ. Mariae* II.1, but in *Pseudo-Matt.* II.1 he is called Ruben and in *Protevangelium* 1.2 Reubel, presumably an error for Ruben. *Leg. Aur.*, Sept. 8, p. 587, does not identify him.

10241–43 All MSS except C soften Wace's "N'ies pas dignes de Dieu servir," 12/15.

10245–89 The discussion with Isachar closely follows Wace 12/18–14/17. In Herman's *Bible*, by contrast, the high priest is a flat, brusque, officious figure: "Ne sés que dit la lois?," l. 2844; "Fui tost hor de cheens!," l. 2855. In *Pseudo-Matt.* II.1, *De Nativ. Mariae* II.1–2, and *Protevangelium* 1.2–4, Joachim does not debate the matter.

10260–62, 10266–67 The curse of barrenness, not found in Herman's *Bible*, is implied in *Pseudo-Matt*. II.1 and explicit in *De Nativ. Mariae* II.1, *Protevangelium* 3.1, and *Leg. Aur.*, Sept. 8, p. 587. The source, however, is Wace 13/12–14, 13/18–19. The poet notwithstanding, neither the laws nor God makes barrenness a curse in the Bible. The divine injunction to procreate ("Crescite, et multiplicamini, et replete terram," *Gen.* 9:1), along with God's promise ("Non erit infecunda, nec sterilis in terra tua," *Ex.* 23:26, cf. *Deut.* 7:14), would easily lead to the association of sterility and God's disfavour. In fact, this association soon assumed the stature of law through the statements of influential patristic authors. See AUGUSTINE, "Illo itaque tempore cum et lex dies Patriarcharum subsequens maledictum dicit qui non excitaret semen in Israel, et qui poterat non promebat, sed tamen habebat," in *De Bono Conjugali*, xxii, *PL* XL 391, and JEROME, "Maledicta sterilis quae non habet semen in Israel," in *In Isaiam*, IV.1, *PL* XXIV 72.

10273–74 The fruitless tree reference, evidently added by the poet, may derive from Christ's cursing of the barren fig tree in *Matt.* 21:19, *Marc.* 11:13–14, or the parable in *Luc.* 13:6–9.

10289–94 Only *Protevangelium* 1.3 has Joachim delay his departure until he verifies in the records of his people that he alone has been without issue. Lines 10291–94 are given a different order from Wace 15/8–10.

10295–99 Wace 15/16–16/4. Several lines on the remoteness and hardships of the desert area (Wace 15/11–14) have been omitted.

10303–05 Fasting is also mentioned in *Protevangelium* 1.4, but both content and expression come from Wace 16/9: "Il a à geune pensé." The fast is at least forty days long in *Protevangelium* 1.4. Cf. Wace 16/10: "Ne ni avoit gaires esté."

10313–72 The annunciation to Joachim, although available in Herman's *Bible*, ll. 2888–2949, is translated and paraphrased from Wace 16/19–19/14. In Herman's *Bible*, Joachim is portrayed as an argumentative, sceptical, and recalcitrant individual: "je nel croi, tant est gregnour folie," l. 2893; "Ne sai . . . se me dis verité," l. 2898; "Non ferai," l. 2939. This is a portrait developed from *Pseudo-Matt*. where Joachim requires a second visitation from the angel and the warning of his men, "Vide ne ultra contemnas angelum Dei" (III.4), before he will obey. By contrast, Wace presents Joachim as properly submissive to God's will (19/19ff.), a trait that will be evident in his daughter in a parallel annunciation scene later. The characterization is consistent with the accepting and reasonable Joachim of the temple scene, ll. 10227–89.

10330 The line in HTLB perverts the intended meaning that parenthood in old age is above the suspicion of lust. CG preserve the proper sense: "Es right born and noght o licheri." Cf. Wace 17/15–16: "Que cil qui naist est d'aventure/De dieu dont vient, non de luxure."

10331–46 The five examples of children born to elderly parents occur in the same order and with the same detail in Wace 17/17–18/11.

10347–50 A translation of Wace 18/12–15. The manner in which Mary is conceived is here made to parallel that of other outstanding Old Testament personages, freed from the taint of lust, and is seen as a prelude to her own miraculous virginal conception of Christ.

10352–56 Wace 18/17–21, with slight changes in sequence. The passage states unequivocally that Mary was conceived in the normal way. See also ll. 10571–72. Her begetting is exceptional only in that it occurs to a couple hitherto unable to procreate, the wife now being past the age of childbearing. Herman's *Bible*, l. 2945, is likewise explicit about Mary's thoroughly human conception. The desire to normalize the conception was strong enough in *Pseudo-Matt*. III.2 to prompt the addition of "ex semine tuo," referring to Joachim, in spite of the angel's promise that Joachim would find Anna "habentem in utero: excitavit enim Deus semen in ea." See *Pseudo-Matt.*, p. 289n.

"Fulfilde wiþ goddis g*race*," 1. 10356, may intimate what is more clearly expressed in other treatments: that Mary was filled with the Holy Spirit from the moment of conception. See Herman's *Bible*, 1. 2946; *Leg. Aur.*, Sept. 8, p. 588; and *De Nativ. Mariae* III.3. *Pseudo-Matt.* III.2 mentions the indwelling of the Holy Spirit, but only inconclusively in conjunction with Mary's life as a temple virgin.

The details about the manner of Mary's conception and of God's grace in her are important in the controversy over the conflicting doctrines of original sin and the Immaculate Conception. AUGUSTINE, *De Natura et Gratia*, xxxvi, *PL* XLIV 267, felt it best not to speculate on the matter. Bernard of Clairvaux, however, argued that Mary was conceived in original sin, in "Epistola clxxiv: Ad Canonicos Lugdunensis, de conceptione S. Mariae," *PL* CLXXXII 332–36. Aquinas, adopting a more moderate position, conceded that her conception was tainted by original sin but concluded that God removed this stain prior to her birth; see *Summa Theologica* 3a, 27.2 ad 2, and E. D. O'CONNOR, "Immaculate Conception," *New Cath. Enc.*

10358   Only in Wace 18/23–19/1 does the angel instruct Joachim as to when Mary should be presented to the temple.

10375–84   Neither the angel's command nor the sacrifice appears in Herman's *Bible*, *Leg. Aur.*, or *De Nativ. Mariae*. The notion of an angelically-enjoined offering is ultimately derived from *Pseudo-Matt.* III.3; the number and kinds of victims, from *Protevangelium* 4.3. The immediate source, however, remains Wace 19/17–20/3.

10385–88   The votive intentions parallel those in Wace 20/1–4.

10391–408   The *significatio* closely follows Wace 20/10–21/12 except for the omission of 21/9–12 explaining Joachim's unconsciousness of the communion of saints.

10419–94   In terms of poignancy and overall effectiveness, the *CM*'s treatment of Anna's grief is fully as powerful as that of the source, Wace 22/3–24/20. The entire episode receives only twelve lines in Herman's *Bible*, ll. 2864–75, while *De Nativ. Mariae* completely disregards Anna's feelings, and *Leg. Aur.*, Sept. 8, p. 588, notes only that she wept bitterly.

10451   The minims in "mi" could easily be construed as "un," thus leading to MS H's "daunsele."

10461   The problematic nature of the line is evident from the various readings: "þat nu mai be, thar þe noght wene" C; "I mak na mirthe, thar ye noght wene" G; "To myrthe me dare the not wene" L. The agreement on "þar"/behoove, need, suggests some such intended meaning as "You need not expect to jolly me." The corresponding passage in Wace 23/10–11 is: "dois me tu dire/Que joie face ne liée soie?"

10471–94   The ultimate source of Anna's lamentation is *Protevangelium* 2.4–3.3. The *CM* poet's immediate debt, however, is to Wace 23/21–24/20. *CM*'s l. 10494 alters the sense of the original "Diex! pourquoi fui brehaingne née?" (24/20).

10495–550   The angel's visitation to Anna closely follows Wace 24/21–27/8.

10497–98   See ll. 10306–76.

10517–18   Although *Gen.* 17:17 makes Sarah ninety years old, *De Nativ. Mariae* III.2, the source for Wace 25/21, puts her age at eighty and the *CM* poet follows this rather than the biblical version. *Leg. Aur.*, normally content to follow *De Nativ. Mariae*, here corrects the figure to ninety, p. 588.

10521   GB's "ferly" is possible but probably an error through metathesis. Joseph is less "wonderful" than "noble," as in CHTL.

10529   See note to ll. 10352–56.

10531–32   Lines 10648–51 and Wace 31/13 make it clear that Mary remained in the temple *until* she was fourteen, not *for* fourteen years. The source for the present passage, "Jusques quatorze anz iert gardée" (Wace 26/15), is not without ambiguity, however. A variant reading in Wace, "Et.xiiij.anz illec gardée," further illustrates the confusion over the length of Mary's temple service.

10550   The poet's addition.

10552–55   The episode of the messengers derives immediately from Wace 27/11–15 and ultimately from *Protevangelium* 4.2.

10564–66   MSS CG read "gastli game," l. 10564, against HTLB's "gladnes of gamen." Cf. the source, Wace 27/21–22: "Mult doucement se saluerent;/A l'encontrer grant joïe firent."

10573–74   The date of Mary's conception, December 8, is the poet's addition. Although the feast occurs in pre-Conquest calendars, it did not begin to be widely observed until 1129 when it was formally sanctioned by a council of English bishops. See M. R. JAMES, ed., *Latin Infancy Gospels*, p. xxxiii; Hilda GRAEF, *Mary: A History of Doctrine and Devotion*, I, 210–306; and E. D. O'CONNOR, "Immaculate Conception," *New Cath. Enc.* Lines 24759–968 provide a stirring account of how the feast was established.

10577–78   See l. 10526.

10579–610   The temple presentation of Mary closely follows Wace 28/10–29/20.

10589–90   The couplet, missing in HTLB, translates Wace's observation that Mary's ascent started from the bottom step, 28/16–17. In *Protevangelium* 7.3 she begins on the third step and dances to the top.

10595–96   Wace 29/5–6: "Illec vout Diex avant mostrer/Qu'ele doit croistre et haut monter."

10611–54   The account of Mary's temple service is paraphrased and translated from Wace 29/20–31/17. In l. 10611, "mirþful may" is the poet's addition.

10619–20   The source is Wace 30/5–6, which follows the same tradition as Herman's *Bible*, ll. 3116–17 and *De Nativ. Mariae* VII.1 in which the angels are merely visitors. In *Pseudo-Matt.* VI.2 they bring food.

10655–718   Wace 31/18–34/14.

10698   The line in HTLB is unsatisfactory. By marrying, Mary will *not* be keeping her "avowe of chastite," l. 10692. The context requires the sense "and still" which is expressed in CG: "Sco moght hir mari and hald hir vou."

10714   The solution to the dilemma created by Mary's vow of perpetual virginity varies. In *Pseudo-Matt.* VIII.1–3, both God and an angel offer guidance; in *Protevangelium* 8.2–3, only the latter does so. In the main tradition, followed by Wace 34/10, a voice solves the problem: "Une voiz desus aus oïrent." See also Herman's *Bible*, ll. 3280ff., *De Nativ. Mariae* VII.3, and *Leg. Aur.*, Sept. 8, p. 589.

10719ff.   *Is.* 11:1–2 ultimately, but the immediate source is Wace 34/15ff.

10733–36   Wace 35/7–8. The use of a miraculously flourishing rod as a selection procedure closely parallels that employed in the confirmation of Aaron to the priesthood in *Num.* 17:1ff. Joseph, like Aaron, is divinely chosen.

10745–80   The account of Joseph's selection is taken from Wace 35/17–37/7, with minor changes.

10749–57   Joseph's advanced age, widowhood, and sons older than Mary are uncanonical details from Wace 36/2–4, ultimately from the second-century *Prot-evangelium* 9.2 and popularized by *Pseudo-Matt.* VIII.4. They may be the result of an attempt to explain Jesus' "brothers" in *Marc.* 3:31, *Luc.* 8:19.

It was Joseph's age, however, which became the central feature of the tradition, perhaps to strengthen belief in Joseph as Mary's chaste guardian. Cf. *De Nativ. Mariae* VIII.1; Herman's *Bible*, l. 3294; *Leg. Aur.*, Sept. 8, p. 589. See *Protevangelium*, pp. 38, 52, and Joseph's claim in *Chester Plays*, IX 214–15: "[I have been] keeper of her virginitie/. . . manye a daye."

The influence of Jerome's related concern, expressed in *De Perpetua Virginitate B. Mariae*, *PL* XXIII 213, to establish Joseph as a life-long virgin can occasionally be found in Middle English drama: "I haue be maydon evyr and evyr more wele ben," *Lud. Cov.* 88/179. More often, however, Joseph's age is the occasion for bawdy humour: "though I would,/I might not playe noe playe" in *Chester Plays* VI 135–36; Mary is entrusted to him only when he is no longer able "sinne for to assaye" (*Chester Plays* IX 211); and

> What heylyght þi leggys now to be lame
> Þou dedyst hem put ryght freschly owte
> Whan þou dedyst pley with ȝon ȝonge dame. (*Lud. Cov.* 131/230–32)

I have found no reference to the "prior marriage" aspect of the Joseph tradition in English mystery plays.

10758–60   Only in *Protevangelium* 9.1, where Joseph throws down his axe at the heralds' approach, is there a trace of eagerness on his part.

10766–74   The statement in Wace 36/12 concerning Joseph's attempt to escape selection reads: "La verge que il tint muça." The *CM* poet here reverts briefly to Herman's *Bible*, l. 3298: "Honteus derier les autres commenche a retourner." Joseph's detection, by a careful rod-count (ll. 10767–72), likewise draws on Herman's *Bible*, ll. 3299–304. In Wace 36/16–18, God is petitioned for advice. No such complications arise in *Protevangelium* 9.1. In *Pseudo-Matt.* VIII.3 the high priest overlooks Joseph's small wand on the altar, whereas in *De Nativ. Mariae* VIII.1 Joseph forgets his wand and in *Leg. Aur.*, Sept. 8, p. 589, he avoids putting it with the others.

10775–76   In Herman's *Bible*, ll. 3299–305, the dove plays no role in the miracle, and in *Protevangelium* 9.1 and *Pseudo-Matt.* VIII.3 the bird appears from the wand. The poet here returns to Wace 37/3: "Une colombe del ciel vint." *De Nativ. Mariae* VIII.1 and *Leg. Aur.*, Sept. 8, p. 589 follow the "columba de caelo" tradition. This feature of the miracle is probably influenced by the accounts of Christ's baptism in *Matt.* 3:16 and *Marc.* 1:9–10.

10781–814   The three reasons for Christ's being born to a married virgin do not appear together in any of the poet's usual sources.

10785–98   This "ad daemonum confusionem" explanation enjoyed wide acceptance. See *Leg. Aur.*, Dec. 25, p. 46; March 25, p. 216; "Geburt Jesus," ll. 263–68, cited by HAENISCH, *CM*, p. 20*; *SE Nativity*, ll. 185–86; *Mirk's Festial*, 108/23–24; and *Hist. Schol.* iii, *PL* CXCVIII 1539: "ut diabolo occultaretur Dei partus."

10799–808   Marriage to avoid the death-penalty for unwed mothers (*Deut.* 22:20–21) occurs as an explanation in JEROME, *De Perpetua Virginitate B. Mariae*, *PL* XXIII 196 and *Mirk's Festial*, 108/13–15.

10809–14   Companionship or help as a reason for the Virgin's marriage appears in JEROME, *De Perpetua Virginitate B. Mariae*, *PL* XXIII 196 and *Hist. Schol.* iii, *PL* CXCVIII 1539. See also l. 11174.

10815–16   The *CM* poet's homage to Mary is in keeping with his earlier, lengthier veneration, ll. 69ff., and the dedication of his poem to her, ll. 111–14.

10817–34   The *CM* poet once more returns to Wace, 37/9–38/1. *De Nativ. Mariae* VIII.2 and *Leg. Aur.*, Sept. 8, p. 589 also furnish Mary with seven attendant virgins, as in ll. 10819–20. *Protevangelium* mentions no female companions and is vague about Mary's travels after the miracle of the flourishing rod; see 9.2, 10.2. *De Nativ. Mariae* VIII.2, *Leg. Aur.*, Sept. 8, p. 589, and Herman's *Bible*, l. 3311 agree that she went to her parents, the last-mentioned differing only in giving her three companions (l. 3313). In *Pseudo-Matt.* VIII.5, Mary goes directly to Joseph's house but Joseph then spends the next nine months away working (X.1). Here the companions number five, and are named Rebecca, Sephora, Susanna, Abigea, and Zahel (VIII.5).

Polemically, the virgin attendants play an important role in the narrative. They are Mary's constant companions and hence key witnesses to her spotless conduct, despite her incriminating condition.

10835–906   The southern redactor has here omitted seventy lines of the original poem and substituted sixty lines of his own (here numbered A1–A60). While CG show that the poet continued to translate Wace 37/23–39/14, the lines in the southern version are a close translation of *Luc.* 1:26–38. The transition is awkward, for ll. 10833–34 have stated that Gabriel appeared to Mary before she joined Joseph, but ll. A1–A11 say that the Annunciation took place when Mary was at Joseph's house in Nazareth. Furthermore, the introductory explanatory manner of ll. A7 and A9–10 is incongruous in the course of a narrative in which such basics as the couple's name and marital status have already been clearly established.

The reasons for the substitution in the southern version are obscure. The northern MSS emphasize the virgin birth more than the Gospel does, but this was surely not a controversial theological point. Perhaps the southern redactor was attracted by the higher authority of the biblical account, or perhaps there was a lacuna in his exemplar (seventy lines is almost the equivalent of two columns in most of the *CM* MSS).

A11   Neither Luke nor the *CM* poet specifies Mary's activity at the time of the Annunciation. Most often she was depicted as being indoors, meditating or weaving for the temple. Less frequently, she was pictured as fetching water outdoors. In *Protevangelium*, 11.1–2, the source of these traditions, the Annunciation is begun by a mysterious voice outdoors and completed by an angel when she returns to her weaving indoors. The double visitation is repeated in *Pseudo-Matt.* IX.1–2 but *De Nativ. Mariae* IX.1 records only the "indoors" version.

A35   Haenisch's claim in *CM*, p. 17*, that MSS CG abandon Wace here (l. 10869) and turn to the Lucan account is in error: both manuscripts continue to follow Wace 39/15–40/16 until l. 10890.

A47   In *Luc.* 1:36, Elizabeth is less precisely called Mary's *cognata*. Since Ismeria and Anna were sisters, Elizabeth and Mary would be first cousins.

A48   *Luc.* 1:36. Surprisingly, the figure is seven in Herman's *Bible*, l. 3364.

A55–A56   An elaboration of *Luc.* 1:37: ". . . non erit impossibile apud Deum omne verbum."

10907–24   The poet now abandons Luke and returns to Wace, 41/9–42/7.

10925–30   Apparently the *CM* poet's addition.

10927–30   As *Leg. Aur.*, Dec. 25, p. 40, notes, there was disagreement over the interval between the creation of the world and the Incarnation and birth of Christ:

5199, 5228, and 6000 years. BEDE, *De Temporibus Liber, PL* XC 290, also remarks on the diversity of opinion and cites 5099 as one estimate. The *Stanzaic Life*, ll. 57–61, specifies 5196 years. I cannot explain why the *CM*'s figure is six months longer. MSS GTLB agree with "elde" in H, l. 10930. C reads "hele." Since "elde" makes no sense as "age," we must view the word either as an alternate spelling (along with "heild," "hald," "hil") of "hele"/salvation, or as a corruption of "hele."

10931–97   *Luc.* 1:5–25, with changes of detail and sequence as well as additions from Herman's *Bible*. In the Lucan account, 1:5–38, the angel appears first to Zachary and then to Mary six months later. The *CM* poet, however, reverses this clear sequence, ll. 10833ff., 10931ff. Since Herman's *Bible*, ll. 3154ff., 3318ff., observes the biblical chronology and Wace omits the Zachary episode entirely, one can only speculate that the *CM* poet opted for narrative continuity in his Marian account at the expense of strict fidelity to the Bible.

10941   The sadness of Elizabeth and Zachary at being childless is not part of the Lucan narrative. The poet may have assumed it or been influenced by the double reference in Herman's *Bible*, ll. 3162, 3164.

10943   The phrasing comes closest to Herman's *Bible*, l. 3160: "bien près tot leur aage."

10948   CG's reading "on ald wise" is probably original.

10951   In *Luc.* 1:10, the people are already outside. Cf. Herman's *Bible*, l. 3170: "La gent en fist issir."

10959–61   Based on Herman's *Bible*, ll. 3174–75.

10982   *OED* "cider" points out that in biblical contexts "siþer" preserves its original broad sense of "strong drink." Line 12679 is cited in illustration of this point. Cf. Wace 55/18: "Onques ne but sidre ne vin."

10999   The date of John's conception, September 24, has been added by the poet.

11012   *Luc.* 1:36 specifies six months, the time between the Annunciation, March 25, and John's conception, September 24. The poet's extra week is puzzling.

11023–56   Wace 43/10–44/18. Cf. *Luc.* 1:39ff.

11029–30   The suggestion here of a "praying" posture for John is made explicit in *Lud. Cov.* 117/55: "[he] turnyd down on his knes · to oure god reverently."

11059–64   The chronology in *Luc.* 1:56–57 implies that Mary left before John was born. However, M. E. MCIVER, "Visitation of Mary," *New Cath. Enc.*, warns that "Luke had a stylistic habit of finishing one incident before beginning the narrative of another," and thus that it is unlikely that Mary would have left before John's birth since the purpose of her visit was to help Elizabeth. This is the view adopted in *Leg. Aur.*, June 24, p. 358, where Mary acts as Elizabeth's midwife. John's privilege of being lifted off the ground by Mary is mentioned both in *Hist. Schol., PL* CXCVIII 1538 and *Leg. Aur.*, p. 358. The wording of the latter — "ministrans ei natumque puerum suis sanctis manibus de terra levavit" — is closer to that of ll. 11062–64.

11072–74   Herman's *Bible*, l. 3207, likewise includes "Paien et sarazin" among the peoples observing the feast of John's birth. The statement may have been prompted by *Luc.* 1:14.

11077–78   *Matt.* 11:11.

11079–81   The rejoicing at John's birth may derive from Luke's "congratulabantur ei," 1:58, but is more probably due to Herman's *Bible*: "Grant leeche en demainnent et ami et parent" (l. 3204) and "Tout firent grant leeche, quant sains Jehans fu nés" (l. 3211).

11086ff.   *Luc.* 1:59ff.

11095–100 In *Luc.* 1:63–64 Zachary recovers his speech by writing John's name. The events are likewise linked in Herman's *Bible*, 1. 3218. An additional change is that Zachary's prophecies have been considerably shortened from those in the Lucan account, 1:67–79.

11102–14 The Bible does not indicate when John began his desert existence. Herman's *Bible*, 1. 3222, puts the leave-taking age at seven. This and other correspondences in this section indicate that the poet is now following Herman's *Bible*, ll. 3222–26d.

11108–12 *Luc.* 1:15 mentions John's avoidance of strong drink and *Matt.* 3:4 supplies details of the camel clothing and desert diet. The poet's additional details are from Herman's *Bible*: "ne de pain n'i menga" (1. 3226) and "Onques lingne ne laingne ne vesti n'en usa" (1. 3226d).

11118–80 The *CM* poet once more turns to Wace, 44/21–47/21.

11125 Luke makes no mention of either Joseph's absence or Mary's extra-marital pregnancy, and *Matt.* 1:18 is vague on the subject. The poet's "þre moneþes & more" translates the statement in Wace 45/8 that Joseph returned "quant li quarz mois entra."

11133–34 Wace 45/12–13. In Herman's *Bible*, ll. 3426–33, the discovery is far less delicately handled. Joseph feels Mary's stomach and exclaims: "Dame, vous estes grosse" (1. 3433).

11143–53 In *Matt.* 1:19, *Protevangelium* 14.1, and *De Nativ. Mariae* X.1, Joseph's decision is to put Mary away secretly. The notion of fleeing derives ultimately from *Pseudo-Matt.* X.2 but the poet's immediate source was Wace 46/9–11. Joseph's concern not to betray his suspicions is peculiar to Wace 45/21–46/2.

11161–71 The scriptural basis is *Matt.* 1:20–25. The rhyme word in 1. 11161 seems to have been problematic (see the variants). The meaning of 1. 11167 is clearer in MSS CG: "Hir sunne and fader sal he be bath." The awkward syntax of "mayden one" (also in TL) possibly arose from dittography of the -an suffix in "maidan," the form of the word in CG.

11172–76 *Matt.* 1:25, *De Nativ. Mariae* X.2, and Herman's *Bible*, 1. 3460 likewise note the chasteness of the relationship. The poet's closely-followed source, however, continues to be Wace 47/13–17.

11181–84 Such Jewish slanders provided an important polemical reason for the composition of the apocryphal infancy gospels. See O. CULLMANN, "The Motives for the Composition of the Apocryphal Infancy Narratives," in Hennecke, *NT Apocrypha*, I. 366–69. In *Protevangelium* 15.1–16.2 and *Pseudo-Matt.* XII.1–5, the accusations lead to the ordeal of the "testing waters" (cf. *Num.* 5:11–31) in which the sceptical Jews unintentionally provide another proof of the couple's chaste life and of the Immaculate Conception. The trial scene received dramatic treatment in the *Lud. Cov.* play, "The Trial of Joseph and Mary." The uncanonical flight to Bethlehem to escape the suspicions of the Jews derives from Herman's *Bible*, ll. 3463–68.

11185–204 The passage combines Herman's *Bible*, ll. 3469–79a and *Luc.* 2:1–5.

11191 Although MSS GHTLB agree on "kyng," the context suggests that "kin," C's "kynd," rather than "king" is the appropriate meaning. The same variation is found in 1. 22010 where "king" (C) is used when "kinde" (F) or "kin" (GHTLB) is clearly intended.

11209–32 Wace 48/1–4; 48/17–49/15.

11213–16 The allusion seems to be to the miracle of Joseph's flourishing wand, ll. 10763–74, although Wace 48/11 relates it to Aaron's rod. *Mirk's Festial*, ll. 1003–04, however, claims that plants bore witness to Christ's coming by putting forth leaves and fruit in less than an hour.

11222　CG retain Wace's allusion to the "dumb asse" (49/1), presumably a reference to the story of Balaam and Balak in *Num.* 22:21–35.

11227–32　Cf. l. 10093. This analogy occurs in HILDEFONSE OF TOLEDO, "Sermo xiii: In Diem Sanctae Mariae," *PL* XCVI 282; GODEFRIDI ADMONTENSIS, "Homilia lxv," *PL* CLXXIV 965; and *Lud. Cov.* 181/97–100. It has also been found on fol. 40 of Geffroi of Paris' *Bible* (see Jean BONNARD, *Les Traductions de la Bible en vers français au moyen âge*, p. 46) and in the Irish work *Lebar Brecc* (see M. R. JAMES, ed., *Latin Infancy Gospels*, p. 106). The *CM* poet's immediate source, however, was Wace 49/8–15. For a study of the image see Yrjö HIRN, *The Sacred Shrine*, pp. 343–45. Hirn concludes: "The window and the rays of light become, therefore, perpetually recurring similes by the aid of which Christian poetry illustrated both the Conception and the Birth" (p. 344).

Interestingly, Wace's "soutilment" (49/12), as a description of the Incarnation and Virgin Birth, appears in *CM* l. 11231 as "sililiker" in MS G, "Qwayntylere ȝit" in Add, but as "kyndely" in HTLB and "flescheliker" in C. The two groups of readings reflect basically different theological positions. One views Christ's birth as extraordinary: "sine sorde et sine dolore," *Elucid.* I.126. Cf. "Nulla pollutio sanguinis," "nullus dolor," in *Pseudo-Matt.* XIII.3. The other stresses, as far as possible, the naturalness of the birth as indicative of Christ's humanity.

11233–37　The vagueness surrounding the circumstances of Christ's birth parallels that of the biblical accounts in *Matt.* 2:1 and *Luc.* 2:7. Other treatments, however, show less restraint. *Protevangelium* 18.1–20.3, for example, introduced the notion that Christ was born in a cave and that a "doubting-Thomas" midwife, arriving after the fact, physically examined Mary to verify her postpartum virginity. Whatever the indelicacy of the matter, the episode attained its theological goal of providing another witness to Mary's virginity. *Pseudo-Matt.* XIII.2–XIV retained the cave and midwife but attempted to reconcile its narrative with that of the Bible by having Jesus transferred, at three days old, to a stable.

11238–40　Herman's *Bible*, ll. 3486–90 also notes the simplicity of the Christ-child's clothing. MS H's "greyþe greyde" conveys basically the same meaning as "gere greide" (CGTLB) but is a suspiciously unpoetic combination quite possibly produced through dittography.

11241–76　The *CM* poet seems to have drawn on both *Luc.* 2:8–19 and Herman's *Bible*, ll. 3498–513.

11253–54　The tethered donkey does not form part of the "tokenyngis" in *Luc.* 2:12. Generally, however, the *CM* poet is faithful to the Lucan nativity account. See note to l. 11272.

11263–65　*Luc.* 2:9 simply records the shepherds' fears; Herman's *Bible* explains: "De tel visetement ne sont acoustumés" (l. 3513).

11272　The tradition of the ox and ass derives from *Pseudo-Matt.* XIV in response to the prophecies of *Is.* 1:3 — "Cognovit bos possessorem suum, et asinus praesepe domini sui" — and of *Hab.* 3:2, which reads as follows in *Pseudo-Matt.* XIV: "In medio duorum animalium innotesceris." Jerome's translation was based on the Hebrew, not the Greek, and so differs markedly. See his remarks on the subject in *Commentariorum in Abacuc*, *PL* XXV 1309.

11287–88　*Luc.* 2:22 supplemented with *Lev.* 12:2–4.

11293–305　*Lev.* 12:1–8.

11307　MS H's "wiþ" was probably copied from the preceding line in the exemplar. CGTL all read "for."

11309–12   The poet's moralizing aside on the virtues of poverty.

11313–70   *Luc.* 2:25–35 with minor changes in the narrative order. Simeon's age, unspecified in *Luc.*, is given as 112 in *Pseudo-Matt.* XV.2 and the *SE Nativity*, l. 582 but as 120 in *CM*, l. 11315. In another tradition, however, Simeon was regarded as having been crucified under Trajan at the age of 120 years. See M. R. JAMES, ed., *Latin Infancy Gospels*, p. xxix.

11321–22   These lines, present only in MSS HTLB, translate part of *Luc.* 2:26 and may therefore be original.

11345–46   In MS C the widowhood is three days longer.

11373–594   Cf. *Matt.* 2:1–13.

11373   The meaning is "Thirteen days after he was born." "For" in HT is possibly the result of metathesis in copying "Fra," as in CAddGB. Matthew, the sole evangelist to deal with the Magi, is vague concerning the time of their visit. The number "thirteen" appears in *Leg. Aur.*, Jan. 6, p. 87; *Stanzaic Life*, l. 1772; and *Hist. Schol.* vii, *PL* CXCVIII 1541. It was the interval between the traditional dates which emerged for Christmas and the Epiphany. By the fourth century, January 6 was already associated with the Magi's visit. See C. SMITH, "Epiphany, Feast of," *New Cath. Enc.*

11376–79   Such speculations about the time of the Magi's visit were invited both by Matthew's silence and by the need to explain why Herod set the cut-off age at two (*Matt.* 2:16) if the visit occurred only shortly after Christ's birth. One solution to the problem came from Comestor (*Hist. Schol.* vii, *PL* CXCVIII 1543), who suggested that immediately following the Magi's visit, Herod had to leave on urgent business and was only able to deal with the matter upon his return nearly two years later. The explanation was repeated in *Leg. Aur.*, Dec. 28, p. 64. *Pseudo-Matt.* XVI.1 would be among the works referred to in ll. 11378–79 which adopt the "two-year" theory.

11380–428   *Hist. Schol.* vii, *PL* CXCVIII 1541 and *Leg. Aur.*, Jan. 6, p. 88 both cite Chrysostom in connection with their accounts of the Magi. The *CM* poet, however, cites more of the work than either of the other two. The reference is to the *Opus Imperfectum in Matthaeum*, *PG* LVI 637–38, a work erroneously attributed to Chrysostom in the Middle Ages. The obvious alternative to having the Magi arrive up to two years after the Nativity was to allow them an early start. *Opus Imperf.*, *PG* LVI 638 specifies two years, not one as in *CM* l. 11383 (cf. l. 11422). *Leg. Aur.*, Jan. 6, p. 89, following the lead of *Hist. Schol.*, reconciled the problem of time and distance thus: the Magi "super dromedarios venerunt, qui sunt animalia velocissima, qui tantum currunt una die, quantum equus in tribus." In the "Adoration of the Magi," *Chester Plays*, VIII.160/105–08, the camels are capable of travelling one hundred miles per day.

11388–89   Balaam's prophecy originates in *Num.* 24:17.

11398   The Book of Seth is mentioned in *Opus Imperf.*, *PG* LVI 637.

11405   *Opus Imperf.*, *PG* LVI 637 identifies the place as Mount Victorialis.

11418–19   "habens in se formam quasi pueri parvuli, et super se similitudinem crucis," *Opus Imperf.*, *PG* LVI 638.

11424–26   "et neque esca, neque potus defecit in peris eorum," *Opus Imperf.*, *PG* LVI 638.

11430   Cf. *Luc.* 1:32–33: "et regnabit in domo Iacob in aeternum, et regni eius non erit finis."

11435–40   *Leg. Aur.*, Jan. 6, p. 90 also claims that the star ceased to shine when the Magi entered Jerusalem, but explains the phenomenon as having forced the wise men to make inquiries, thereby publicizing Christ's miraculous birth. *The Three*

Kings of Cologne, 52/26–27 adds that the star vanished two miles out of Jerusalem in a "derk cloude." The star's temporary disappearance, although not explicit in the Bible, is easily inferrēd from the Magi's having to ask directions in Jerusalem; see *Matt.* 2:2.

11444–65   Basically *Matt.* 2:1–3 with supplemental detail from Herman's *Bible*, ll. 3551–613.

11467–72   The prophecy is from *Mich.* 5:2.

11483–84   "hit semeþ to me" probably signals a personal observation because the poet's usual sources offer no such speculation.

11493–506   The names of the Wise Men are not traceable beyond the eighth century; see E. J. JOYCE, "Magi in the Bible," *New Cath. Enc.* They occur in this order in Herman's *Bible*, ll. 3644–46, but with a reversal of the last two in *Leg. Aur.*, Jan. 6, p. 88. MSS CAddG, however, call the third Wise Man Attropa, l. 11502.

The same significance is attached to gold and incense in Herman's *Bible*, ll. 3671–72, but myrrh is left unexplained despite the intention of completeness: "Si a en ces.III.dons.III.senefiemens," l. 3670. However, the association of myrrh with Christ's humanity and death (*CM*, ll. 11505–06) was a commonplace of scriptural exegesis. See *Leg. Aur.*, Jan. 6, p. 91; *Metrical Life*, ll. 463–74; *Chester Plays*, IX 178/81–87, 102; and *The Three Kings of Cologne*, 79/1–3.

11507–36   Matthew's silence about where the Magi spent the night allowed the assumption that it was with Mary and Joseph, hence in humble fashion. The absence of straw beds and other luxuries is pointed out in Herman's *Bible*, ll. 3675–78, which also provides the detail of the Kings' exhaustion, l. 3680. Cf. *CM*, l. 11521.

11541   Herod's use of spies comes from *Pseudo-Matt.* XVII.1.

11578–79   Matthew's account of the massacre (2:16–18) leaves the number unspecified. The poet's figure of 144,000 derives from *Rev.* 7:4, probably by way of Herman's *Bible*, l. 3737, some versions of which, however, read 44,000. A misprint in the summary headnote in *CM* makes the death toll 14,400. From a literary point of view, it is worth noting how strong the contrast is between the poet's avoidance of grisly detail in the narrative of the slaughter and Herman's gruesome details of infants "detrenchiés, . . . decolpés, /As mameles leurs meres parmi le cuer boutés," ll. 3718–41.

11582   I have found no source for the poet's placing of Joseph's warning dream seven days before the massacre. The timing of these events in *Matt.* 2:13–16 is entirely vague and *Pseudo-Matt.* XVII.2 separates them by only a day.

11590   MSS TLB likewise read "wete" as opposed to CG's "wildrin," and Add's "foreste." Both directives make sense: follow water holes or stick to the wilder (less well-travelled) routes.

11595–12576   With the exception of ll. 11797–926, this lengthy section is devoted to the "enfances" of Jesus, in three major parts: (1) en route to Egypt; (2) Egyptian sojourn; (3) residence in Galilee. The complete silence of the Bible concerning the childhood of Christ from the time of the flight into Egypt until the temple episode when He was twelve (*Luc.* 2:42–50) made this an attractive area for speculation. The *Gospel of Thomas*, written in Greek in the second century A.D., contains stories of miracles worked by the infant Jesus. These were re-told in Latin in the *Gospel of Pseudo-Matthew* (eighth or ninth century), the *CM* poet's immediate source. Other ME versions are printed in Carl HORSTMANN, ed., *Altenglische Legenden* (1875), pp. 3–61 and *Sammlung Altenglischer Legenden* (1878), pp. 101–23. The classic study of the Old French versions is Robert REINSCH, *Die Pseudo-Evangelien von Jesu.* For a modern list of the Old French versions see Maureen BOULTON, ed., *The Old French Evangile de l'enfance*, pp. 4–6. The *CM* poet follows *Pseudo-Matt*. very closely, often simply translating large portions. Herman's *Bible*, ll. 3731a–b alludes to these "wonder-child" exploits but refrains from relating any of them.

The two motives of curiosity (what did Christ do as a child?) and polemics (showing that Christ's divine nature was present from infancy) are important to an understanding of the particular treatment the subject matter received. As Amann has pointed out, however, the major attraction of such apocryphal stories in western Christendom was "moins leur aspect dogmatique que leur aspect historique"; see *Protevangelium*, p. 14.

11597–600 The details of the attendants are drawn from *Pseudo-Matt*. XVIII.1.

11615–18 The reference, also in *Pseudo-Matt*. XVIII.2, is to *Ps.* 148:7.

11641–42 On the uncanonical ox and ass, see note to l. 11272. Concerning these animals, VINCENT DE BEAUVAIS gives valuable testimony about the channels for popular transmission of such details: "Et in picturis ecclesiarum quae sunt libri laicorum, sic representatur nobis," *Speculum Historiale*, VI, 89.

11647–52 *Pseudo-Matt*. XIX.2 cites the passage but does not name the prophet. The *CM* poet wrongly identifies him as Jeremiah. The source is *Is.* 11:6–9, 65:25.

11658–730 The episode of the obedient palm tree follows *Pseudo-Matt*. XX–XXI closely.

11674–80 Joseph's reply emphasizes the human impossibility of obtaining the fruit and the precariousness of their situation because of lack of water. Jesus' double miracle of fruit and water is thus given a dramatic context.

11716ff. Christ's anachronistic and interruptive blessing of the palm as a future symbol of victory (*Pseudo-Matt*. XXI) was judiciously disregarded by the poet.

11731–46 *Pseudo-Matt*. XXII.

11759–62 The poet omits the number involved (365) given in *Pseudo-Matt*. XXII.2. The figure, suggesting worship of a different idol every day of the year, is reduced to 345 in the *SE Nativity*, ll. 729–30. The source's *idola*, *Pseudo-Matt*. XXII.2, is translated "idels" in CG and "mawmettes" in FAdd, but "deueles" in HTLB. A dilatory couplet, ll. 11761–62, on how the idols broke their necks in falling, occurs only in F.

11764–68 The poet's version of the prophecy combines *Is.* 19:1 (cf. I *Reg.* 5:1–7) and *Pseudo-Matt*. XXIII.

11769–90 *Pseudo-Matt*. XXIV.

11769 As he earlier omitted the name of the city (l. 11746 — Sotinen in *Pseudo-Matt*. XXII.2), here too the poet disregards the insignificant detail of the ruler's name (Aphrodosius in *Pseudo-Matt*. XXIV).

11773 By changing what was merely the priests' interpretation of the lord's action ("putabant se vindictam videre in eos quorum causa dii corruerant," *Pseudo-Matt*. XXIV) into his actual intention, the poet heightens the suspense of the situation.

11785–86 Missing in MSS HTLB. Morris wrongly indicates the gap in TL as ll. 11787–88.

11789–94 The story is told in *Ex.* 14:5–29. The sudden belief of the ruler parallels the renewed conviction of the Israelites in *Ex.* 14:31 after God's demonstration of power.

11797–926 For the account of Herod's death, the poet generally relied on Herman's *Bible*, ll. 3742ff. Certain details, such as Herod's reign of thirty-seven years (ll. 11799–801), do not come from Herman; cf. "Longes regna Herodes," l. 3742. These are derived instead from *Hist. Schol.*, xviii, *PL* CXCVIII 1547. MSS

GHTLB's reign of "þryes seuen" years after Christ's birth would make Him twenty-one when He returned from Egypt. The correct reading, "yeres seuen," is found in MSS CFAdd. *Leg. Aur.*, Dec. 28, p. 64, *The Three Kings of Cologne* 90/30, and the *SE Nativity*, ll. 745–46 also limit Herod's rule to seven years after the Incarnation.

11802–15   Based on Herman's *Bible*, ll. 3743–48, but the vilification is much more pronounced in *CM*. The accusation in l. 11810 stems from the tradition that Herod killed his plotting sons, Alexander and Aristobulus, and perhaps includes a reference to the accidental slaying of a younger son who happened to be in Bethlehem during the massacre. See *Leg. Aur.*, Dec. 28, p. 65. In the *Metrical Life*, ll. 714–29, Herod has this son killed in his presence.

11816–36   The catalogue of Herod's afflictions closely follows Herman's *Bible*, ll. 3747–60.

11843–96   Herman's *Bible*, ll. 3762–92.

11879   Herod is also foul-tongued in Herman's *Bible*, l. 3781: "Que queïstes cheens, fil a putain glouton?" Cf. l. 3788.

11884   A popular colloquial expression of the period. *CM* provides the earliest reference cited by B. J. and H. W. WHITING, *Proverbs, Sentences, and Proverbial Phrases*, T485. The saying remained in use at least until the seventeenth century. See M. P. TILLEY, *A Dictionary of the Proverbs in England in the Sixteenth and Seventeenth Centuries*, T536.

11900–04   This general reference to Herod's fate in hell replaces the graphic account of pitchforks, chains, flames, and a strangling serpent found in Herman's *Bible*, ll. 3797–806.

11911–26   Cf. *Matt.* 2:19–22.

11929–84   The poet now returns to *Pseudo-Matt.* The dam incident follows chapter XXVI closely.

11940   Cf. "filius diaboli," *Pseudo-Matt.* XXVI.1.

11941   MSS TLB agree with H's "erþe." The line, however, does not make much sense with "erþe," and the notion of malice is stronger in C through the consistent use of abstractions: "With nith and enst and iuel witt." G repeats C's triple listing but substitutes "erd" for "nith." In *Pseudo-Matt.* XXVI.1, the passage runs: "Tunc unus ex infantibus illis, filius diaboli, animo invido clausit aditus qui ministrabant aquas in lacus . . . ."

11975–76   Christ's spiteful treatment of the corpse follows *Pseudo-Matt.* XXVI.3: "pede suo dextro percutiens nates mortui."

11985–12014   The account of the miraculous mud-sparrows faithfully reproduces *Pseudo-Matt.* XXVII.

11992   The accusation of breaking the Sabbath as a child was doubtless inspired by the same charges against the adult Christ. See *Luc.* 6:1–11, 13:10–16; *Ioan.* 5:9–16.

12015–28   The episode of the Christ-child's withering curse is virtually a translation of *Pseudo-Matt.* XXVIII. A minor difference is that in l. 12015 the poet leaves vague the identity of the father, "filius Annae." A two-line rubric introduces this section in MS F.

12029–78   A close paraphrase, in places a translation, of *Pseudo-Matt.* XXIX.

12032–33   MS H's "ryse" is supported by TLB. The better and perhaps original reading is preserved in C's "resis"/rush. G has "rase"/hasten. In the next line "childer" means shoulder: cf. "Wit scholdur gaf he him a scou" (C) and "*and* shulderred ih*e*su w*ith* grete enuy" (F) (l. 12034 in this MS).

12039   The corresponding passage in *Pseudo-Matt.* XXIX reads "parentes mortui."

12041–44 The puzzlement over the child's nature serves the polemical goal of asserting Christ's supra-human powers from infancy. See A. F. FINDLAY, *Byways in Early Christian Literature*, p. 177. The Bible's silence about any demonstration of divinity through miracles prior to manhood left the subject open to controversy.

12053 "wedis" is not the noun "clothes" but the verb "to grow angry."

12072 MS F reads "bi þe arme." In *Pseudo-Matt*. XXIX Christ lifts the body "ad aure."

12079–167 The heated words between Christ and the first teacher provide an appropriate introduction to the more dramatic pedagogical dispute which occurs later. The poet, despite such changes as expunging the teacher's name, Zaccheus, and adding ll. 12089–90, sticks closely to his source, *Pseudo-Matt*. XXX. Unlike the earlier feats, Christ's confounding of learned men as a child has a biblical basis in *Luc*. 2:40–47.

12094–95 The accusation has a slightly different character in *Pseudo-Matt*. XXX.1, in that it is Joseph and Mary who are said to be more concerned with their son than with the traditions of the people.

12118 The form of the utterance is reminiscent of *Ioan*. 8:58.

12136 MSS CAddGHTLB have "fiue." F has "vij."

12151–53 *Pseudo-Matt*. XXX.4, which in turn draws on *Ioan*. 8:53–58.

12168–252 In presenting Christ's disputation with Levi, the poet continues to paraphrase and translate his source, *Pseudo-Matt*. XXXI.1–3.

12180 The identity of the letter, Aleph in *Pseudo-Matt*. XXXI.1, has been omitted.

12183 The poet suppresses "virgam storatinam," *Pseudo-Matt*. XXXI.1, as neither necessary nor meaningful to his audience.

12188 The poet simplifies and personalizes the corresponding generalization in *Pseudo-Matt*. XXXI.2: "In veritate scias quia ipse qui percutitur magis docet percutientem se quam ab eo doceatur."

12191–92 The lines do not make satisfactory sense in H. Their purpose is not to contrast Christ's omniscience with human teachers' limited knowledge but to characterize as blind those teachers who attempt to teach what they do not know themselves: "caecus autem si caeco ducatum praestet, ambo in foveam cadunt" (*Matt*. 15:14).

MSS CFG agree on "feris" as a verb ("is appropriate"), with a corresponding slight change in meaning: "And wat noght q*uat* thing þe*r*to feris."

12193–96 The imagery of the indictment recalls that of I *Cor*. 13:1.

12199–200 The poet here (and later) replaces or confuses the Hebrew "aleph" of his source, *Pseudo-Matt*. XXXI.2, with the more familiar Greek "alpha."

MSS HTLB read "sew" in l. 12200. The literal sense of the lines seems to be that different people view the various letters differently. However, "dispositione discernitur," *Pseudo-Matt*. XXXI.2, and the different rhyme words "taw/knau" in CFG argue that the poet's intended meaning is that the letters are recognized by their diverse appearances, as is clear in Add: "Off dyu*er*se schappe men may þam knawe."

12211 The following, presumably esoteric, bit of lore has wisely not been reproduced by the poet: "Dicat magister legis, prima littera quid sit, vel quare triangulos habeat multos gradatos, subacutos, mediatos, obductos, productos, erectos, stratos, curvistratos." See *Pseudo-Matt*. XXXI.2.

12220 *Pseudo-Matt*. XXXI.3, "et alia deludere tormenta," favours the reading in MSS CG: "And oþer þin." If F's "I note how best is to be-gyn" is meant to convey the teacher's exasperation — "I don't know where to begin!" — the altered form of the line can plausibly be attributed to a misreading of "be-gyn" as "begin" instead of "beguile," the meaning of the word in MSS CGHTLB.

12230   MS T agrees with H, but CG read "I wend i moght me w*it* hi*m* stere," while F has "ellis ne may na man him stere."

12244   The line is acceptable as it stands. "Not many can communicate with him." The reading in MSS CFAddG, however — "þat he wit man has na co*mm*un" — is closer to the Latin: "nihil cum hominibus commune videtur habere," *Pseudo-Matt.* XXXI.3.

12253–67   *Pseudo-Matt.* XXXI.4.

12257–61   The lines look forward to the public adult life of Christ.

12268   The poet's addition.

12269–305   A more attractive side of the Christ-child emerges in this episode. He demonstrates the same absolute control over life and death, but this time for someone else's victim. There are only minor deviations from the source, *Pseudo-Matt.* XXXII.

12273–74   The poet's addition.

12276   Cf. *Pseudo-Matt.* XXXII, "una sabbati."

12281   "His frendis" is not in strict harmony with the filial relationships of l. 12285. The reading in *Pseudo-Matt.* XXXII, "parentes mortui," suits the context better. As a result of this change, the scene loses some of its effectiveness: aggrieved friends are less emotionally gripping than bereft parents. The poet also softens the strong implication in his source that Jesus' reputation for nasty behaviour makes His absent parents immediately suspect Him.

12285–86   "stryf" and "felou*n*ly" are the poet's additions to the emotionally flat accusation of the parents in *Pseudo-Matt.* XXXII.

12297–98   In *Pseudo-Matt.* XXXII, the source, Jesus proceeds to establish His innocence directly.

12303–22   All *CM* MSS begin a new narrative section here. F also has an introductory two-line rubric. The division in *Pseudo-Matt.* seems less natural, the next chapter in the printed edition (XXXIII) not beginning until l. 12306.

12307–08   The child's obedience is not mentioned in *Pseudo-Matt.* XXXIII. The emphasis on Christ's submissiveness indicates that MS H's "he" is a mistake for "þei," the form found in CFGT.

12313   One leaf is missing at this point in MS H. The lacuna is remedied from T. H resumes at l. 12474.

12315   MS F's "wiþ-outen witte a reklis dint" transforms the act into a mere blunder devoid of deliberate malice. MSS CGHTLB allow for either possibility. *Pseudo-Matt.* XXXIII, like Add, shows no interest in this aspect of the incident.

12317   I do not know the poet's source for this detail. *Pseudo-Matt.* XXXIII states only that Christ carried the water home in His cloak.

12319–20   *Pseudo-Matt.* XXXIII, which in turn draws on *Luc.* 2:19, 51.

12321–22   The Marian tribute is the poet's addition.

12323–32   *Pseudo-Matt.* XXXIV, with minor changes.

12326   This detail, apparently the poet's addition, makes the event miraculous in speed as well as yield. The relevant phrase in *Pseudo-Matt.* XXXIV is "Et factum est denique."

12330   The hundredfold yield is not found in *Pseudo-Matt.* XXXIV: "collegit fructus ex eo tres choros." It does, however, appear in another apocryphal work, *The Infancy Gospel of Thomas*, 12.2, for the same miracle; see Hennecke, *NT Apoc-*

rypha. A more probable source for the number, however, is *Marc*. 4:8 and, in a totally different context, *Luc*. 16:7.

The miracle is reminiscent of another in which the Holy Family, on the flight into Egypt, comes across peasants sowing wheat. Mary, leaving instructions that anyone inquiring about the family should be told that the time of passage coincided with the seeding, pressed on with the group. Immediately, the wheat sprang up, ready for harvesting. Herod's troops, arriving moments later and learning that their quarry had passed by at seedtime, gave up the pursuit in despair. See Adey HORTON, *The Child Jesus*, pp. 109–10. Here, however, the miracle serves a primarily narrative, suspense-creating function, differing markedly from the *CM* poet's employment of it to demonstrate the Christ-child's amazing powers.

12332   MS Add is more specific about the wheat's distribution: "And [y]manges þe pore men it delt."

12333–74   *Pseudo-Matt*. XXXV. Like Daniel, *Dan*. 6:16–23, Christ is safe in the lions' den, not because "Deus meus misit angelum suum, et conclusit ora leonum" (*Dan*. 6:22), but because of Christ's divine character.

12334   The versions found in MS Add, "Hawntede strete þan was þer nane," and F, "Lay þer na way bot on," offer a more plausible explanation for Christ's choice of a dangerous route: there was no alternative. The reading in CFHT, however, makes acceptable sense.

12335   *Pseudo-Matt*. XXXV adds: "ibi arca testamenti dicitur resedisse."

12343–54   Like the earlier dragon episode, ll. 11603–56, the lion incident illustrates Christ's claim: "Alle þo beestis þat are wylde/To me shul be tame & mylde," ll. 11627–28. A possible biblical influence would be "[Laudate Dominum] Bestiae . . . ," *Ps*. 148:10.

12357–60   *Pseudo-Matt*. XXXV reads: "Hic nisi gravia fecisset peccata aut parentes eius, non se ultro leonibus obtulisset." None of the manuscripts conveys the notion of desperate sinfulness as a motive for the apparent suicidal entrance to the lions' den. Although different from the Latin, and variously expressed, the thought in CF is that the lions would not honour a sinful person. GHTLB, however, garble the idea to mean the opposite: the lions would show obedience *only* if the person were sinful. The episode has affinities with other accounts (such as the story of the virgin and the unicorn) in which holiness, nobility, or purity has a subduing effect on wild animals.

12368–74   The complaint of lack of recognition is incongruous from a child who was eight years old according to *Pseudo-Matt*. XXXV and who was not to bid for public notice for another twenty-two years.

12375–84   The brief episode of the parting of the waters and dismissal of the lions draws heavily on *Pseudo-Matt*. XXXVI. Lines 12377–78 recall Moses and the passage through the Red Sea in *Ex*. 14:8–29. Indeed, "as wal vp stode" (l. 12378) is more indebted to "erat enim aqua quasi murus" (*Ex*. 14:22) than to "et aqua Iordanis divisa est ad dextram et ad sinistram" (*Pseudo-Matt*. XXXVI). Moses, however, is merely an agent through whom the miracle is wrought and he is unable to perform it of his own accord as Christ could. The later miracles of calming the stormy sea (*Matt*. 8:23–27), walking on the water (*Matt*. 14:25; *Marc*. 6:48–51), and changing water to wine (*Ioan*. 2:1–11) are all prefigured here.

12385–86   In *Pseudo-Matt*., the detail occurs early in the lions' den episode, XXXV. MSS CAddG put Christ's age at eight but "namar." FHT fix it at eight "& more."

12387–414   *Pseudo-Matt*. XXXVII. There is no strictly comparable adult miracle for this childhood feat of stretching wood. The closest is the miracle of the multiplication of loaves and fishes (*Matt.* 14:13–21), in which quantity likewise miraculously changes to suit the circumstances. See also, however, the account of the expanding and shrinking rood-beam in *CM*, ll. 8777–820.

12393   The poet transforms the six cubits of his source, *Pseudo-Matt.* XXXVII.1, into their rough equivalent in English measure. See note to ll. 1675–76 in Horrall, *SVCM*.

12402   This line, not found in *Pseudo-Matt.*, is clearest in MS F: "oft laide he hit doun & toke up agayn"; CG are similar. Here Joseph's distraught state, seen in his repeated desperate attempts to make the short beam fit, is as skilfully suggested as it is poorly presented in HTLB.

12403   In *Pseudo-Matt.* XXXVII.1, Joseph's reaction is much stronger: "aestuando cogitare."

12404   MSS CFG stress the awkwardness of the situation through "vngainand tre." MSS HTLB's "ilke forseide" is tautologous.

12415–48   For the most part, this additional pedagogical disputation is accurately translated from *Pseudo-Matt.* XXXVIII.

12422   Cf. *Pseudo-Matt.* XXXVIII.1: "Et tunc coepit magister imperiose eum docere."

12423–25   "alpha" and "betha" appear in *Pseudo-Matt.* XXXVIII.1, in contrast to the Hebrew letters found in XXXI. This discrepancy led B. H. Cowper, ed., *The Apocryphal Gospels*, p. 79n, to assume that chapter XXXVIII was a later addition. *The Infancy Gospel of Thomas*, 14.2, in Hennecke, *NT Apocrypha*, consistently uses the Greek letters.

12439–40   The couplet, present only in MS F, repeats the content and some of the vocabulary of ll. 12435–36.

12442   The theological reminder of the divine nature of the child is the poet's addition.

12446   The intended meaning is that God the Father will protect the Son "from" wicked men, the reading which is preserved in MSS CFAddG.

12448   *Pseudo-Matt.* XXXVIII.2 has "a malo," while MSS CFG include "site" as well as "shame."

12449–84   The third pedagogical episode is distinguished by its fidelity to, and sober development of, the Lucan account of Christ and the doctors, *Luc.* 2:40–47. However, the *CM* poet's immediate source, which he follows closely, is still *Pseudo-Matt.*, XXXIX.

12453–55   The poet does not retain the Latin explanation of why Joseph and Mary comply so readily: fear of the people, the insolence of the princes, and the threats of the priests (*Pseudo-Matt.* XXXIX.1).

12484   In *Pseudo-Matt.* XXXIX.2, the conclusion to the episode returns to the earlier metaphorical language of springs and rivers, *CM*, ll. 12468–70, as a fulfilment of the psalmist's words: "Flumen dei repletum est aquis" (64:10). The *CM* poet retained the metaphorical diction but not the prophetic interpretation of the event found in his source. Except for minor differences in word order, MSS CF agree on "To lere him oght i claim þe quit," T supports H, and G's "a chaime þe quite" indicates scribal corruption but basic agreement with CF.

12487–516   The revival of the deceased burgess was no doubt inspired by such canonical accounts as the raising of Lazarus (*Ioan.* 11:39–44), the widow's son (*Luc.* 7:12–15), and Jairus' daughter (*Luc.* 8:41–55). The episode follows *Pseudo-Matt.* XXXX closely.

12488   Capernaum, the site of many of Christ's miracles, is a natural choice for a specific location; see *Matt.* 11:23; *Luc.* 4:23.

12491 *Pseudo-Matt.* XXXX does not specify the man's rank: "quidam homo . . . dives valde."

12510 Joseph is less casual in the source: "statim abiit . . . currens," *Pseudo-Matt.* XXXX.

12515 MS C's reading is puzzling: "þat lik liknes to bere." If not a meaningless reading through haplography, the sense would be: "the corpse took on the likeness [of a living person]."

12516 The poet omits the revived man's curiosity about the identity of Jesus, *Pseudo-Matt.* XXXX.

12517–42 The viper episode, although rich in potential symbolism, remains a simple, literal narrative of wonder-working, as it is in the source, *Pseudo-Matt.* XLI. Although there is no strict canonical parallel for the miracle, Christ's healing of the withered hand (*Marc.* 3:1–5; *Luc.* 6:6–10) is probably close enough to have been an influence. Also worth consideration is an episode in *Pseudo-Matt.* XIII.3–5, in which a midwife, in "doubting-Thomas" fashion, grotesquely examines the Virgin to ascertain her postpartum virginity and suffers a withered hand for her lack of faith. Restoration occurs when she touches the edge of Christ's swaddling clothes. (Cf. 3 *Reg.* 13:1–6 for a parallel miracle.)

12517 The brevity of the stay in Capernaum is the poet's addition.

12521 The tradition of James as a son of Joseph arose, at least in part, from *Matt.* 13:55: "Nonne mater ejus [i.e. Jesus'] dicitur Maria, et fratres ejus, Jacobus, et Joseph, et Simon, et Judas?" These latter, however, could also be the children of Mary Cleophas, sister of the Virgin (*Ioan.* 19:25) and still warrant the designation "brethren" according to the social conventions of the time. Wace 55/8–9 claims only two sons, Joseph and Jacobus, for Mary Cleophas, while *Leg. Aur.*, Sept. 8, p. 586, adds two more, Simon and Jude, in keeping with *Matt.* 13:55.

12523 The poet particularizes the indefinite "olera" of *Pseudo-Matt.* XLI.1.

12528 The source is less explicit: "percussit manum Iacobi," *Pseudo-Matt.* XLI.1.

12531 The source does not mention this reaction.

12542 The poet has omitted matter, thus making James and Christ the antecedents of "þei" and consequently the somewhat awkward "discoverers" of the dead serpent. In *Pseudo-Matt.* XLI.2, it is Joseph and Mary who investigate the commotion and "invenerunt serpentum mortuum."

12543–76 The source is *Pseudo-Matt.* XLII.

12546 The names of Joseph's four sons are taken from *Matt.* 13:55. In *Leg. Aur.*, Sept. 8, p. 586, these sons are the offspring of Mary Cleophas, described as the Virgin's half-sister, and Alpheus. *Leg. Aur.*, Sept. 8, p. 586 cites the following verse to summarize the relationships:

Anna solet dici tres concepisse Marias,
Quas genuere viri Joachim, Cleophas, Salomeque
Has duxere viri Joseph, Alpheus, Zebedaeus.
Prima parit Christum, Jacobum secunda minorem,
Et Joseph justum peperit cum Simone Judam,
Tertia majorem Jacobum volucremque Joannem.

Herman's *Bible*, ll. 3147c–d concurs in making John and James the sons of Mary and Zebedeus, but associates this Mary with Anna's second marriage rather than the third.

12547 *Matt.* 13:56 mentions the daughters but does not specify their number.

12548–51 "mary cleophe" is identified as the Virgin's sister in *Ioan*. 19:25. Both Wace 54/10–55/7 and *Leg. Aur.*, Sept. 8, p. 586 record the tradition of Anna's three marriages — to Joachim, Cleophas, and Salome — each of which produced a daughter called Mary. Herman's *Bible*, ll. 3123–53 agrees substantially with these versions except for reversing the order of the second and third husbands. See Max FÖRSTER, "Die Legende vom Trinubium der hl. Anna," pp. 105–30.

M. R. JAMES, "The Salomites," pp. 218–19, dated this motif to the late eleventh century and suggested that it was originally Norman or Anglo-Norman. However, it was known to Haymo of Auxerre in the ninth century; see *Historiae Sacrae Epitome*, *PL* CXVIII 823–24 (where it is printed under the name of Haymo of Halberstadt). For the motif in *Hist. Schol.*, see chapter xlvii, *PL* CXCVIII 1563.

12573–74 The divine light that attends the Christ-child may have been inspired by the transfiguration of the adult Christ. See *Matt*. 17:1–5; *Marc*. 9:1–6; *Luc*. 9:28–35.

12576 The "A" version of *Pseudo-Matt.* — the letter designations were established by TISCHENDORF in his edition of *Evangelia Apocrypha* — ends at this point, XLII.2, with the familiar "laus et gloria" formula, while "B" terminates with the assurance that the work was written by the apostle John and translated by St. Jerome, of all people. See *De Perpetua Virginitate B. Mariae: Adversus Helvidium*, *PL* XXIII 200–01 for his strong opposition to apocryphal writings. The headnote in "A" just as confidently — and as truthfully — credits Matthew with the authorship.

12577–655 Having finished with the period of Christ's life about which the Bible is silent, from the flight into Egypt when He was an infant to the disputation with the doctors when He was twelve, the poet now turns to *Luc*. 2:42–52 for the sole scriptural account of an event in Christ's youth.

12582 It is noteworthy that the poet's claim of truthfulness for his source is not one he made when drawing on apocryphal materials.

12593–94 The poet has added these details to Luke's sparse account in 2:43–44.

12598 Either MSS GHTLB's "ansuerd" or CFAdd's "asked" is acceptable, for in *Luc*. 2:46–47 Christ listens, questions, and replies.

12611–12 In *Luc*. 2:45–46, both parents seek Jesus, but nothing is said of Mary's exhaustion, a humanizing touch by the poet of the same kind as the observations that Mary was "flesshy and sumdele/broune" and the infant Jesus "sumdele fatte" in *The Three Kings of Cologne*, 70/13–17.

12636–40 An amplification of "et erat subditus illis," *Luc*. 2:51.

12645 *Luc*. 2:52: "Et Iesus proficiebat . . . gratia apud Deum."

12648 *Luc*. 3:23.

12653–54 Herman's *Bible*, l. 3821: "Adonc s'est porpensés, baptisier se fera."

12659–712 Chronologically, Christ's maternal background is out of place at this point in the narrative. In Wace 54/10ff., the information is similarly located after the birth of Christ. By contrast, in Herman's *Bible*, ll. 3123–53, this material is included in the account of Mary's temple service where it forms an appropriate closing chapter to the lengthy marital history of Mary's illustrious parents. The location in *CM* can be defended on literary grounds, however, for it effects a clear separation of Christ's adolescent and adult stages. The separation receives additional emphasis in MS F which introduces the section with the rubric "þe kinradin of saint Anne & hir/þre housbandis," and in Add, where the rubric reads "The Genelogye of Anna and hir Sist*e*rs/and thaire housebaundes."

In addition to the different location, Herman's *Bible* alters the usual sequence of Anna's second and third husbands (Cleophas, Salome) and otherwise differs too greatly in detail to have been the source. Actually, the *CM* poet here returns to Wace, 54/10–57/7 and is largely content to translate and paraphrase.

12659–61 Translated from Wace 54/22–55/3.

12673–74 The second line is variously written. The couplet in Wace 55/12–13 — "Frere fu dit par parenté,/Et par valor et par bonté" — shows that F omitted a term (CG's "wirschip," Add's "honoure") and that HTLB misread "bunte" as "beauty."

12675–76 The couplet, missing in MSS FHTLB, translates "Auques li sambloit de façon./Si fu de grant religion" (Wace 55/14–15) and is therefore original. This is the only place in *CM* where FHTLB share a common loss against all other manuscripts.

James's resemblance to Christ is noted in *Leg. Aur.*, May 1, p. 295, and again at ll. 12687–88.

12678–92 Wace 55/16–56/6 provides the hagiographical details about James. *Leg. Aur.*, May 1, p. 297, adds that he anointed himself with oil, did not cut his hair, and never bathed.

12683–86 According to *Leg. Aur.*, May 1, p. 297, James's difficulty in walking was not due to his swollen knees but rather to lameness suffered when he was pushed off a high platform. Cf. Wace 55/23–56/2:

Et tant ora agenoillons,
Que la char fu créuë grant
Deseur les.ij.genouz devant.

Wace makes no mention of lameness, however.

12691 Wace 56/5: "Fu en Jherusalem ocis." *Leg. Aur.*, May 1, p. 298, specifies the manner: he was thrust off the temple pinnacle, stoned, and brained.

12693–708 The details of Anna's third marriage are largely translated from Wace 56/7–57/7.

12700 The distinguishing epithets "Great" and "Less" (*Marc.* 15:40) were applied respectively to James, son of Zebedee, and James, son of Alpheus.

12701 This comes ultimately from *Act.* 12:2, but the immediate source is Wace 56/15: "Qu'Erodes fist martirier."

12704–12 The portrait of John as intimate companion and favourite apostle of Christ arises ultimately from New Testament situations and inferences. Thus, John is privileged to witness the transfiguration (*Matt.* 17:1–2), the agony in the garden (*Marc.* 14:32–34), the revival of Jairus' daughter (*Luc.* 8:51), and to ask Christ questions on Olivet (*Marc.* 13:3). So too, however, are both Peter and James. What singled John out was his identification as "illum discipulum, quem diligebat Iesus" and, more importantly, as the man chosen by the Saviour to look after the Virgin (*Ioan.* 19:25–26); as the one "recumbens . . . in sinu Iesu" at the Last Supper (*Ioan.* 13:23); and as the first disciple to recognize the risen Christ (*Ioan.* 21:7). All these passages employ the "quem diligebat Iesus" phrase. The *CM* poet's direct source, however, was clearly Wace 56/21–57/7.

APPENDIX A

Errors in Morris' Texts

9233   heard]G herd.
9239   aȝor]T azor.
9260   criste]F criste.
9266   I say]T Isay.
9275   þat]G þat.
9277   till]C til.
9304   Again]G Agayn.
9361   loke]L loke.
9371   take]L take.
9376   ȝe]G þe.
9387   Þat]C Þat.
9404   fleȝely]T sleȝely.
9420   neuer]C neuer.
9422   the]C þe.
9429   that]C þat.
9503   widuten]G widuten.
9504   helden]G halden.
9533   she]T he.
9549   lauerdhede]C lauerdhele.
9558   him]T him.
9598   this]L þis.
9641   his]L his.
9669   laste]T lafte.
9757   þinges]T þing es.
9789   my]T ny.
9807   laste]T lafte.
9834   with]T wiþ.
9914   gound]T ground.
9916   grenis]L grevis.
9917   grenis]L grevis.
9956   lend]T lende.
9976   hert]G herte.
9990   [Of]]G Of. al]G all.
9996   day]L dai.
10020   graithli]C grathli.
10145   Þat]G Þat.
10150   widuten]G widvuten.
10192   his]L his.
10236   [To I]]C To I.
10237   [Bifor]]C Bifor.
10238   [I bid]]C I bid.

10243 [Þin]]C Þin.
10244 [Ga]]C Ga.
10253 vnderstand]G vnderstand.
10272 not]T mot.
10304 wild]C wald.
10317 Þe]T He.
10393 sone]T done.
10420 her]G hir.
10495 menid]L mevid.
10574 þat]G þat.
10610 ilkand]G ilkane.
10629 hou]G hu.
10730 kindred]G kinred.
10771 whenne]T whenne.
10868 þaim]G þaim.
10894 her]G hir.
10917 þat]G þat.
10958 He]T Þe.
10967 quat]G quat.
10996 ledd]G ledde. house]T hous.
11001 annunciacoune]G annunciacioune.
11021 Not]G Noght.
11050 þe]G om.
11054 divers]G diuers.
11058 Til]G Till.
11092 was]G ws.
11093 said]G sayd.
11114 crist]G cristi.
11151 tok]G toke.
11154 be]T he.
11193 þing]G þing.
11203 gan]G gane.
11235 as]G als.
11239 ne]T no.
11291 on]G of.
11336 bi-fore]G bi-for.
11341 eyen]T eȝen.
11343 was]T was an.
11349 scho bune]G bune scho.
11357 propheci]G propheci.
11358 lauedi]G leuedi.
11368 and]G and.
11380 mowþ]L mowþe.
11399 sterrie]T sterne.
11412 mounteyn]T nounteyn.
11502 Balchisor]T Balthisor.
11541 by]G bi.
11578 childe]T childre.
11594 yon]L you.
11603 was]G was.
11650 com]T com to.

11655 þan]G þai.
11669 fayne]T fayn.
11673 þer-to]F þer-to.
11694 vp]G up.
11696 plantyd]T planted.
11742 day]G dai.
11770 tiþing]G tiþ[i]ng.
11807 þat]G þat.
11812 mi]G nu.
11818 pride]G pride.
11828 fever]G feuer.
11842 for]F to for, to cancelled.
11865 on]F of.
11867 get]T gete.
11881 Medicine]G Medecine.
11887 it]T hit.
11912 com]G come.
11958 warne]T warne.
11975 þere]CG þar; F þer.
11996 mak]G make.
12005 held]T helde.
12008 the]G þe.
12013 com]T coom.
12020 þat]T þat.
12102 the]F þe.
12118 funden]G funden.
12149 moderis]G moderis.
12189 oþer]G oþer.
12192 and]F and.
12237 childe]G child.
12278 a-noþer]F a-noþer.
12286 broght]G br[o]ght.
12288 awey]T alwey.
12301 þat]C þat.
12310 water]G water.
12333 flum]T flum.
12341 This line in C is found on leaf 68, back, col. 1.
12366 leonis]G leons.
12402 Oft]G Ofte.
12426 þe]G þe sai.
12441 Na]G Nai.
12447 þat]T þat.
12467 can]C gan.
12472 ʒing]G ʒung.
12493 Pat]C Pat.
12595 ʒede]G ʒode.
12601 so]F sa.
12624 this]C þis.
12636 vnderlute]C vnderlute.
12664 gode]G god.
12672 broþer]G broþer.

12674   worschip]G worchip.
12682   neu*er*]T neu*er* on.
12683   Him þouȝte himself neu*er* wery]C Sua haunted he on knes to lij.
12684   On god on knees for to cry]C And for to prai sua Iþenli.
12700   þat]G þat.
12701   herodes]G h*er*odes.
12702   toþer]G toþer.

APPENDIX B

Cursor Mundi from MS BL Additional 31042
(The Thornton Manuscript)

[At the time of her death, Dr. Horrall had not completed the proofreading of the text which forms Appendix B. Professor George Kaiser, Kansas State University, graciously offered to check the transcription against his microfilm of the manuscript. He subsequently brought to my attention a point on which I have had to make an editorial decision. At the time of copying MS BL Additional 31042, the scribe, Robert Thornton, was evidently in the process of altering certain features of his hand. He frequently reverted to his old habits, however, and often produced a "þ" when he clearly intended a "y." I have signified such slips by emending the "þ" to "y" in square brackets. Except for this one change, the transcription faithfully reproduces the text of the manuscript.]

Scho was & that was sone appon hir sene	10630 fol. 3r col. 1
F⟨or⟩ godd hy*m*selfe in hir he lighte	
And his wonnyng stede in hir he dighte	
And hereby may men wele see	
That ⟨in⟩ hir was grete bounte	
For it es funden als we rede	10635
Þat oure lorde wolde hy*m* neu*er* bede	
To saule þat solsede was with synn	
To make his wonnyng stede thereInn	
Þan moste this mayden be clene & brighte	
W*ith*owtten playnt & w*ith*owtten plighte	10640
In whayme þe kyng þ*at* alle may make	
Wolde lighte manhede for to take	
In þe temple es scho wonnande ay	
And seruys godd bothe nyghte & day	
W*ith* alle hir myghte & hir entent	10645
To goddes seruys was scho went	
Swa lange this mayden þ*er* hase bene	
Þat scho elde was ʒeris fourtene	
Þan dide þe Bischoppe co*m*mande thare	
Þ*at* alle þe maydones þ*at* there ware	10650
In þe elde of fourtene ʒere	
Solde be sent vnto þayre frendis dere	
For to mary & for to spouse	
⟨ j⟩lkane to thaire awenn house	
⟨Many⟩ of þam þat thare ware stadd	10655
Bote als þe Bischoppe þam bedde	
Bot marie wolde no maryinge	
Bot mayden be till hir endynge	
When men till hyre of housebande spakke	

Scho sayd scho wolde nane take 10660
To godd I hafe gyffen mee
I ne maye to no man maryede bee
Othere housebande I may ha⟨fe nane⟩
For my lemmane I hafe hym tane
My maydenhede till hym I highte 10665
I sall be swa at alle my myghte
I sall neuer it vndoo
Þat I hym hafe highte vntoo
To godd I was gyffen are fol. 3r col. 2
Are my modir me of hir body bare 10670
In his seruys I thynke to lende
Righte vnto my lyues ende

The Bischoppe noghte what to speke
Wold noȝt late hir hir vowe breke
It was byfore many a daye 10675
Comande in þe alde laye
To holde and ȝelde withowtten bade
Þe vowe that thou haues made
One owthere syde he was dowtande
To brynge a newe custome one hande 10680
Þe mayden frendis for to lett
In maryage hir for to sett
For it was boden in thaire lede
With mariage þe folke to sprede
Þerefore garte þe bischoppe fett 10685
Þe wyseste men þat he myghte gett
Off alle þat was in that conutree
And in þe temple made a semble
When all were comen ȝonge & alde
Þe prelate to thaym þe resone talde 10690
Whi he þam garte assemblede bee
For þe vowe of the chastyte
And for to wete at thaym rede
If scho walde halde till hir dede
Off this matir solde þay speke 10695
Whethir scho vow solde halde or breke
And depely solde þay luk howe
The beste to ordayne for this vowe
For vowe þat is made rightwysse
Men sall it halde one alle wyse 10700
Are it be made it comes of will
Bot made nede wayes men moste fulfill
Bot þar was nane at þis gederynge
Þat couthe giffe consell of þis thynge
Other consaill couthe they gyffe nane 10705
Bot calle & crye one godd allane
Þat he solde þam some taken schewe
Whareby þat þay myghte knawee
What þay solde do of that maye fol. 3v col. 1

To do hir breke vowe or naye   10710
Þan lay þay alle in knelynge downn
Makand to godd þaire Orysoun
Whils þat þay in prayers laye
A voyce þey herde vnto þam saye
Lokes he sayd þe prophecye   10715
Þat was sayde of [Y]say
And by the prophecy ȝe schall see
To whaym þat may schall spoused be
[Y]say þat alde prophete
Lang sythen that he byhete   10720
Off þe rote of Iesse ther solde sprynge
A wande þat solde a floure forthe brynge
Bathe floure & fruyte owte solde breste
Þe haly gaste þerone solde reste
Thurgh þat voyce þat þay gan here   10725
Þay sayd þat wande solde floure bere
Þare solde a rote of Iesse sprynge
Þan ware þay putt in grete wetynge
And hastily þay garte forthe calle
Off Dauit þe progeny alle   10730
Whase ffader thane was Iesse
Þare ware þay spredde in þat contree
Ilkane of þam in thaire hand
Bedyn was to bere a wande
And whilke of thaym als bare burioune   10735
Solde wedde þat maye in his baundoun
With this thay sent vp and downn
And bad þam at a daye be boune
Alle þat of Dauit kynde ware bredde
And þat no woman wedde   10740
And alle þat thedir ware calde
Solde in þaire handes a wande halde
And whase wande so bare a blome
Marie solde wedde this was þe dome

The day come sone of this semble   10745
Þay come alle of that contree
Within þe temple alle were þay ȝare
Alle bot men that spoused ware
Ioseph come to Ierusalem   fol. 3v col. 2
A man wonnande in Bedlem   10750
His wyfe was dede hymselfe was alde
[Y]manges thase men þat I of talde
He come for to bere his wande
Als þe biddyng was in lande
Ane alde mane was he ane   10755
Wyfe to hafe couayte he righte nane
He was a mane of halynes
Did he to na man na wrangwisnes
In that þat he moghte he droghe on bakke

He was in will na wyfe to take   10760
If he droghe hy*m* neu*er* swa awaye
Þay garte hy*m* come vnto this daye
When Ilkane w*ith* his wande forthe lepe
Þan on bakke hym droghe Iosephe
When þat þayre wandes vp ȝalde   10765
Byhynde standis Ioseph þe alde
Than badde þe prestis þam forth calle
To offre vp þaire wandis alle
Þe preste þam talde & sone he fande
Þat thare was wanttande a wande   10770
When Ioseph saghe no hydynge doghte
Þan he forthe his wande broghte
And al sone als it was sene
W*ith* lefe & flo*ur* þay fande it gren
A dowe þat fra heuen was sent   10775
One þat wande of Ioseph lent
Þan was þat maye Ioseph bytaghte
And in spowsayl hir hase he laghte
Whethere so he walde or naye
He moste hir spouse and lede awaye   10780

Why that oure lady was spowsed

Resouns thare are wretyn sere   10783
Whi þat god wolde scho spoused were
Firste þat þe fend sold noghte p*er*ceyue   10785
Þat a mayden solde conceyue
For and he myghte hafe vndirtane   fol. 4r col. 1
A barne be borne of a mayden
Ne wolde he neu*er* hafe gyffen his rede
For to hafe done Ih*esu* to dede
For wele he welde hafe wetyn þan
Þat he solde hafe saued man
Oure lorde þ*er*fore & for resone swilke   10795
Be fedde of a mayden mylke
Þat solde hir maydenhede hafe hidd
Of alle scho were for wedded kydde

Anothir þat men solde noȝte hir stane
If scho w*ith* childe were ouertane   10800
For þe laghe þat tyme was i*n* lande   10805
And a woman had na housebande
And scho funden were with childe
Fra stanyng ne solde hir schilde

Þe thirde resone of hir spousaile
Þat mannes helpe hir solde nan faile   10810
Hir helped Ioseph in hir nede
Whidir so scho rede or ȝede
Þus he hir kepid þat lorde [y]wysse
Þat souereyne kyng of heuens blys   10814

Ioseph spoused þis lady free   10817
And led hir into galile
With hir toke he maydens seuen
Þaire names ne herde I neuer neuen   10820
Alle þaire were of his kynn
And of þat elde þat scho was Inn
Þase seuen þe bischop hir bytaghte
When scho at hym hir leue laghte
WithIn þe lande of Galile   10825
Es nazareth a faire Cite
Þare lefte Ioseph marie his spouse
Till þat he went vnto his house
Vnto bedleme went es hee
To gare his Bridale graythed bee   10830
He garte þare graythe all thynge
Are he his wyfe wolde hame brynge   fol. 4r col. 2
Bot are to Bedlem sho was ffett
With þe angell was scho grett

Saynt Gabriel come fra heuen   10835
And sayd thus with myld steuen
Haile Marie full of grace
God is with the in ilke a place
Ouer alle wymmen blyssed þou bee
And blyssede be þe fruyte of thee   10840
Þis lady ne dowttede noghte þe syghte
Off this angell þat was bryghte
For bifore ofte hade scho sene
Angels þat ware bryghte & schene
Bot of hym this scho was in were   10845
He haylsed hir one swilke manere
Alle bydroved scho was in thoghte
What that he was þis haylesyng broghte
He saughe hir hert & hir will
And one þis wyse he spake hir tyll   10850
Mary he sayd why art þou madde
The ne es no nede for to be radde
Be þou noghte menged in thi mode
Bot hafe hope stedfaste & gude
Ioyfull to be matir hafes thou   10855
Þou art goddes modir chosen nowe
Þe haly gaste in the es lyghte
Goddes wonnyng stede in the es dighte
Oure lorde hase made the his lemman
Þou sall hafe childe & be mayden   10860
Modir and mayden bothe sall þou be
And goddes sone be borne of thee
Off hym ferre mon sprynge þe fame
Kyng of kynges mon be his name
Off all thynge he sall be kynge   10865
Euermore withowtten endynge
His folke saufe þan sall he make

And clense alle of synn & sake
This mayden nothyng dowtted scho   fol. 4v col. 1
Wele scho wyste he moghte alle doo   10870
Bot wete scho wolde one alle manere
How a mayden a childe solde bere
Barne scho sayd how solde I brede
With man I ne dide neuer fleschly dede
Þat man that hafes spowsede mee   10875
Fordide neuer my chastytee
Þe woman þat neuer towchede man
How solde scho concayue thanne
I ne herde it neuer in na lede
Woman bere barne in maydenhede   10880

Gabriel sayd lady nay
How that may be I sall the say
Þe haly gaste in the sall lende
And goddes myghte in the discende
A childe þou sall hafe and hee   10885
Goddes sone sall callede bee
Withowtten synn or solpnes
Þow sall be mayden als þou es
Es and was and sall be clene
Als euer ȝitt thou hafes bene   10890
Þat þou ne be noghte hereof in were
Elezabeth be thi Samplere
Þatt sa ferre intill elde
Godd hase lent grace a childe to welde
In erthe þe whethir was na thynge   10895
Þat scho had of mare ȝernynge
Scho hase consayued of hir housbande
Sex monethes with childe gangande
For it es nathyng þat may falle
Þat ne godd may do alle   10900
This Bodworde gan this lady trowe
To goddis sande scho gan hir bowe   10902
To þe angell scho sayde onane   10905
Loo me here goddes hande mayden
Als þou hase sayde to me byforne
Goddes sone of me be borne
Þat all hafes wroghte and hafes in hande
Mone and sternes See and Sande   10910
Þat euer sall bee & euere hase bene
Es loken in þat mayden clene   10912
With childe scho wexe in þat stownde þare   10903 fol. 4v col. 2
Als neuer swa dide woman are   10904
And þarby may we say alle   10913
Now es þe lorde bycommen thralle
Þe doghtir modir agaynes þe wonne   10915
And the fadir bycommen sone
And he þat firste na dede myghte drye

Now es he able for to dye
Godd þat tyme mane bycome thus
Noghte for na nede he hade of vs 10920
Ne for no thynge bot forthi
Þat he with his grace wolde by
Fra þe powere of the fende
And fra dede withowtten ende
Þe day þat firste was sent þis sande 10925
Was mare & þe fyfte & twentyande
Fra fyve thowsande [y]er was bygonnenn
After þis worlde it was bynomen
Nyghenty and nyghen and monethes sexe
Þat oure helde in this mayden wexe 10930
Lefe we now thatt ladye
And speke we of Zakarye
How þe angel come hym to warne
How þat he solde hafe Iohn to barne 10934

Off the Concepcyon off Iohn þe Baptiste

This zakary þat I of rede 10935
He comen was of leuy sede
Elezabeth his wyfe was alde
Anna sister doghter þat I of talde fol. 5r col. 1
An haly lyfe þay samen ledde
Withowtten barne bytwix þam bredde 10940
And þarefore þay mournande were
Off alle þay toke it with gud chere
Almaste to theire lyves ende
Bot at þe laste god þam sende
Swa felle a feste in that lede 10945
And Zakarye to the temple ȝede
For to do þe folkes seruyse
Als þe laghe was one alde wyse
He reueste hym one his manere
And went hym to his autere 10950
He bad þe folke wende oute ilkane
Wyls he prayede in þe kirke allane
Swa to do þan was he wont
And thare he prayed a grete stount
He luked one his righte hande 10955
And þare he saghe an angel stande
For hym in mode he was al made
Þe angell bad hym noghte be radde
And sayd hym þat he was sent
Till hym thare fra þe firmament 10960
Hym to comforthe oute of syte
A barne he sayde þou sall hafe tyte
And of þat barne þou may be blythe
For goddes werkes sone sall he kythe
His name men sall calle Iohan 10965

Þus hase godd tid the this bon
Do waye he sayde what says þow
Thi tythandes forsothe may I noȝte trow
Þat I & my wyfe nowe in oure elde
Sold any barne welde   10970
Þou sall hafe ane forsothe I saye
And þerfore ioye now make þou maye
Men sall be blythe in his birthe
For he sall be man of mekill myrthe
Bot for þat þou wolde noghte me trowe   10975
Þou sall be dombe forthe fra nowe
Till that he be borne that ȝonge   fol. 5r col. 2
And he sall gare þe hafe thi tonge
Byfore allemyghty godd he sall
Be a man of mekyll tale   10980
He sall be man of mekill swynke
Wyne ne Cesare sall he nane drynke
In his modir wambe sall hee
With the haly gaste fulffilled be
Þou sall be doumbe for thi mistrounne   10985
Vntill þe tyme of his circumsisiounne
Zakarie haue now gude daye
For þou sall fynde als þou heres me saye
Þe folkes owtwith stode & habade
And thoghte grete ferly what he made   10990
For þay habade till þay ware irke
And than þay went into þe kyrke
And alle madde sir Zakarye þay fande
Till þam ne couthe he telle na tythande
Na seruyce doo swaa was he madde   10995
And dombe þay till his house hym ledde

Þe Concepcyon of Saynt Iohn of Baptiste

Now bredys barne Elezabeth
In Septembire in þat moneth
In þe foure & twenty nyghte
Was Iohn getyn thurghe goddes myght   11000
Byfore þe anucyacyoun
Off Criste þat gatte vs alle pardoun
For righte it was þat þe puruayoure
Solde come byfore þe Saueoure
He þat broghte vs alle oure hele   11005
Sent byfore hym his bedelle
Forthi sent Ihesus Iohn forthwith
Are he wolde shewe hymselfe in kythe
And bathe theire modirs þat were mylde
At anes ȝode thay with childe   11010
Bot Elezabeth was forthir gane
By sex monethes and a woke ane   fol. 5v col. 1
Fra Saynt Iohn Concepcyoune
Vnto the anuncyacyounne

Sone oure lady was mett 11015
With þe angell þat hir grett
Scho went oute of Nazareth
For to speke with Elezabeth
Þat lange was gelde and ane alde wyfe
And nowe scho es with barne one lyfe 11020
Noghte ferre from childynge in a syquare
And marye come vnto hir thare
When þay mett thase ladys twynn
Þat ware bathe cosyns þam withInn
At þe metyng Saynt Marie spakke 11025
And hir haylsynge bygane to make
Till Elezabethe that woman
Hir childe in hir wambe to glade bygane
And in hir wambe it satt vpryghte
Alle for þe Ioye of godd of myghte 11030
And made a gladnesse & a glewe
Righte als he his lorde wele knewe
Loo he knewe his lorde byforne
Are he was of his modir borne
Þe man his lorde þe mayster his clerke 11035
Þe makere knewe his handewerke
Elezabeth in that Ilke place
Thare scho stode full of grace
Bygane & sayde a prophecye
Blyssede be thou euere Marye 11040
And blyssede be þe fruyte of the
Þat thou walde thus come to vesete me
Þe modire of my lorde so dere
Þe childe withInn my wambe gan here
Þe hailsyng that thou to me made 11045
And it for Ioye bygane to glade
Blyssede be thou þat mystrowede noghte
Þe bodworde that was to the broghte
Thou may be trayste & þou will byde
Alle þat is bihighte to þe sall betyde 11050

Thir ladys menskede þam Imelle
Their wills ayther till oþer gan tell
Bot their menskyng þam bytwene
Dyuerse was somwhat es sene fol. 5v col. 2
Þe tane was lady & mayden clene 11055
Þe toþer his handwoman seruynge
Thare duellede oure lady with hir nece
To Iohn was borne a gude pece
At hir childynge scho was helpand⟨e⟩
And als in some bokes we fande 11060
Scho was hirselfe þe firste woman 11063
Þat euer layde hande one saynt Iohn 11064
When Iohn was borne þat Ilke sythe 11065
His frendis were bothe gladde & blythe 11066

And hade of hir full mekill myrthe
Þat was so lange withowtten byrthe
Noghte allane Ierusalem burghe
Bot also alle the contreth thurgh   11070
His fest es in Somyrs tyme
Bothe Iewes it honowrs a Sarazyne
Thurghe alle þe landis þer heythyn lyfes
Alls ferre als þe sounne hym ryses
Forthi of hym wittnesse vs   11075
Oure lorde and Saueoure Ihesus
Off wyfe he sayde was neuer borne ane
Grettere barne þan saynt Iohn
Alle made þay myrth of his berynge
Fadir and modir and thayre kythynge   11080
And gadirde þam togedir alle
Þay ne wiste neuer whatt hym to calle
Sir Zakarye þay forthe broghte
Bot he with þam myghte speke righte noghte
Þe resoune byfore ȝee hafe herde why   11085
Þan countenance made he sir Zakarye
After tabills and poyntell tytt
And he bygane þe name to wrytt
And sayd als þe angell bygane
And gaffe hym Iohn vnto name   11090
His frendis thoghte þerof selcouthe
Of this name that was vncouthe
And saide þat þay ne couthe noghte fynde
Swilke a name in alle his kynde
When he was circumcysede Saynt Iohn   11095
His fadir þe speche hadde anone
And swilke a prophecye gonn he mele
Blyssed be godd of Israel   fol. 6r col. 1
That vesittyng till his folke hase sent
And rawnsonyng till vs hase lent   11100
Þis barne þat was fosterde dere
Whan he come at seuen ȝere
He lafte his kynn & alle his thede
And into wildirnesse he ȝede
For that he wolde flye synn   11105
He lefte his kythe & alle his kynn
And in that wildirnesse he bade
And lange he ledde thare harde lyfelade
And lyffede with rotes & with gresse
And also with hony in that wildirnesse   11110
He ne ete no brede ne dranke no wyne
Ne wered noþer wolle ne lyne
This was Iohn þe Baptiste
Þat aftirwarde crystende Ihesu Criste
When þat Iohn was borne in hy   11115
Þan Saynt Marie oure lady
Bykenned to godde Elezabeth

And went hirselfe vnto Nazareth
With this bygane to come to þe sythe
Hir wombe itselfe bygane to kythe   11120
Þat men was somedele perceyuede
Þat this mayden hadd conceyuede
Aftir Ioseph wedded this maye
Certanely þe sothe to saye
He duellide mare thane monethes three   11125
In his awenn kyndely countree
At þe income of þe ferthe monethe
Ioseph went to Nazareth
Þat lady when he come nerehande
With hir to speke als dose housebande   11130
To speke of nedis þat felle to house
Als men dose þat delis with spouse
He saghe withowtten any warne
Þat þis woman was with barne
And when he knewe hir in this state   11135 fol. 6r col. 2
Was neuer no man halfe so mate
Swa sary ne was he neuer in his lyfe
With barne when he saghe his wyfe
Þat he neuer ne towchide till
Ne hafed at doo within wanttone will   11140
Þat wonder nane ne was for he
Ne wiste noghte of hir preuatee
Bot whatso þat he thoghte
To hir þat tyme ne sayde he noghte
Bot helde in herte full wondir stylle   11145
And was in purpose and in will
Pryualy awaye for to stele
Fra þat ladye gude and lele
Off hir ne wolde he for noo thynge
Late any ⟨k⟩yn worde vppe sprynge   11150
Bot toke his redde aye for to flee
Fra hir awaye & late hir bee
Gude will he hade to flye hir fraa
Þat nyghte he solde hafe donne swaa
Bot till hym slepande als he laye   11155
An angell come þat þus gane saye
Ioseph he sayde tell me nowe why
Will þou leue thi spouse Marie
Þat ba[r]ne scho hase in hir body breedde
Þarefore be þou noghte adradd   11160
Be þou in trayste and sekirnes
Þat þe haly gaste within hir esse
It is þe haly gastes myghte
Withowtten part of mannes plyghte
Þe childe þat scho gaa with alle   11165
Ihesus men sall it calle
He sall be godde & mane bathe
And al mankynge mon he were fra wathe

Fra this tyme hade Ioseph nane
Euelle hope to that womane   11170
Full kyndely kepe till hir toke hee
And dwellyde with hir in chastytee
With menske and wirchippe hir to ȝeme   fol. 6v col. 1
And hir he seruede aye to queme
And swaa forthe withowtten fayle   11175
Samen helde thaye thaire spowsaile

The tyme that brynnges alle to fyne
Ranne with this to monethes nyne
Ioseph dighte hym to gaa
Till Bedlem and did alswaa   11180
Thare wolde he noghte late hir dwelle
For drede of þe Iewes felle
For drede of sclandere & of fame
To Bedleme he ledde hir hame
In that menetyme þat þay dide thus   11185
Was Emperoure Sir Augustus
A man men hadde off full mekill dowte
For he was dowtted alle þe werlde abowte
Till alle þis werlde he made statut
Þat alle solde be his vndirlout   11190
And þat alle men solde be boune
To come vnto þaire kyndly townne
To make hym homage with some thynge
Till sir augustus þat was þaire kynge
A mane tuke þis note one hande   11195
Þe wittyeste of alle that lande
Alle thaire names gane he wrytte
And ay als þay gaffe he made þam quyte
Ioseph come in þat menetyme thare
To Bedleme als I sayd are   11200
Right vntill his awenn house
Broghte he marie his dere spouse
Þan was that mayden mylde
Almaste at þe tyme of childe
And are aftir lange reghte þare   11205
Þat blyssede barne Ihesu scho bare
Mayden & modir wemlesse
Þat woman full of alle mekenes
Þat goddis myghte knawes witterly
Hym thare thynke þeroffe no ferly   11210
Mary bare þat barne in chastitee
Godd wolde it solde so bee   fol. 6v col. 2
He þat moghte Ioseph wande gare
In a nyghte fruyte & lefe bere
Withowtten werke of erthe aboute   11215
And in a nyghte so garre it sprowte
And floreste faire als I hafe sayde
Þan moghte þat þis puruayede

Be borne of a mayden ethe
Within þe terme of nyne monethe 11220
He þat alle hase made of noghte
And to þe dombe his speche broghte
And the see cleue in twaa
His enymys for to slaa
Wele moghte he withowtten steme 11225
Garre a mayden bere withowtten wemme
Þe lyknes of þis barneteme
Righte als þou sees þe sonnes beme
Gaaes thurgh þe glasse & commes agayne
Withowten breke clene and playne 11230
Qwayntylyere ȝit come criste & ȝede
Sauande his modir maydenhede
And thus scho bare hir barneteme
Þat blyssede birde in Bedleme
Swilke clothes als scho had in hande 11235
Scho wappede abowte hym & wande
In symple cloutes scho hym layde
Was thare no riche wedes graythede
Was thare no pride of couerlite
Chambrere curtyns ne no tapite 11240
Þe hirdis þat were wounte to bee
Sittande one þe feldes ȝemande þaire fee
Thare come aungells fra heuen
Syngande with full mylde steuen
We brynge ȝow worde of ioye & blysse 11245
This nyghte oure lorde borne es
And this to taken we ȝow saye
Ȝe gaa to morne when it es daye
To Bedleme and fynd ȝe schalle
Ihesu borne the lorde of alle 11250 fol. 7r col. 1
Þat is kyng of alle kynges
Es borne this nyghte by thire takenynges
In a cribbe he sall be funden
Liggande thare als an asse is bounden 11254
And ane noxe feste hym by
This schall ȝe fynde sekirly
Honowres hym for whi he sall 11255
Be sett in Dauit kyng stalle
Whils þe angels this tythandes tolde
Othir come downne full thik folde
And loued godd with swilke saughe
One heghe be ioye & pese one laughe 11260
When þay hadde sayde þat þay wolde saye
Thire angells went þam þaire waye
Radde were thire hirdes of that lyghte
Þat þay saghe of thase angels bryghte
For þay saghe neuer swilke a syghte 11265
Na visytynge byfore þat nyghte
Þay sayd to Bedleme gaa we

And luke if thir tythandes sothe be
When þay come thare thay marie fande
And with hir Ioseph hir housebande   11270
And þe childe þat swadilled was
Liggande in a cribbe byfore þe asse
And þe oxe als I ȝow talde
Þareof þay meruayllede ȝonge & alde
Alle helde Marie in hir herte full still   11275
And thanked godd of all his will
In August tyme þe Emper*our*
Till he was borne oure Saueoure
When þat this werlde was beste i*n* pese
One a wyntt*er* nyghte w*ith*owtten lese   11280
And þe same ȝere was saynt Iohn
Borne byfore in flesche & bone
Sone aft*er* þat Criste was borne
Circumzisede he was and schorne
Ih*esus* one hym to name þay layde   11285 fol. 7r col. 2
Als þe angelle byfore had sayde

How Ih*esus* was offrede to the temple

S one aftir aboute fourty dayes
Als þe gospel til vs says
Þay bare þe childe fra Bedleme
To the temple of Ierusalem   11290
For to do of hym that daye
The costome of þe alde laye
Þe lawe of moyses thus wilde
A woman þat had a knawe childe
Hir firste birthe solde scho   11295
Offre þe haly temple vntoo
After þat scho hade lyne
Fourty dayes in gysern
For mayden childe efte als lange
To þe temple or scho solde gange   11300
And with hir childe solde offre thare
A lambe and scho so ryche ware
And whaso ne myghte doo swaa
Þay solde gyffe turtill doufes twaa
Or of doufes double bredde   11305
Þis laughe with Ih*esus* Marie dide   11306
Of pouere no disdeyne hase hee   11309
That biddis vs lyffe in pouerte   11310
Off pore thare na mane myslyke   fol. 7v col. 1
In gode thoghte þat es sa ryke
Thare was a gud haly man   11313
Wonnande in the temple thane
Off sex skore ȝere highte symyon   11315
Þat many haly dedis hade done
And hade p*r*ayede godd þat he myghte i*n* hele

See þe comforthe of Israel
Þat mannes rawnsone solde bere
And godd hym hadd sende answere 11320
Þat he ne solde neu*er* dye 11323
Or þat he Criste hade sene w*ith* eghe
Forthi when Marie modire milde 11325
Into the temple broghte hir childe
ʒitte this Symeon hade his taste
Touched with the haly gaste
Off this childes come so fayne
He was þat he went hym agayne 11330
And for gladnes he keste a cry
Þat alle herde that stode hym by
Godd þ*at* is mekill of myghte
Hase sent þe folke þ*at* he þam highte
Þan he ranne to Ih*esu* swete 11335
And felle down byfore his fete
And hono*ur*red hy*m* þat sely man
And in his armes tuke hym þan
And kiste his fete & sayd dryghtyne
In pese leue thou s*eruau*nt thyne 11340
For nowe myn eghne hase sene the hele
Þat is graythed till Israel
Þare was alsua ane alde woman
Anna þat was w*ith* elde forthe gane
Þat hadde lyffed þan foure skore ʒere 11345
In wodowhed & in p*ra*yere
And full lele scho was i*n* hir lede
Neuyre owte of þe temple scho ʒede
Bot thare was scho eu*ere* more bownne
In almousdede and orysoune 11350 fol. 7v col. 2
And when þat scho Ih*esu* gane see
Scho honored hym on hir knee
And sayde forsothe this is hee
Thurgh whayme þe worlde sall saued bee
Off p*ro*phecye this worde es 11355
For anna was a p*ro*phetys
Ilke a daye a p*ro*phecye
Sayd Symeone of oure lady
And of hir dere sone Ih*esu*
Þe whilke þ*at* I sall to ʒowe 11360
This childe he sayde byfore þam alle
Sall be to many dounefalle
And to many vprysynge
Dampny*n*g to some & to some sauynge
Dounefalle ʒe schall vndirstande 11365
To men þat are mysbyleuande
And vprysesynge vnto fele
To men þat are in trouthe lele
Till hir he sayd thyne awenn hert
A swerde of sorowe sall stikke ou*er*thwert 11370

Þe swerde thurgh hir herte stode
When his sone hange one þe rode

How the three kynges made offerande

Fra he was borne þe daye thrittende
Hym offred þe thre kynges hende
Riche gyftes þay hym broghte   11375
Þat ȝere þat he was borne noghte   fol. 8r col. 1
Some says þe secounde ȝere
And some sayse one other manere
Þat twa ȝere aftir þay come
Sayne Iohn þareof gyffes dome   11380
Þat he fande in a boke
Thir kynges thre þaire wayes toke
A twelmoneth are the natyuite
For ells moghte noghte þe kynges three
Haue ouergane sa longe a waye   11385
And come to criste þat ilke daye
He says þat in the boke he fande
Off a prophete of estren lande
Balaam þan was he calde
Off astronomye mekill he talde   11390
And of sterne þat was schene
Was neuer swilke ane are sene
And Iohn with þe gildyn mouthe
Vs telles of a folke vncouthe
Full ferre by esten þay are wonnande   11395
Byȝonde þam wonnes nane lyuande
[Y]manges thase men was broghte a writ
Seth was þe name þay layde one itt
Þis writt of þe sterne it spakke
And of þe offerandes þe kynges sold make   11400
Þe writt was kepide fra kyn to kyn
Þat beste couthe þerone myn
And at þe laste [y]mange þamselfe
Þay hafe þam ordeyned twelue
Þat ilke daye ȝode till a hill derne   11405
For to wayte aftir this sterne
When any dyede of þat dussayne
His sone was sett hym agayne
Or his nexte frende þat was hym dere
Swa þat euer ilke a ȝere   11410
When þaire cornes were in done   fol. 8r col. 2
To þe mountayne went þay sone
Thare þay offerde & prayed & swanke
& thre dayes noþer ete ne dranke
Þis custome full lange þay dide   11415
And at þe laste þe sterne it kydde
Þat ilke sterne þam come to warne
One þat mounte in forme of barne

And bare one it taken of þe croyce
And to þam spake in mannes voyce   11420
Þat þay solde wende to Iewes lande
And twa ȝere þay ware walkande
Full graythly þe sterne þam ledde
And selcouthely þan were þay fedde
Þaire scrippes whethir þay rade or ȝode   11425
Ware neuermare withowtten fode
Thir kynges whareso þay rade
Þe sterne euer byfore þam glade
Thay sayde gaa we to the kynge
Þat hafes in erthe nane euynynge   11430
Þis kynge we sall bere offrande newe
And honour hym with trebut & trewe
Alle þe kynges of this werlde
For hym sall be quakande & ferde
And ay þay folowed þis sternes beme   11435
Till þay come to Ierusalem
Bot fra þay come thare als swythe
Þe sterne to þam no mare wold kythe   11438
When þay come in heraude lande
Na sterne þay saghe schynande
Þe kynges were þan in mekill thoghte   11441
& wende þay had funden þat þay soghte
Þay toke þaire giftes in þat tounne
And went sekande vp & doune
Bot þe burges of þat cite   11445
Thoghte wondir what þay myghte bee
And askede what þay soghte & thaye   fol. 8v col. 1
Saide a barne that alle maye
He sall be kyng of kynges alle
Till handes and fete we sall hym falle   11450
Sewe þe sterne þat ledde vs hedire
Þan þay gadirde þam togedir
And spake hereof with grete wounderyng
And worde come till herode kyng
Þat swilke thre kynges ware ther commen   11455
And in þe toune þaire herbere nommen
When he this tyraunte vndirstode
Hym thoghte it noþer faire ne gude
For he wend þan withowtten swyke
For to tyne his kyngrike   11460
And in haste garte samen calle
Þe mayster of his lande alle
And spirrede at thaym if þay wiste
Whare he was borne þat ilke Criste
Þat þe kyng of Iewes solde be   11465
And þay sayde in Bedleme Iudee
For a prophete sayde swaa
A thow lande of Iuda
A littill towune if þat þou bee

Þow arte noghte lefte in dygnytee   11470
In the than sall he brede
Þe folke of Israel þat sall lede
Kyng heraude called þam in derne
And spirrede at thaym of this sterne
Gase he sayd and spirres garne   11475
Till ȝe hafe funden that barne
When he is funden commes till mee
I will hym with honoure see
Sir þay sayde that sall be ȝare
And ordayned thaym forthe to fare   11480
When þay were fra heroude gane
Þe sterne þam ledde sone onane
It semys hereby als thynkes mee
Nane saghe it bot thire kynges three
Bitwix þe lyfte & þe erthe it glade   11485
And sa faire was neuer made
Reghte fra þe burgh of Ierusalem
It ledde þam into Ierusalem   fol. 8v col. 2
Euen oure þat house stode þe sterne
Þat Criste & his modir in warne   11490
Þay kneled downn & with thaire handes
Gaffe vnto Criste dyuerse offrandes
Þe firste of thayme þat Iaspare highte
Offerde golde with resone righte
And that was in takynnynge   11495
Off kynges alle þat he was kynge
Melchiore hym come thare nexte
He kidd he was bathe godde & priste
With rekills byfore hym he felle
Þat giffes in þe kirke swaa swete a smelle   11500
And that do the gomme þat commes of fire
Attropa hym offerde mirre
Ane smerelle of selcouthe bitternesse
Þat dede men corps with ennoyntted es
For rotynge es na bettir rede   11505
In sygne that he man solde be dede
Thir thre thynges als says þe boke
At anes Criste in his armes toke
Full swetely and with mylde chere
Byhelde he thase giftes sere   11510

How the angel warnned þe thre kynges
to ga noghte by heraude

Ioseph and marie his spouse   11511
Full faire þay called thir kynges til house
Thayre sopere garte þay sone dighte
And with þe childe þay laye all þat nyghte   fol. 9r col. 1
Withowtten pride forsothe to telle   11515
Hadde þay no bedde spredde with pelle
Bot þay toke swilke als þay fande

And loued godde alle his sande
And hadd þay hade so wele spedde
Now are þay slepande broghte in bedde   11520
Thre wery kynges of thaire waye
The ferthe a kynge mare than thaye
Thay wiste þay wele & kydde in dede
Þat he solde aquyte þam þaire mede
Þaire ware in will þat ilke nyghte   11525
To wende b[y] heraude als þay highte
Bot whils þay slepande laye in bedde
Ane angelle come & thaym forbedde
To wende by hym by any waye
For he es false & hase bene aye   11530
Anothir waye þan gane þay fare
One þe morne when þay resyn ware
Thay take þaire lefe at þat childe
And at Mary his modir mylde
And thankkede Ioseph full curtasely   11535
His esement & his herbery
Þe kynges are went anothir waye
When þat heraude herde þat saye
Þan wonder wrathe þan was þat kynge
And thoghte hym dreuyn full to hethynge   11540
He sett men waytande by þe strette
If þat þay myghte those kynges mete
He commande þay solde be tane
And withowtten mercy slayne
Bot heraud men mett noghte þam with   11545
Full harmeles come þay to þaire kythe
When heraude herde that he mourdnede sare
Þat þase kynges swa passede ware
And for his ill will myghte noghte ryse
Venge hym wolde he one oþer wyse   11550
Þan he made a vowe in hye
Þat made a vowe in hye
Þat many sakles þerfore solde dye   11552
For he moghte do þase kynges no schame
Thase it boghte þat neuer seruede blame   fol. 9r col. 2
Wha herde euer of any slyke   11555
Ordynance swa full of swyke
Þat for þe lufe of a barne
Swa many solde þe lyfe tharne
He commande his knyghtis kene
To slaa þe childire alle by dene   11560
Withþin þe townne of Bedleem
And owtwith many a barnetem
Þan gart þat tyraunt losse þe lyffe
And full wafull made many a wyfe
Within þe launde he ne lefte nane   11565
Off twa 3ere þat ne þay were slayne
Off twa 3ere or lesse I tell 3owe
For swa he wende to slaa Ihesu

Bot alle for noghte þat he dide swaa
For Ihesu myghte he noghte slaa   11570
Vs alle þat garres þe lyfe hafe
Hymseluen fra dede may he wele saffe
Are hymseluen wolde þat kynge
Right nane hym moghte to dede brynge
Þere es no noþer for to saye   11575
Als þat he ordeyned it was sa aye

How Ioseph fledd intill Egipt with Marie and Ihesu

Itt es rewthe for to rede
Off thir childir þat thus ware dede
An hundreth & fourty & foure thowsande
Thurgh Ihesu come to lyfe lastande   11580 fol. 9v col. 1
Bot seuen dayes byfore fynde I
Are heraude gart þose barnes dy
Als Ioseph in a slepyng laye
Ane angell till hym gane saye
Ryse vp Ioseph and hethyn gaa   11585
With marie & hir sonne alswaa
For ȝow byhoues alle three
Vnto þe lande of Egipt flee
Ryse vp þerfore are it be daye
And gaa forthe by þe foreste waye   11590
For kyng heraude sekes too & fraa
Mary hir sone and the to slaa
And in Egipt duelle still with þe barne
Vnto þe tyme þat I ȝow warne
Sone was Ioseph redy bounne   11595
By nyghttertale went owt of tounne
With marie and þaire menȝe
A mayden and knaues three
Þat with þam was in seruyce
Þat ware warre & wondir wyse   11600
One a mule rade mary mylde
And in hir arme bare scho hir childe
Till þay come till a caue depe
Thare they þam ordeynede to riste & slepe
Þare þay þam ordeynned to riste & slepe
And thare garte þay mary lyghte   11605
Bot sone scho saughe a selly syghte
Als þay lokede þam besyde
Out of þat kaue þan saughe þay glide
Many dragouns right sodaynely
Þe knaues þan bygane to crye   11610
Bot when Ihesus saughe þam radd be
He satt vpp appon his modir knee
And spakke vnto those bestis grym
Þan mare & lesse þay honored hym

Comen es þe prophecye þan clere   11615
Þat is sayde in the psaltere
Dragouns wonnande in þaire koue
Þaire lorde þay sall honoure & loue
Ihesu went byfore þam thanne
And badde thaym harme vnto no mane   11620 fol. 9v col. 2
Mary and Ioseph na forthy
For the childe were full sary
And Ihesu to þam saide onane
Drede for me ne hafe ȝe nane
For me ne hafe ȝe care ne syte   11625
For I man [y]noghe perfite
And alle þe bestes þat beris name
I may make thayme wilde or tame
Lyouns mekely ȝode þam [y]myde
And alswaa þe dragouns dide   11630
Byfore mary faire þay ȝede
In righte waye hir for to lede
When mary saughe of bestis þat route
Firste scho was in grete dowte
Bot hir sone hir bade be blythe   11635
And nakyns ferdenes for to kythe
Modir he sayde hafe ȝe na warde
Nowthir of dragoune ne of lybarde
For þay come vs no harme to doo
Bot þay come vs to serue vntoo   11640
Bathe oxe & asse þerwith þam ware
And oþer bestes þat þaire harnays bare
Oute of Ierusalem þaire kythe
Thies bestes mekely went þam with
Lyouns noghte harmed oxe ne asse   11645
Ne oþer bestis þat there wasse
Than was fulffillede þe prophecye
Þat was sayde of Ieremye
Wolfe and wethir lyone and oxe
Sall come samen and lambe & foxe   11650
In a wayne þaire gere was inn   11653
Þat drawen was with oxen twynn   11654

How the Tree Bowede downn at þe biddyng
of Ihesu

Mary forthirmare scho rade   11657
In wildernes grete hete it made
Faynte scho wexe and wery   fol. 10r col. 1
A palme tree scho sawe hir by   11660
Ioseph scho sayde fayne wolde I reste
And vndir this tree thynke me beste
Gladly he sayde that is resoune
And he belyne toke hir downne
When scho hadd sytten thare a thrawe   11665

Þis palme tree sone scho sawe
Fruyte scho saughe þerone hyngande
Þat dates are callede in this lande
Ioseph scho sayd fayne wolde I ete
Off ȝone fruyte and I myghte it gete   11670
Me thynke he sayde wondir of the
Now byhalde þe heghte of ȝone tree
May na man wynn þe fruyte vntill
And it to clymbe es wondir ille
Bot I mornne for anothir thynge   11675
Þat we of watir hafe wanttynge
Oure watir purueance es nowe gane
And in this wildirnes es righte nane
Noþer for vs ne for oure fee   11679
Ihesu satte appone his modir knee   11681
Full swettly than sayd hee
Boughe down till vs þou tree
And of thi fruyte gyffe vs plentee
And vnnethes was this worde sayde   11685
To bowe down þe tre hym graythed
Righte vnto Marye fotte
Þe croppe euen vnto þe rote
And when þay had etyn fruyte [y]noghe
Ȝitt it bewede ilke a boughe   11690
Vnto he commande it to ryse
It bowed down to þaire seruyce
Vnto þat tree þan sayd Ihesu
Ryse vpe & righte the nowe
I will þat þou fra now forewarde   11695
Plantted be in myn orcherde
Imanges my trees in paradyse
Þat þou & þay be of a pryce
Vnder thi rote þare es a sprynge   fol. 10r col. 2
And thereoffe I will þe watir owt wrynge   11700
Make vs a welle for my sake
Þat alle theroffe may watir take
In this tree stirte vpe faste
Owte of the rote a welle vp braste
With strandis swete clere and calde   11705
Thay dranke [y]noghe alle þat walde
And alle that was in that place
Thay thankede godd so full of grace
And one þe morne when it was daye
Þay ordeyned þam to wende þair waye   11710
Ihesu hym turnede to the tree
And sayde palme I comande the
Þat of thi brawnches ane be schorne
And with myn angell awaye borne
Vnto þe place of paradise   11715
Þare my fadirs mirthe es
And vnnethes was this worde spoken
Þare come an angelle & hase broken

A boughe & bare it thethyn sone
Full tyte his commandement was done 11720
Þe boughe away with hym he bere
In swyme þan felle alle þat there were
For þe angell þay ware so made
And Ihesu sayde whi are ȝe radde
Whi es swaa ne wate ȝe noghte 11725
Þat with my handis this tre I wroghte
And I will that this ilke tree
In paradyse now standande bee
Vnto my sayntes in stede of fode
Als it till vs in the waye stode 11730

How the mawmettis Felle when Ihesu come intill Egipt

S[y]then forthe þay wente þaire waye
And Ioseph gane to Ihesu saye
A lorde this es a mekill hete
It greues vs huggely it es so grete fol. 10v col. 1
And if þou rede that it swaa bee 11735
Late vs wende awaye by þe see
For there are townnes we may in reste
And so to wende me thynke es beste
Drede the noghte Ioseph I the praye
I sall abrigge ȝow the waye 11740
That þat is thritty dayes iournee lange
In a daye ȝe schall it gange
And als þay went samen talkand swa
Þay one ferrome loked thaym fraa
And sone bygane þay for to see 11745
Þe walles of Egipt þat faire cite
Þan were þay full wondir blythe
And vnto þat cite come þay full swythe
Bot there than hafed þay na knaweynge
Þat þay myghte aske at any gestenynge 11750
And sone after þat þay come to townn
Þe pristes of þe lawe made þam bownn
To doo þe folkes þaire seryuse
And to þaire mawmettes to make sacrafyce
Marye to þe temple gane faree 11755
And with hir thedire hir sone scho bare
And within þe kirke whils þat scho was
Men myghte see a selcouthe case
Alle þaire mawmettes within a stounde
Wyd opynne felle vnto þe grounde 11760
And doune at þe erthe ware þay layde 11763
For þan come þe prophecye þat was sayde
Þat says þat a lorde salle 11765
Comme till Egipt and sall gare falle
Þaire goddes & garre þam dwyne to noghte
Þat þay with þaire handes hafe wroghte

And in þat townne was a lordynge
And when he herde this tythynge 11770
He gadrede men bothe grete & smalle
And to þe temple broghte þam alle
And for to venge þam made þam bownn
Off hym þat keste þayre goddes doun
In hert he was full sary 11775
When he saughe swaa his mawmetes ly
He come to Marie withowtten harme fol. 10v col. 2
Thare scho hir childe bare in hir arme
And one knes doune he felle
And to þe folke he gane thus telle 11780
Ne hadde this barne bene godde of myghte
Oure goddes hadde bene standande vprighte
For he es godd & lorde of alle
Oure goddes agaynes hym dose falle
Oure goddes ne may noghte till hym doo 11785
Vengeance I hope mon come vs to
Off wrake full sare we may vs drede
Als it es tolde in olde dede
How it byfelle of Pharahonn
He & his folkes ware fordonne 11790
For þat þay ne wolde noghte trowe
In his myghte & in his v[ir]towe
Alle þay drownnede in the see
I trowe one hym and swa do ȝee
Off alle þe temples in thate townn 11795
Alle þe mawmettry felle adownne
In Egipt leue we Ihesu now stille
And of kynge heraude speke I will
Þis heraude had regned thritty ȝere
When þat mary Ihesu did bere 11800
Sythen he regnede ȝeris seuen
His wranges god on hym sall euynn
Þat false þat felle þat goddes faa
Þat soghte oure lorde for to slaa
How hade he will to spill þaire blodde 11805
Þat neuer to hym ne dide bot gude
Þat wyly wolfe þat foxe so false
Agaynes frendis & fremmed als
Off carefull costes to vnknawen
And manquellere vnto his awenn 11810
Þat gredy gerarde als a grippe
His vnrighte bygane to ryppe
And for his seruys of many a daye
Þe tyme nere to take his paye
Þat misdoere so vnmeke 11815
Now bygynnes he to be seke fol. 11r col. 1
Þe parlesy es in his syde
Þat garres hym poke in all his pryde
One his hede he hade þe skalle

Þe scabbe ouere his body alle   11820
In his syde he hafes þe stake
His men sawe hym sorowe make
With þe clawe hym toke þe scorfe
Alle his body was lyke a torfe
Þe gowte potagre es ill to bete   11825
Downne it felle into his fete
Ouer alle was he meselle playne
And hade þerwith þe feuere quartayne
Þe dropsye in hym swa was feste
Þat he was ay in poynte to breste   11830
Þe fallande gowte he hade [y]melle
His tethe owte of his hede þay felle
Ouere alle his body he felide sare
Mighte na mare suffre in erthe mare
His wambe was full of venym   11835
Withowtten nombere wormes were in hym
This caytefe combred full of care
Sekes hym leches here and thare
And þay come to hym ferre and nere
Connande men of that mistere   11840
Bot for þay myghte noghte slake his waa
Ilkane euer he gart þam slaa
Hys barnes his wyfe fledde hym fraa
And alle his menȝe þay dide alswa
Fremmed and sybbe fra hym þay fledde   11845
Mighte nane for stynke neghe his bedde
And thus fra hym þay went awaye
Iskande ilkane sare his endynge day
And when his awenn sone archilaus
Saughe his fadir fare thus   11850
To þe baronage he sent
To make a preue perlement
Gode men he sayd what holde ȝe beste   fol. 11r col. 2
Off my fadir þat neuer hafes reste   11854
He es swa stadde in sorowe & waa   11857
Was neuer no man in this worlde swa
Swilke venym fra hym rynnes owte
Dare nane come hym nere aboute   11860
Leche hym hele ne can nane
Forthi he garres sla þam ilkane
And he es in swa carefull state   11864
Þat what he dose he ne wate   11863
He ne bese neuer hale saunse fayle   11855
Says me now ȝoure consayle   11856
Sen he ne schall neuer couer his waa   11865
I rede and ȝee doo swaa
Þat we gete vs leches twynn
Þat we may sauely trayste inn
To make a newe bathe and proue
Off pyke and oyle to his byhoue   11870

And when it es wele broghte one hete
Caste hym þerin & garre hym swete
Þay sayde this was a noble rede
Almous it ware þat he were dede
And twa leches forthe þan gart þay brynge   11875
And sone þay spak vnto þe kynge
He lyftyde vp his lothely chynn
And one þam gane he loke full grymme
Fy herlottes he sayd whatt are ȝee
Thay said sir leches to hele the   11880
Medcyne sall þou of vs take
A noble bathe we sall the make
Þou sall are þou þerof come owtte
Be als hale als any troute
Þay filde a lede of pyke & oyle   11885
And wonder faste þay garte it boyle
When it was to þayre will dighte
Vp þay toke þat wafull wighte
Say traytours he saide I sale
Confounde ȝowe bot ȝe me hale   11890
Nay sir godd wate said þay bathe   fol. 11v col. 1
Þou ne sall neuer do man more skathe
We sall or we fra the fare
Ordeyne þat þou ne sall fele na sare
Þan in that bathe þay lete hym doune   11895
And scaldid hym als a capoun
Þay hym helde þat þay hym hete
In þay helde hym by þe fete
And drownkend hym in pike & terre
And sent hym þare he faris werre   11900
Werre þan he ferrede euer are
For þare es mournynge foreuermare
For he soiournes with sathanas
And with þat traytour Iudas
When he was dede þat gerade grym   11905
Archilaus come aftir hym   11906
In his tyme was done many selcouthe   11907
And some of þam telle I couthe   11908
When heraude thus was forfaren   11911
An angel come Ioseph to warne
And sayd tyme es to wende nowe
Hethen with marie & Ihesew
Vnto ȝour kythe one goddes name   11915
I bidde ȝow þat ȝe wende hame
For he þat soghte þe childe to quelle
Dede he es þe sothe to telle
Ioseph was of þis tythande fayne
And ordeyned hym to wende agayne   11920
Bot vnto þat ilke lande
Thare archelaus was regnande
Bot tyll a lande þat highte Iudee
Inn for to come righte radde was he

Bot went hy*m* vnto galilee   11925
Thurghe burghe townnes & many citee

Off þe Barnehede of Ih*es*u Crist

Þat Ih*es*u dide in his barnehede
With gud will now will I rede
It byfelle appon ane holy daye   fol. 11v col. 2
Þay calle þe Sabot in þat lay   11930
Ih*es*u and other barnes samen
Went by þe watir makand þaire gamen
Ih*es*u satt and in his playe
Lakes seuen he made of claye
Vntill ilkane a furre he made   11935
And rowme to rynne þe watir hade
Þe watir ranne fra & till
Oute of þe flode at his will
Imanges thase barnes þ*er* was ane
Þat full was of the Sathane   11940
And for wanttones of witt
Hy*m* garte ane of þe lakes ditt
Þat þe watir in was broghte
And spilt alle þat Ih*es*u wroghte
Þan spake Ih*es*u þat barne vntoo   11945
Say childe whi dide þ*o*u soo
Þat I hafe done þ*o*u fordose
Þareof sall þ*o*u make na rose
Þare was no langare of to mote
Bot dede he felle at Ih*esu*s fote   11950
His frendis than bygane to kry
Appon Ioseph and Marye
ȝoure sone þ*at* wanttone ladde & wilde
With banny*ng* hase slayne oure childe
When þay hade sayde þaire resou*n*e   11955
Ioseph and marie dred tresone
Off þe frendis of that barne
Ih*es*u fayne þan walde he warne
Þan sayd Ioseph to Marye
Speke þ*o*u till hy*m* preualy   11960
And aske hy*m* why þat he garres
Vs hated be thus w*ith* his afferes
Þe men one vs þay will take wreke
And I ne dare noghte w*ith* hym speke
Marie soghte þan till hym sone   11965
And sayd to hy*m* whatte hase þ*o*u done   fol. 12r col. 1
Why sall this childe dede bee
For worthy to dy es hee
For he walde noghte thole stande
Þe werke I made w*ith* my hande   11970
Scho sayde wirke þ*o*u one this wyse
Thay will alle agaynes vs ryse

Ihesu þan hym vmbythoghte
Þat he his modir wolde greue noghte
Bot þe dede corps thare it laye   11975
Touchede with his fote & gan saye
Ryse vp þou full of felony
For þou was neuer worthy
Part of my fadir blysse to gete
For þou thus my werke hase lett   11980
Þis corps rase vp when sayd swa
And frekly fledd he Ihesu fra
Ihesus in þe same stede
Þare þe watir in þe lakes ȝede
He made alle of layre itselfe   11985
With his handes sparous twelfe
One þaire Saboth this dide he thare
And many barnes þer with hym ware
When þe Iewes this myghte here
Þay spake to Ioseph one this manere   11990
Seese þou noghte Ioseph by thi fay
Howe Ihesu brekes oure haly day
Apon oure Saboth þe sothe to say
Sparouse twelffe he made of clay
Ioseph þan to Ihesu spakke   11995
& said ilke man on þe playnte þay make
For thi wirkynge one oure Saboth
And Ihesus samen his handes smate
And he said in þaire allere sighte
Now rysses vp & takes ȝour flighte   12000
Fleghes forthe & lyffes in þe werlde
With þat worde þay toke a flyght & thethyn ferde   fol. 12r col. 2
When þay this saughe þat by hym stode
Some said euyll & some said gude
Some hym lakked & some gan hym prayse   12005
Bot demyde was he many wayes
Some þat this selcouthe sawe
Sayde he dide agayne þe lawe
Many spake of Ioseph sonne
Whatkyns maystres he hade done   12010
Byfore þe folkes of Israel
Þat ware ful selcouthe for to telle
And at þe laste come this tythande
To þe twelue kynrednes of þat lande

A prestes sone þer was standande   12015
Þat with a wande he bare in hande
For grete enmyte & tene
He brake þase lakes all bydene
He brake thase demmynges þat ware made
Þat Ihesu dide fordon he hade   12020
Þan Ihesu sayd till hym in hy
Þou fole so full of felony

Werke of drede sone of Sathan
Off thi fruyte sall sede be nane
For thi rotes are alle dry 12025
Sall neu*er* thi sede multiply
With this he droghe awaye onane
And felle doun dede any stane

Ioseph Ih*esu* bygan to lede
Marie and þay sone hame 3ede 12030
Þare come a childe a cursed wighte
Anensthe Ih*esu* he come righte
And faste brounted þis cursed Iewe
Fayne he wolde hafe felled Ih*esu*
Þan said Ih*esu* to þat feloune 12035
Þ*ou* ne sall not come i*n* querte to toune
And vnnethes remoued he þat stede fol. 12v, col. 1
Bot felle downn thare starke dede
Othere barnes that þare ware
Saw this & mornede sare 12040
And saide whatt es he this
Alle is done þat his will es
What so he biddes it es done
Withowten taryinge also sone
To Ioseph with this playnte 3ode þay 12045
And thus gates gane þay till hy*m* say
Do away Ih*esu* thi sone
For hym in na towne dare we wonne
Othere þ*ou* moste teche hym thanne
Blyssyng to hannte & noghte to banne 12050
Þan saide Ioseph w*ith* mo*ur*nande chere
Sone why dose thou one this manere
Alle þat in þe gates gase
For thi dedis mo*ur*ny*ng* mase
Þay hatte vs alle & thretis to sla 12055
Leue sone whi dose þ*ou* swaa
Ih*esu* to Ioseph gaffe ansuere
It es na wyfe sone nowrewhere
Bot he be þat his fadir hafes lerede
Aftir þe wisdome of the werlde 12060
Off fadir his bannyng deris noghte
Bot to that sone þat mys hase wroghte
Thir maisters thoghte grete tene
And agaynes Ih*esu* þay rase bydene
And playnte one hym made co*m*monly 12065
Bathe to Ioseph & to Marie
Þan Ioseph bygane to doute
Treso*u*ne of þe Iewes sa stoute
Þan blamed hym Ioseph & Marie
And Ih*esu* went to that body 12070
Þat lay dede þam imange
And by þe hare þ*at* one hym hange

Þat alle myghte hym speke hym to
Als fadir solde to sone doo
And þe spirit þat was fledde 12075
Come agayne into that stede
And he þat was dede was hale & sere fol. 12v col. 2
And alle wondrede þat þere were

How they ledd Ihesu to the Scole at lere

Pare was a preste was somedele kene
Þat at Ihesu was wonder tene 12080
And for he spake swa skilfully
Vnto hym he had envie
Envie hym bolnede at þe hert
And vnto Ioseph he spake ouerthwert
Wordes of full grete dispite 12085
And thus he spake vntil hym tyte
If þou luffed wele thi sonne
Till other maners þou solde hym wonne
He bygynnes to be a fole
Garre hym somewhare ga to þe scole 12090
Some conandenes þat he myghte knawe
For of na man hym standes awe
Bot it semys wele therby
Þat bathe thou and Marie
Ne lered hym neuer landis lawe 12095
Off vs maisters he ne hase nane awe
Ware ʒe connande ʒe scholde hym kenne
To honoure prestis and aldere men
Till other childir swilke als hee
Haffe parfit luffe and charyte 12100
And mekely with þam to duelle
And þaire lawe leren ay [y]melle
Ioseph said one whate manere
May any man þis barne lere
Now leren hym righte als þou will 12105 fol. 13r col. 1
I giffe the righte gude leue þertill
And sett hym hardily to þe lare
Þan Ihesu to þat preste spake thare
Thou semys a maister of the lawe
Swa herde I righte now be þi sawe 12110
Þou and other are holden too
To do þe thynge I will noghte do
I am bownden þe sothe to say
Na thynge vnto ʒoure lay
Fra ʒoure lawes I am owt tane 12115
Erthely fadir had I neuer nane
Bot þou till þe lawe es bounden
And I was or þe lawe was funden
And if þat þou a mayster bee
And wenes þat nane kane kenne the 12120
I kan teche the þat þou ne kan

Thyng I ne lered neuer at man
For þou wiste noghte when þou was borne
What awntirs were layde the byforne
Þou kan on thynke þat is paste   12125
Bot how lange sall thi lyfe laste
How lange sall þou lyffe in þe worlde
And alle had wonder þat this herde

Than bygane þay alle to crye
Wha herde euer swilke ferly   12130
Oþer ȝong man or alde þat couthe
Putt forthe a mare selcouthe
And than they spake vnto Ihesu
A wondirfull thynge art þou
Off thyn elde we are in were   12135
Þou arte noghte ȝitt ouer fyve ȝere
And we ne herde of neuer nane so ȝynge
Schewe to man swilke talkynge
Ilkane sayde als mote þay thryue
Þay saughe neuer swylke ane one lyue   12140

Þan Ihesu gaffe þam ansuere   fol. 13r col. 2
Till alle þe Iewes þat þare were
Alle he sayde ȝow thynke selcouthe
Swilke wordis to here of barne mouthe
And wharefore ne will ȝe noghte trow   12145
Sother thynge þat I tolde ȝow   12146
Þat I knewe wele bothe when & whare
Þe wombe þat ȝow in ȝour modir bare
And ȝa forsothe ȝit sayd I mare   12150
When þat I spakke to ȝowe langare
Off ane þat ȝe Abraham calle   12151
Þat solde be ȝoure faderis alle
I hym saughe and with hym spakke als
And ȝitt ȝe wene þat I ame false
When Ihesu thus hade sayde his will   12155
Als a stane stode stode þay still
Nane þat þer was alde ne ȝonge
Durste noghte speke ne styrre þaire tounge
Vnto þam þan spake Ihesu
I hafe bene als a barne with ȝowe   12160
And als a barne I with ȝow spakke
& knaweynge to me will ȝe nane take
[Y]manges wyse I spakke wisdome with
And ȝe with me ne wolde noghte kyth
Noghte ȝe vndirstode forthy   12165
And ȝe are wonder lesse þan I
Ȝee are of full lyttill faye
A maister than bygane to saye
We haue a maister þat highte leuy   12170
Sayd he to Ioseph & to Marie   12169

Till hym sall ȝe sende ȝoure barne
He kan ken hym we ȝow warne
Þan ȝode Mary & Ioseph
With Ihesu þaire sone for to speke
To þe scole hym gaue þay till   12175
He ansuerde nowþer with gude ne ille   12178
With þam he wente forthe full still   12177
And sir leuy þay broghte hym till   fol. 13v col. 1
Mayster leuy that mayster man
Kende Ihesu a letter than   12180
And badde hym answere þarto
And Ihesu smartly swa gane do
Leuy was wrathe a wande vp hent
And gaffe Ihesu a grete dynt
Þan saide Ihesu to sir leuy   12185
Why betys þou me so velansly
Maister leuy I warne the nowe
Þou smyttes hym kane mare þan þou
For þou teches oþere men
Thyn awenn worde I kane þe ken   12190
Bot at þam forsothe me tenys
Þat spekes & wate neuer what it menes
Als a chyme or a belle
Þat kan noghte vndirstande ne telle
What it by menys þaire awenn sownn   12195
Þam wanttes wit and resoune
Ihesu þan thus bygan to speke
And his resone for to eke
Þe lettirs fra alpha to thau
Off dyuerse schappe men may þam knawe   12200
Wha so alpha say þou me
& I sall than vndo to þe
He þat alpha ne kane noghte see
Full lewede of thau þan is he
Ippocrites I calle ȝow swa   12205
Telles me what es alpha
And I sall telle ȝow [y]wisse
Whatt thyng þat than es
Ihesu gaffe hym thare his taske
Off alle þe lettirs for to aske   12210
He þam vndide ilkane by name
Þan thoght Sir leuy full mekill schame
He was concludide in alle manere
Thurghe þe schappe of many lettirs sere
And bygane a kry to gyffe   12215
Þis barne [y]manges vs may noghte lyffe
Abown erthe he lyffes ouer lange
Worthi it ware hym to hange
For it na fire hym brenne
And wrathely he spake to Ihesu þan   12220 fol. 13v col. 2
I trowe þat þis ilke fode

Was borne byfore Noye flode
Whare es þe wambe he in was bredde
Whare are þe pappes þat hy*m* fedde
Faste now will I fle hym fra 12225
Off his wordes ne will I thole na maa
My hert es clomsed hy*m* to here
May na man his wordes lere
I wende langare als hafe I hele
Þat na man couthe w*ith* me mele 12230
Bot nowe a barne als ȝe may see
In clergy hafes concluded mee
I wende hafe wonnen þe maystry
Bot he kan mare þan kan I
Allas he sayde what may I say 12235
My manhed es tynt for ay
A barne a wighte þ*at* es vnwelde
Me hafes ouercomen in mannes elde
He me apposses of swilke a thynge
Þat I ne knawe of na bygynnynge 12240
In witt clere es he sa balde
One hym ne dare I noghte byhalde
My thynke þ*er*fore by resoune
With man ne may he noghte comoune
Nothyng kan I hy*m* discryve 12245
Was neu*er* nane swilke one lyve
Some tregeto*ur* I hope he be
Or ells godd hy*m*seluen es he
Or ells some angell w*ith* hy*m* delys
And led is þe wordes þat he melys 12250
A whythyn come he now whatt es he
Þ*at* thusgates hase ouercomen me
When Ih*esu* had hy*m* herde a while
He bygan for to smyle
A co*m*mandeme*n*t I make now here 12255
I will alle þat ȝe it here
Þat we foundande frendis fynde
Þat þay hafe sighte þ*at* is blynde
And þat þe pore gete some bote
And gangande þat are lame on fote 12260 fol. 14r col. 1
Þe dede to ryse and othere ilkane
Be sett into thaire state one ane
To be lastande in hym that es
Bote of lyffe lastande swetnes
When Ih*esu* hafed sayd swaa 12265
Alle hafed bote þat ware in wa
And na mare ne saye ne wolde þay
Bot stilly stale þay alle away

Ioseph and mary þan made þa*m* boune
To wende till anoþ*er* tow*n*ne 12270
W*ith* þaire menȝe mylde & methe

Thay went vnto nazareth
Thare was mary wonnande
When Gabryel hir broghte tythande
Ihesu went hym for to play   12275
With barnnes on an halyday
In a loufe was in the toune
A childe keste anoþer doune
Sa sadde he felle vnto þe grounde
Pat dede he was within a stounde   12280
His frendis þeroffe herde worde in hy
And kalde one Ioseph and marye
And lowde one þam gonne þay krye
Whi hafe ȝe latyn oure sone dye
Ȝoure sone oure sone in grete stryffe   12285
Vnconandely gart lose his lyffe
Off Ihesu sayd þay mekill ill
And Ihesu lete þam saye þaire will
Na worde þan wolde he speke
Till marie come and Ioseph   12290
Pan saide marie leue sone me say
If þou sloghe this childe or nay
He ne sayde noþer ille ne gude
Bot downe of þe lofte he ȝode
Till he come there the body lay   12295
And thus till it bygane to say
O ȝee he said how fares thou
And he said lorde wele fare I nowe
If I the putt thou vs saye   fol. 14r col. 2
He ansuerde and sayde naye   12300
The barne frendis þat were thare
Fra þan forth honoured Ihesu euermare

Ioseph went al sone onane   12304
To Ieryco þan es he gane   12303
And marye with hym wend scho wolde   12305
And Ihesu was than sexe ȝere olde
Full mekely he bewede þam vntoo
Alle þaire biddynges for to do
His modir gaffe hym a pott
One a day watir for to fott   12310
With oþer barnes of þe toune
With his watir when he was boune
Oþer barnes that there ware
Brake þe pott that Ihesu bare
Broken it was alle at a dynt   12315
And Ihesus vp þe watir hent
And bare it hame alle in a balle
And present his modir withalle
When Marie saghe this maystry
In hert scho hidd it full preualy   12320

For scho was traiste & doutted noghte
Þat alle thynges do he moghte

Intill a berne als Ihesu ȝode
Ane ere of whete he fande gode spede
And in þe felde he it sewe   12325
And that ilke same day it grewe
So thikke þat wonder was to see
And multiplied full grete plente
& wondere wele it to þam ȝalde
Off þaire mesures an hundrethfalde   12330
Crist toke þis corne þat I of melt
And [y]manges þe pore men it delt

Fra Ieryco to þe flome Iourdane
Hawntede strete þan was þer nane
For a lyonesse that tyde   12336
That laye righte by þe watir syde   12335
Þare laye scho and hir welpes twa
Ne durste there nane for hir gaa   fol. 14v col. 1
Towarde þe flome þe righte way
Ihesu went appon a day   12340
He sawe þe welpes whare þay stode
And to þe lyoune doune he ȝode
Bot fra that þe lyouns hym sawe
Wele þay couthe þaire lorde knawe
Alle þay gane agaynes hym ryse   12345
And honowred hym appon þaire wyse
Ihesu hym sett bisyde þam thane
Þe welpes aboute his fete rane
And with hym played one þaire manere
And fawned hym with ful faire chere   12350
Oþer lyonns þat wer alde
Hym honourred also many falde
And byfor hym went thay
With þaire tailes swepande þe waye
Men stode one ferrome & loked to   12355
Saughe þay thase bestes neuer so do
And ilkane saide vnto other
ȝone es a wondir thyng leue brothir
Þat ȝone bestes one swilke a wyse
Tyll hym profers þaire seruyce   12360
Þus thies lyouns went hym aboute   12362
And als þaire lorde hym gane loute
Þe welpes felle doune till his fete
To playe with hym þam thoght full swete
& many men byhelde one ferre   12365
And durste nane come þam nerre
Þan said Ihesu now may ȝe see
Þat bestes are bettir þan are ȝe

Þaire lorde þay honowre & kenne
Bot ȝe þat solde be witty men   12370
And are made lyke to myn [y]mage
Off me ne hafe ȝe na knawlage
Thies bestes wilde þay knawe me
A man vnnethes me knawes he
Þe flode than gane he passe   12375
With alle þe lyouns þat þare wasse
Þe watir gaffe hym gate full gude   fol. 14v col. 2
One aythir syde þe watir stode
Þe lyouns thane hym comveyed swa
Ham in pes he badde þam gaa   12380
And noy na man ne na man þaim
And thus in pes þay went agayne
Þare he þaim lefte with gude entent
And till his modir es he went
Whils Ihesus wonned with þam thare   12385
Bot aughte ȝere alde he was na mare
Ioseph was a party wrighte
Ploughes and harowres couthe he dighte
Troughes beddis couthe he make
Swilke note couthe he vndertake   12390
Byfelle Ioseph hadde vndirtane
To make a werke vntill a mane
Þe brede þe lengthe he garte hym hafe
And Ioseph þan badde his knafe
Þat he solde hym tymbir felle   12395
And þe mesure he gane hym telle
Þe knafe þat þe tymbir felde
Wele his mesure noghte he helde
Bot ouerschorte he felde a tree
When Ioseph come þam to see   12400
Þis tree ofte he toke in hande
And þarefore was he myslykande
When Ihesu saghe hym murnande be
For þat ilke vngaynande tree
A fadir he sayde murne þou noghte swa   12405
Wee sall þat tree bytwene vs twa
If þat it be neuer so toughe
We sall it make lange [y]noghe
This tree þay drewe þam bytwene
And sone þer was a meruelle sene   12410
Þat was firste þe frawardeste
Tre to þat werke now is it beste
When alle was wele als hym thoghte
Forthe his werke þan Ioseph wroghte

Ȝitt þe folkes that there ware   12415
Sett Ihesu efte vnto lare
And of that Mary thaym bysoughte   fol. 15r col. 1
And Ioseph hym ne lettide noghte

Vnto þe scole þan is he broghte
And thus þe maister with hym wroghte   12420
He bygane hym for to lere
Righte appon a full manere
What is alpha for to saye
Ihesu ansuerde & sayde per faye
Say þou me what es Betha   12425
And thou sall wete what es alpha
This maister vp a wande gane take
And gaffe Ihesu a grete strake
And for he hym strake withowtten resoun
Starke dede þare felle he doun   12430
Þar laye he dede with mekill schame
And to his modir Ihesu went hame
Þan was Ioseph full sary
For Ihesu and swa was Mary
Ofte þay saide vs es wa   12435
We hope thir men oure barne wil sla
Na wonder if þam lyked ille
Ihesus saide to þam bese stille   12438
For to mornne 3ow es no nede   12441
For me ne hafe 3e nankyn drede
For he þat sent me to this place   12444
He will me were fra alle my fas
Þat me sent hedir in his name   12447
Kan me defende fra alkyn schame

Ihesu was in þe thrid siquare
Ordayned for to sett to lare   12450
Þe Iewes wolde algates þat he
Off þaire lare solde leride be
Ioseph and Marye that will nott warne
Vnto þe scole þay ledde þaire barne
With saghyng & with speche mylde   12455
Vnto þe scole þay ledde þis childe
Witty [y]noghe he was of lare
Was neuer man swilke wisdome bare
Ihesus come into the scole
If he were 3onge he was no fole   12460 fol. 15r col. 2
With þe haly gaste was he ledde
A boke in hande þay hym bedde
A boke þat spake of þe Iewes laghe
Many stode & herde and sawe
How he vndide þat he fande thare   12465
And other qwayntese mekill mare
Als þe haly gaste hym gun telle
Off alle wisdome þat es welle
Euer mare full of witt Iwysse
And neuer mare þe lesse it es   12470
Swilke selcouthes thare he talde
Swilke herde neuer man 3onge ne alde

Swilke tales þare gane he telle
Þat þe maister doune felle
And honoured hym & felle hym vnder   12475
& alle þe scole on hym gan wondir
Þan was Ioseph will of rede
& wende þat mayster hade bene dede
Als oþer ware þat I of melt
Þat byfore with Ihesu delt   12480
Þe maister saide to Ioseph thare
Þou hase me broghte na barne to lere
He es worthy to halde þe scole
I by hym ame bot a fole
[Sett hym to lere elleswhare   12485
For of me leres he neuer mare]

Intill a toune þay remowed þan
Þat called was Capharname
Þare wonned Ioseph and mary
For þe Iewes felonye   12490
A man wonned in that wyke
Þat Ioseph highte & was a burgesse ryke
Þat laye in langoure many day
And dede þan in his bedde he lay
When Ihesus herde þe mournyng   12495
Þay made for hym bothe alde & ȝynge
Off þaire care criste hade pyte
And thus to Ioseph þan sayde he
Ioseph wondir hafe I nowe
Þat to this man þat highte als thou   12500 fol. 15v col. 1
Þou schewes grace ne mercy nane
Whi what grace hafe I in wane
Þou sall hafe grace sayde Criste full gude
Gange & one his face thou laye thi hode
And when þat þou hase done swa   12505
Say thusgates or þou thethyn gaa
In Ihesu name I rayse thee
Lyffande agayne þou sall hym see
When Ioseph herde this commandement
Vnto þe dede corps he went   12510
And layde his hode appon his face
And sone he rase thurgh goddes grace
Vnnethes was þe worde sayde   12514
And þe hode appon hym layde   12513
When þe dede corps one the bere   12515
Vp rase bothe hale and fere

Land thare noghte þay habade
Bot to Bedlem flittyng þay made
Thare with Ihesu wonned þay
Ioseph hym calde appon a day   12520
His eldeste sone was calde Iame

And hy*m* he sent to þe gardyn one ane
For to gadir þam herbis & kale
And Ih*esu* forth w*ith* hym stale
Ioseph and Mary vnwetande   12525
Þat Ih*esu* herbis was gadirande
A neddir stirt owte of þe sande
And stangede Iames reght i*n* þe hande
Þis neddir hurt hy*m* selly sare
Þ*at* he rewfully bygane to rare   12530
And hurte he was so bittirly
Þat nere he was i*n* poynte to dy
And down ofte he hy*m* layde
And waylayway many tyme he saide
He graued & cried sarily   12535
Þat vnto Ih*esu* come þe cry
Þat this mangede man made
& Criste ʒode to hy*m* w*ith*owtten bade
Other qwayntis do wolde he nane
Bot toke his hande & blewe þerone   12540
And ou*er*all hale he made his hande   fol. 15v col. 2
And dede þe worme thare þay fande

W̲hen þ*at* Ioseph owrewhare wolde wende
For to ete w*ith* any frende
W*ith* hy*m* to gaa his sonnes ware bownn   12545
Iames: Ioseph: Iude: and Symeoun
Mary with Ih*esu* come alsua   12548
And alsua Ioseph doghtirs twa   12547
Thedir went Marie Cleophe
Þat was ane of þe sistirs thre   12550
For oure lady had sistirs twyn
Als ʒe schall here this boke w*ith*in
When thir men were gadirde samen
In hert had þay nanekyns gamen
To Ih*esu* co*m*men was in place   12555
To comforthe þam w*ith* his grace
Byfore þat he was w*ith* þam sett
Wolde þay nothire drynke ne ete
Ne breke þaire brede ne taste no mese
Till he ware sett at the dese   12560
And gyffen þaire mete þe blyssynge
Ne wolde þay ete nankyn thynge
And if he ware fra þam þ*at* tyde
Till he come þay wolde habyde
And when þay solde ourewhare ga   12565
Mary Ioseph þase barnes alswa
Ouer alle þay dide hym reuerence
And made till hym obedyence
And helde his lyfe bothe day & nyghte
Byfore þam als a candill lighte   12570
Þay hy*m* loued nyghte & day

Whare þat he was by wode or way
Þe vertu of his mekill myghte
Schane als dose þe sone bryghte   12574

Alle þe dedis þat I hafe talde   12577
Criste dide are he was twelue ʒere alde
Bot now of some sall ʒe here
He dide are he was twelue ʒere   12580
Als lucas sayse in his gosepell   fol. 16r col. 1
Þat says of hym nothynge bot lele
In Ier*usale*m þat heghe citee
Þar was ordeynnede a grete semble
A grete feste was þare made   12585
Ioseph & Marie was thedir hade
Þair frendis thedir w*ith* þam soghte
And ʒong Ih*esu* þay with þam broghte
Ay [y]whils þis feste was lastande
In that townne þaire ware duellande   12590
When it was done thethyn þay went
Vnto Ih*esu* noghte þay ne tent
For at þe comynge forthe of the ʒate
He turned agayne & þay forgate
Vnto þe Iewes scole he ʒode   12595
And loked one bokes of þaire lede
Dispyutande w*ith* thaym he satte
And þay hy*m* askede many whatte
And alle þat in þat scole ware stadde
W*ith* clene clergie he made þam madde   12600
This ilke childe þat was so ʒonge
For to answere nane hadde na tou*n*ge
Thus with thase mayst*er*s satt Ih*esu* thare
And Marye hy*m* soghte here and thare
Off hym full grete thoghte hade scho   12605
Full grete mournynge was co*m*men hir to
Als mased men and vnfayne
Ioseph and Marie to*ur*nede agayne
Hym to seke and moo þam with
Alle abowte in that kythe   12610
Swa lange aboute hade scho gane
Grete werynes hase scho tane
Scho hym soghte eu*er* ay whare
For hy*m* hir hert was selly sare
Into þe scole scho come gangande   12615
And a grete gaderyng scho þ*er* fande
Off maist*er*s of þe Iewes lawe
Sittand w*ith* þam hir son scho sawe
Þe beste mayst*er* of that townn
Ih*esu* with clergie hade broghte dou*n*ne   12620
Thane saide his modir till hym thus   fol. 16r col. 2
Sone þ*ou* hafes gloppynde vs
Thi fadir and I many wayes

Hafes the soghte thir three dayes
With heuy hert & mournande chere   12625
Leue sone what dose þou here
Modir he sayde whi soughte ȝe me
And whi sall ȝe for me mournande bee
Wele wate ȝe nedelynges I moste do
Thynges þat falles my fader too   12630
Bot þay ne knewe the entent   12632
And with þam Ihesu went þan hame   12634
Off hym full wyde þan sprange þe fame   12633
Thethyn þay hy ledde for doute   12635
Off þe Iewes so kene & stowtte
Þan are þay wente to Nazarethe   12638
Thedir þam to wynn was ethe   12637
Alle that his modir wolde hym bydde
Full louely & lawly he it didd   12640
In hert his modir helde it ay
Þat scho sawe hym do & saye
Neuer ȝitt ne didde he ill
And full he was of luffe & skille
And full also of the holy gaste   12645
In Nazarethe þare lende he maste
Ay till he was comen nere
To þe elde of twenty ȝere
Þan thoghte hym that he
In Cristyn lawe wolde baptiste bee
For to garre þe lawe sprede   12655
Als I sall sythyn till ȝowe rede
Bot are I thereof oghte begynn
Ȝe schall here of his kynn

**The Genelogye of Anna and hir Sisters
and thaire housebaundes**

When þat Ioachym was dede
Anna with hir frendis rede   12660
Tuke anoþer husbande   fol. 16v col. 1
A noble man of alle þat lande
Cleophas þan was his name
Þat was a man of full gude fame
A dogheter sone of hir he gatte   12665
Þat marye als hir sistir hatte
And sythen a man þis Marie toke
Þat highte Alpheus als says þe boke
Twa sonnes gatt he this Alpheus
Þat were Ioseph and Iacobus   12670
Þis Iacob þat I telle of nowe
Was callede þe brother of Ihesu
Ihesu brothir called was he
For sibreden honoure & bounte
Full lyke hym was he of facyownn   12675

He was of full grete deuocyoun
Haly lyfe he ledd always
Whils he lyffede als þe storye says
He dranke neuer ceser ne wyne
Ne weride clothe þat was of lyne   12680
Flesche ȝitte ne ete he neuer
Appon Criste he callede euer
Swa haunted he one knes to lye
For to praye stedfastlye
Þat his knes were bolned swaa   12685
Þat vnnethes moghte he a fote ga
Þis Iacob hadde all lyknes
Of Ihesu bathe in mare & lesse
Þis Iacob þat I of telle
Stode one a day to preche a spelle   12690
In Ierusalem & þare was he slayne
Till heuen þan was his soule tane
When he was dede this Cleophas
Anna: þan wedded: Salomas
Scho was with childe & þat in hye   12695
With a mayden þat hight Marye
Scho was sythen gyuen to Zebede
A doghety man of Galyle
Off hir gatte he childir twa
Iames þe mare highte ane of tha   12700
Þat kyng heraude gart sla   fol. 16v col. 2
Þe toþer broþer of thase twa
Highte Iohn þe Euangelist
Þat so wele was luffed with Crist
For his grete gudnes   12705
And of his maydenhod þe clennes
Alle þe appostils he ouerpaste
In gudnes was he so stedfaste
In ilke place satt he Ihesu nexte
& att his maunde slepand on his breste   12710
And saghe þer þe preuates of heuen
Þat ma were þan I kane neuen

BIBLIOGRAPHY

PRIMARY SOURCES

ADAMS, J. Q., ed. *Chief Pre-Shakespearean Dramas*. Cambridge, Mass.: Riverside, 1924.
AILRED OF RIEVAULX. "In Assumptione Beatae Mariae: Sermo xvii." *PL* CXCV.
AMANN, Emile, ed. *Le Protévangile de Jacques et ses remaniements latins*. Paris: Letouzey et Ané, 1910.
ANSELM. "De Conceptu Virginali: Homilia ix." *PL* CLVIII.
AQUINAS, Thomas. *Summa Theologica*. Trans. Fathers of the Dominican Province. 3 vols. New York: Benzigen Brothers, 1947.
AUGUSTINE. *Contra Faustum*. *PL* XLII.
————. *De Bono Conjugali*. *PL* XL.
————. *De Civitate Dei*. *PL* XLI.
————. *De Natura et Gratia*. *PL* XLIV.
————. *In Psalmum*. *PL* XXXVII.
————. *Quaestiones ex Novo Testamento*. *PL* XXXV.

BEDE. *Chronicon Breve*. *PL* XCIV.
————. *De Temporibus Liber*. *PL* XC.
————. *De Temporum Ratione*. *PL* XC.
BERNARD OF CLAIRVAUX. "Epistola clxxiv: Ad Canonicos Lugdunensis, de conceptione S. Mariae." *PL* CLXXXII.
————. "In Festo Annuntiationis Beatae Mariae Virginis: Sermo I." *PL* CLXXXIII.
BLOCK, K. S., ed. *Ludus Coventriae or the Plaie called Corpus Christi*. London: Oxford University Press, 1922. EETS ES 120.
BOULTON, Maureen, ed. *The Old French Evangile de l'enfance*. Toronto: Pontifical Institute of Mediaeval Studies, 1984. Studies and Texts, 70.

COWPER, B. Harris, ed. and trans. *The Apocryphal Gospels and Other Documents Relating to the History of Christ Translated from the Originals in Greek, Latin, Syriac, etc.* London: Williams and Norgate, 1867.
COWPER, J. M., ed. *Meditations on the Supper of Our Lord, and the Hours of the Passion*. London, 1875. EETS OS 60.

De Nativitate Mariae, in Emile Amann, ed., *Le Protévangile de Jacques et ses remaniements latins*. Paris: Letouzey et Ané, 1910.
D'EVELYN, Charlotte, ed. *Meditations on the Life and Passion of Christ*. London: Oxford University Press, 1921. EETS OS 158.
DICKINS, Bruce, and R. M. WILSON, eds. *Early Middle English Texts*. London: Bowes, 1951.

FOSTER, F. A., ed. *A Stanzaic Life of Christ*. London: Oxford University Press, 1926. EETS OS 166.
FOWLER, Roger R., ed. *An Edition of Lines 9229–12712 of Cursor Mundi*. Diss. University of Ottawa, 1981.
FULBERT OF CHARTRES. *Sermo i: De Nativitate Mariae*. *PL* CXLII.
FURNIVALL, F. J., ed. *The Minor Poems of the Vernon Manuscript*. Part II. London: Kegan Paul, Trench, Trübner, 1901. EETS OS 117.

GELASIUS, I. *De Libris non Recipiendis. PL* LIX.
GODEFRIDI ADMONTENSIS. "Homilia lxv." *PL* CLXXIV.
GROSSETESTE, Robert. *Le Château d'amour de Robert Grosseteste, Évêque de Lincoln.* Ed. J. Murray. Paris: Champion, 1918.

HAYMO OF HALBERSTADT. *Historiae Sacrae Epitome. PL* CXVIII.
HENNECKE, E., and W. SCHNEEMELCHER, eds. *New Testament Apocrypha.* 3rd ed. 2 vols. Trans. R. McL. Wilson. Philadelphia: Westminster Press, 1963.
HERMAN DE VALENCIENNES. *La Bible von Herman de Valenciennes.* II. Ed. Otto Moldenhauer. III. Ed. Hans Burkowitz. Griefswald: Hans Adler, 1914.
──────. *Li Romanz de Dieu et de sa mère.* Ed. Ina Spiele. Leyden: Presse Universitaire de Leyden, 1975.
HILDEFONSE OF TOLEDO. "Sermo xiii: In Diem Sanctae Mariae." *PL* XCVI.
HOLTHAUSEN, F., ed. *Vices and Virtues.* London: Oxford University Press, 1888, 1921. EETS OS 89, 159.
HONORIUS AUGUSTODUNENSIS. *Elucidarium.* Ed. Yves Lefèvre, *L'Elucidarium et les lucidaires.* Paris: de Boccard, 1954.
HORRALL, Sarah M., ed. *An Edition of the Old Testament Section of the Cursor Mundi from MS College of Arms, Arundel LVII.* Diss. University of Ottawa, 1973.
──────. *The Southern Version of Cursor Mundi.* Vol. I. Ottawa: University of Ottawa Press, 1978.
HORSTMANN, C., ed. *Altenglische Legenden.* Paderborn: Ferdinand Schöningh, 1875.
──────, ed. *The Minor Poems of the Vernon Manuscript.* 2 vols. London: Kegan Paul, 1892. EETS OS 98.
──────, ed. *Sammlung Altenglischer Legenden.* 1878; rpt. Hildesheim: Olms, 1969.
──────, ed. *The Three Kings of Cologne.* London: Kegan Paul, 1886. EETS OS 85.
HUGH OF ST. VICTOR. *Miscellanea. PL* CLXXVII.

The Infancy Story of Thomas, in E. Hennecke and W. Schneemelcher, eds., *New Testament Apocrypha.* 3rd ed. Trans. R. McL. Wilson. Vol. I. Philadelphia: Westminster Press, 1963.
INNOCENT I. *Epistola vi. PL* XX.

JACOBUS A VORAGINE. *Legenda Aurea.* Ed. Th. Graesse. Leipzig: Arnold, 1850.
JAMES, M. R., ed. and trans. *The Apocryphal New Testament.* 1924; rpt. Oxford: Clarendon Press, 1972.
──────, ed. *Latin Infancy Gospels: A New Text with a Parallel Version from Irish.* Cambridge: Cambridge University Press, 1927.
JEROME. *Commentariorum in Abacuc. PL* XXV.
──────. *De Perpetua Virginitate B. Mariae: Adversus Helvidium. PL* XXIII.
──────. *In Isaiam. PL* XXIV.
JOHN DAMASCENE. *De Fide Orthodoxa.* Ed. Eligius M. Buytaert. St. Bonaventure, N.Y.: Franciscan Institute, 1955.

LANGLAND, William. *The Vision of William Concerning Piers the Plowman.* Ed. W. W. Skeat. 2 vols. London: Oxford University Press, 1886.
LUMIANSKY, R. M., and David MILLS, eds. *The Chester Mystery Cycle.* London: Oxford University Press, 1974. EETS SS 3.
LURIA, M. S., and R. L. HOFFMAN, eds. *Middle English Lyrics.* New York: Norton, 1974.
LYDGATE, John. *Life of Our Lady.* Ed. J. A. Lauritis *et al.* Pittsburgh: Duquesne University Press, 1961.

MADDEN, F., and S.J.H. HERRTAGE, eds. *The Early English Versions of the Gesta Romanorum.* London: Kegan Paul, 1898. EETS ES 33.
MILTON, John. *Complete Poems and Major Prose.* Ed. Merritt Y. Hughes. New York: Odyssey, 1957.

MIRK, John. *Mirk's Festial: A Collection of Homilies.* Part I. Ed. T. Erbe. London: Kegan Paul, Trench, Trübner, 1905. EETS ES 96.

MORRIS, Richard, ed. *Cursor Mundi.* 1874–93; rpt. London: Oxford University Press, 1961–66. EETS OS 57, 59, 62, 66, 68, 99, 101.

MOUS, P.H.J., ed. *An Edition of the New Testament of the Cursor Mundi (17289–21346) from MS College of Arms, Arundel LVII.* Diss. University of Ottawa, 1980.

———, ed. *The Southern Version of Cursor Mundi.* Vol. IV. Ottawa: University of Ottawa Press, 1986.

ORIGEN. *Contra Celsum. PG* XI.

PETRUS COMESTOR. *Historia Scholastica. PL* CXCVIII.

PICKERING, O. S., ed. *The South-English Nativity of Mary and Christ.* Heidelberg: Carl Winter, 1975. Middle English Texts, 1.

Protevangelium, in Emile Amann, ed., *Le Protévangile de Jacques et ses remaniements latins.* Paris: Letouzey et Ané, 1910.

PSEUDO-AUGUSTINE. *Contra Judaeos. PL* XLII.

———. "Sermo CXCV." *PL* XXXIX.

PSEUDO-CHRYSOSTOM. *Opus Imperfectum in Matthaeum. PG* LVI.

Pseudo-Matthaei Evangelicum, in Emile Amann, ed., *Le Protévangile de Jacques et ses remaniements latins.* Paris: Letouzey et Ané, 1910.

ROBERT MANNYNG OF BRUNNE. *Robert of Brunne's Handlyng Synne.* Ed. F. J. Furnivall. London: Kegan Paul, Trench, Trübner, 1901–03. EETS OS 119, 123.

SAJAVAARA, Kari, ed. *The Middle English Translations of Robert Grosseteste's Château d'amour.* Helsinki: Société Néophilologique, 1967. Mémoires de la Société Néophilologique de Helsinki, 32.

SAUER, Walter, ed. *The Metrical Life of Christ.* Heidelberg: Carl Winter, 1977. Middle English Texts, 5.

SMALL, John, ed. *English Metrical Homilies from Manuscripts of the Fourteenth Century.* 1862; rpt. New York: AMS Press, 1973.

SPINDLER, Robert, ed. *Court of Sapience.* Leipzig: Bernhard Tauchnitz, 1927.

STAUFFENBERG, Henry J., ed. *An Edition of Cursor Mundi 12713–17082 from MS College of Arms, Arundel LVII.* Diss. University of Ottawa, 1977.

———, ed. *The Southern Version of Cursor Mundi.* Vol. III. Ottawa: University of Ottawa Press, 1985.

TESTUZ, Michel, ed. *Papyrus Bodmer V: "Nativité de Marie."* Cologny-Geneve: Bibliotheca Bodmeriana, 1958.

TISCHENDORF, K. von, ed. *Evangelia Apocrypha.* 1876; rpt. Hildesheim: Olms, 1966.

VINCENT DE BEAUVAIS. *Speculum Historiale.* 1624; facsimile edition. Graz: Akademische Druck- und Verlagsanslatt, 1965.

WACE. *L'Établissement de la fête de la conception Notre Dame dite la fête aux normands.* Ed. G. Mancel and G. S. Trebutien. Caen: Mancel, 1842.

SECONDARY SOURCES

ALFORD, John A. "Literature and Law in Medieval England," *PMLA,* XCII (1977), 941–51.

BERGER, Samuel. *La Bible française au moyen âge.* Paris: Imprimerie Nationale, 1884.

———. *Histoire de la Vulgate pendant les premiers siècles du moyen âge.* Paris: Hachette, 1893.

196   THE SOUTHERN VERSION OF *CURSOR MUNDI*

BONNARD, Jean. *Les Traductions de la Bible en vers français au moyen âge*. Paris: Imprimerie Nationale, 1884.

BORLAND, Lois. *The Cursor Mundi and Herman's Bible*. Diss. University of Chicago, 1929.

———. "Herman's *Bible* and the *Cursor Mundi*," *Studies in Philology*, XXX (1933), 427–44.

BOSSUAT, Robert, et al. *Dictionnaire des lettres françaises: le moyen âge*. Paris: Librairie Arthème Fayard, 1964.

BRASWELL, Laurel. *The South English Legendary Collection: A Study in Middle English Religious Literature of the Thirteenth and Fourteenth Centuries*. Diss. University of Toronto, 1964.

BROWN, Carleton. *Register of Middle English Religious and Didactic Verse*. Part I. Oxford: Oxford University Press, 1916–20.

———, and Rossell Hope ROBBINS. *The Index of Middle English Verse*. New York: Columbia University Press, 1943. *Supplement*. Lexington: University of Kentucky Press, 1965.

BUEHLER, P. "The *Cursor Mundi* and Herman's *Bible* — Some Additional Parallels," *Studies in Philology*, LXI (1964), 485–99.

CHARLESWORTH, J. H. *The Pseudepigrapha and Modern Research*. Missoula, Montana: Scholars Press, 1976.

CULLMANN, O. "Infancy Gospels," trans. A.F.B. Higgins, in E. Hennecke and W. Schneemelcher, eds., *New Testament Apocrypha*. 3rd ed. Trans. R. McL. Wilson. Vol. I. Philadelphia: Westminster Press, 1963. Pp. 363–414.

DEANESLY, Margaret. *The Lollard Bible and Other Medieval Biblical Versions*. 1920; rpt. Cambridge: Cambridge University Press, 1966.

ENSLIN, M. S. "The Christian Stories of the Nativity," *Journal of Biblical Literature*, LIX (1940), 317–38.

FINDLAY, A. F. *Byways in Early Christian Literature: Studies in the Uncanonical Gospels and Acts*. Edinburgh: Clark, 1923.

FÖRSTER, Max. "Die Legende vom Trinubium der hl. Anna," in Wolfgang Keller, ed., *Probleme der englischen Sprache und Kultur (Festschrift Johannes Hoops)*. Heidelberg: Carl Winter, 1925. Pp. 105–30.

———. "Die Weltzeitalter bei den Angelsachsen," in *Neusprachliche Studien (Festgabe Luick: Die Neueren Sprachen)*, 6 Beiheft.

FOWLER, David C. *The Bible in Early English Literature*. Seattle: University of Washington Press, 1976.

GRAEF, Hilda. *Mary: A History of Doctrine and Devotion*. 2 vols. London: Sheed and Ward, 1963–65.

HAENISCH, Dr. "Inquiry into the Sources of the *Cursor Mundi*," in Richard Morris, ed., *Cursor Mundi*, VI. London: Kegan Paul, 1893. EETS OS 101. Pp. 1*–56*.

HAMILTON, George L. "Review of Gordon Hall Gerould, *Saints' Legends*," *Modern Language Notes*, XXXVI (1921), 230–42.

HARGREAVES, Henry. "From Bede to Wyclif: Medieval English Bible Translations," *Bulletin of the John Rylands Library*, XLVIII (1965), 118–40.

HEFFERNAN, T. J. Rev. *The Southern Version of Cursor Mundi*, by Sarah M. Horrall. *Speculum*, LV (1980), 801–04.

HERVIEUX, Jacques. *What are Apocryphal Gospels?* Trans. Dom Wulstan Hibberd. London: Hawthorne Books, 1960.

HIRN, Yrjö. *The Sacred Shrine: A Study of the Poetry and Art of the Catholic Church*. London: Macmillan, 1912.

HORTON, Adey. *The Child Jesus*. London: Geoffrey Chapman, 1975.

HUNT, Tony. "'The Four Daughters of God': A Textual Contribution," *Archives d'histoire doctrinale et littéraire au-moyen âge*, XLVIII (1981), 287–316.

HUPE, H. *"Cursor Mundi," Anglia Beiblatt,* I (1890–91), 133–36.

———. *"Cursor Mundi*: Essay on the Manuscripts and Dialect," in Richard Morris, ed., *Cursor Mundi,* VII. 1893; rpt. London: Oxford University Press, 1962. EETS OS 101.

———. "Zum Handschriftenverhältniss und zur Textkritik des *Cursor Mundi," Anglia,* XI (1889), 121–45.

JAMES, M. R. "The Salomites," *Journal of Theological Studies,* XXXV (1934), 287–97.

KAISER, Rolf. *Zur Geographie des mittelenglischen Wortschatzes.* 1937; rpt. New York: Johnson, 1970.

KALUZA, Max. "Zu den Quellen und dem Handschriftenverhältniss des *Cursor Mundi," Englische Studien,* XII (1889), 451–58.

———. "Zum Handschriftenverhältniss und zur Textkritik des *Cursor Mundi," Englische Studien,* XI (1888), 235–75.

KER, N. R. *Medieval Libraries of Great Britain.* 2nd ed. London: Royal Historical Society, 1964.

KURATH, H., and S. KUHN. *Middle English Dictionary: Plan and Bibliography.* Ann Arbor: University of Michigan Press, 1956.

MACGREGOR, G. *A Literary History of the Bible from the Middle Ages to the Present Day.* New York: Abingdon Press, 1968.

MCLINTOCH, J., and J. STRONG, eds. *Cyclopedia of Biblical, Theological, and Ecclesiastical Literature.* Grand Rapids, Michigan, 1867–87.

MCNALLY, Robert E. *The Bible in the Early Middle Ages.* Westminster, Maryland: Newman Press, 1959.

MARDON, Ernest. *The Narrative Unity of the Cursor Mundi.* Glasgow: William MacLellan, 1970.

MEHL, D. *The Middle English Romances of the Thirteenth and Fourteenth Centuries.* London: Routledge and Kegan Paul, 1968.

A New Catholic Commentary on Holy Scripture. Ed. R. C. Fuller. Rev. ed. London: Nelson, 1969.

New Catholic Encyclopedia. McGraw-Hill, 1967.

NICOLAS, Michel. *Études sur les Évangiles apocryphes.* Paris, 1866.

OWST, G. R. *Literature and Pulpit in Medieval England.* 2nd rev. ed. New York: Barnes and Noble, 1961.

PANTIN, W. A. *The English Church in the Fourteenth Century.* Cambridge: Cambridge University Press, 1955.

PÉTAVEL, Emmanuel. *La Bible en France ou les traductions des saintes Ecritures.* Paris, 1864.

REINSCH, Robert. *Die Pseudo-Evangelien von Jesu und Maria's Kindheit in der romanischen und germanischen Literatur.* Halle: Max Niemeyer, 1879.

RENWICK, W. L., and H. ORTON. *The Beginnings of English Literature to Skelton, 1509.* 3rd ed. rev.: M. F. Wakelin. London: Cresset Press, 1966.

SAJAVAARA, Kari. "The Use of Robert Grosseteste's *Château d'amour* as a Source of the *Cursor Mundi*: Additional Evidence," *Neuphilologische Mitteilungen,* LXVIII (1967), 184–93.

SHEPHERD, Geoffrey. "English Versions of the Scriptures before Wyclif," in *Cambridge History of the Bible.* II: *The West from the Fathers to the Reformation.* Ed. G.W.H. Lampe. Cambridge: Cambridge University Press, 1969.

SMALLEY, Beryl. *The Study of the Bible in the Middle Ages.* 1952; rpt. Notre Dame: University of Notre Dame Press, 1964.

SMYTH, M. W. *Biblical Quotations in Middle English Before 1350.* New York: Henry Holt, 1911.

THOMPSON, J. W. *The Medieval Library*. 1939; rpt. New York: Hafner, 1967.

TILLEY, M. P. *A Dictionary of the Proverbs in England in the Sixteenth and Seventeenth Centuries*. Ann Arbor: University of Michigan Press, 1950.

TRAVER, Hope. *The Four Daughters of God: A Study of the Versions of this Allegory with Special Reference to those in Latin, French, and English*. Bryn Mawr: Bryn Mawr College, 1907. Bryn Mawr College Monograph Series, 6.

WHITING, B. J., and Helen Westcott WHITING, eds. *Proverbs, Sentences, and Proverbial Phrases from English Writings Mainly Before 1500*. Cambridge, Mass.: Belknap Press, 1968.

WILSON, R. M. "The Contents of the Medieval Library," in F. Wormald and C. E. Wright, eds., *The English Library before 1700*. London: Athlone Press, 1958. Pp. 85–111.